EMT Manual

ROY G. SOPER, Paramedic

EMT Training Coordinator,
Renton Fire Department, Renton, Washington

STEVEN C. MACDONALD, M.P.H., EMT

Policy Analyst, Department of Health Services
School of Public Health and Community Medicine,
University of Washington, Seattle

MICHAEL K. COPASS, M.D.

Associate Professor, Department of Medicine,
School of Medicine, University of Washington;
Director, Emergency Trauma Center,
Harborview Medical Center;
Deputy Director and Director of Training,
Medic I, Seattle

MICKEY S. EISENBERG, M.D., Ph.D.

Associate Professor, Department of Medicine,
School of Medicine, University of Washington;
Director, Emergency Medicine Service, University Hospital;
Medical Advisor, King County Emergency Medical
Services Division, King County
Department of Health, Seattle

W. B. SAUNDERS COMPANY
Harcourt Brace Jovanovich, Inc.

Philadelphia London Toronto
Montreal Sydney Tokyo

Blue Books Series is a trademark of the W. B. Saunders Company

W. B. Saunders Company: West Washington Square
Philadelphia, PA   19105

1 St. Anne's Road
Eastbourne, East Sussex BN21 3UN, England

1 Goldthorne Avenue
Toronto, Ontario M8Z 5T9, Canada

Apartado 26370—Cedro 512
Mexico 4, D.F., Mexico

Rua Coronel Cabrita, 8
Sao Cristovao Caixa Postal 21176
Rio de Janeiro, Brazil

9 Waltham Street
Artarmon, N.S.W. 2064, Australia

Ichibancho, Central Bldg., 22-1 Ichibancho
Chiyoda-Ku, Tokyo 102, Japan

Library of Congress Cataloging in Publication Data

Soper, Roy G.

EMT manual.

1. Medical emergencies—Handbooks, manuals, etc.
   I. Title.   II. Title: E.M.T. manual. [DNLM:
   1. Emergency medical technician manual.   2. Emergencies—Handbooks.   3. Allied health personnel—
   Handbooks. WB 105 E559]

RC86.7.S69 1984   616'.025   83–15269

ISBN 0–7216–8487–4

EMT Manual   ISBN   0–7216–8487–4

Last digit is the print number: 9   8   7   6   5   4

PREFACE

The purpose of this book will be met if Emergency Medical Technicians find it useful in the performance of their jobs. It is meant to be carried in the pocket (or on the dashboard of an emergency vehicle), which is why the book is small and spiral bound. It is meant to be referred to when some question arises about the recognition or management of a patient's condition. This will probably not occur while emergency patient care is actively ongoing. The book will probably be most useful after an emergency call, as a review of the clinical problem, or it may be used on the way, responding to a call, if the dispatcher can provide specific clinical information (assuming all eyes are not needed to monitor traffic flow). On occasion, a team of EMTs may choose to divide responsibilities in such a way that one EMT reviews material in the manual while the other EMT attends to the patient. This teamwork and division of responsibilities may work particularly well when the patient presents a diagnostic challenge. Diagnostic challenges also occur in patients who present with problems or complaints that are not frequently seen. It might also seem appropriate to the EMT to refer to the manual while en route to hospital with the patient, as a means of verifying the initial impression that has guided patient management to that point. If this manual is useful in these settings, then it has accomplished its purpose.

The EMT instructor/coordinator may also find the book useful as an adjunct to course textbooks. The design of the manual is such that the student will find here all of the essential information about EMT emergency medical care. However, this book cannot serve as a replacement for a textbook. We have intentionally not included physiology or detailed anatomy. Our goal was to keep the material concise, specific, and immediately relevant. In essence, this is a reference manual for the practicing EMT.

Some recommendations for therapy in this book may not agree with local protocol. The authors would like to stress that the EMT should always follow local guidelines and protocols.

The task of an EMT is difficult. He or she must make critical decisions based upon minimal information without the aid of x-rays or diagnostic tests. The EMT often provides emergency care in circumstances that are far from ideal. With good training and good supervision (such as case review), the EMT can make judgments and do the job well. We hope this book can help in the task of providing good emergency care. It is in this spirit that we dedicate this book to Emergency Medical Technicians.

ACKNOWLEDGMENTS

We appreciate our colleagues in the field of emergency training who have forged new paths in the world of EMT and paramedic training and who have helped establish fine emergency programs. A special expression of appreciation goes to Nancy Caroline, M.D., for her outstanding contributions to EMT and paramedic training.

Our approach to behavioral emergencies is based upon principles contained in *Behavioral Emergencies*, by Ellen Bassuk, Sandra Fox and Kevin Prendergast, Little, Brown, 1982. The section on blood pressure monitoring has been graciously provided by Emergency Training from their textbook *Using Anti-Shock Trousers (MAST): A Guide for the EMT*, 1982.

A special thanks goes to the officers, and especially the EMTs, of the Renton Fire Department, Renton, Washington, for allowing us to use them as a test group for many of the approaches put forth in this manual.

A personal thanks from Roy goes to Marilyn Soper for her contributions from the vantage point of an active EMT and as a source of constant encouragement during the writing of this manual; and from Steve to Rita Altamore for much patient understanding of work that often extended late into the nights and weekends.

We appreciate the efforts of Harriet Moles, Judy Prentice, and Treasure Payne, who painstakingly typed numerous versions of the manuscript. Artwork was provided by Dinah Stone, who worked closely with us to get the illustrations "just right." We are also appreciative of the continual editorial support offered by Baxter Venable.

CONTENTS

INTRODUCTORY NOTE

Each volume in the Saunders Blue Books® Series is intended to be a practical aid for primary care physicians, house officers, and medical students in clinical training. Each Blue Book presents the latest diagnostic and therapeutic information pertinent to its clinical field. Above all else, these books are intended to be useful in the real world of providing daily patient care. Their convenient format allows maximal retrieval of relevant information in a minimum of time.

Our Series derives its name from the "Blue Series"—the first books published by the W. B. Saunders Company almost 100 years ago. That Series, like its modern descendant, was intended to sort out important scientific and clinical facts that would aid the physician or the student in training. Today, as medical information grows exponentially, health professionals recognize their obligation both to remain current and to select from the engulfing sea of clinical data those particular pieces that will aid them in their practice. The volumes in Saunders Blue Books® Series will help them achieve these goals. They should be regarded as portable clinical tools—useful, always on call, and ready to help when needed.

MICKEY S. EISENBERG, M.D., PH.D.
Consulting Editor

PATIENT CARE: SKILLS AND PRINCIPLES

1

HOW TO SAVE A LIFE

ATTITUDE

The attitude an EMT brings to his or her performance directly affects care.

1. The EMT must have a strong desire to help people and to provide good care and comfort.

2. The EMT's concern for the patients' needs must be first and foremost. All personal feelings and prejudices must be set aside.

3. The EMT should be professional at all times. Disagreements with coworkers should be settled after the patient is treated.

4. The EMT should take full advantage of all available assistance, using coworkers as part of a team.

5. The EMT should avoid taking unnecessary risks. Injury to the EMT or coworkers only adds to the overall problem.

The demonstration of these attitudes occurs in the following ways:

Contact. Maintain eye-level contact. Make physical contact with the patient quickly. Palpating the radial pulse is helpful for early assessment of the patient and also provides a non-threatening impression that treatment has begun.

Confidence. Conduct the interrogation and physical exam systematically. This indicates to the patient that a specific purpose is in mind. Warn the patient before exposing skin. Protect the patient's modesty from curious onlookers.

Curiosity. Learn as much about the patient's problem as you can. Ask, don't assume. "Why did you call?" "Why do you take this medicine?" "Where do you hurt?"

Compassion. Be soothing and empathetic. Warn the patient before doing anything that will cause pain or anxiety.

Common Sense. Be flexible. Be able to make rapid adjustments in assessment and management based upon minute-to-minute changes in the patient's status and the setting.

RECOGNIZING THE ACUTELY ILL PATIENT

An important EMT skill is the ability to distinguish an acutely ill patient from one who is not. In some instances, the difference will be obvious. Other cases are more difficult. Experience and intuition will help the EMT make this distinction. Table 1–1 presents a guide to signs and symptoms in acutely ill patients.

Table 1-1. GENERAL OBSERVATIONS: ACUTELY ILL PATIENT

Posture	Slumped or leaning forward
	Leaning to the side
	Stiff neck
Skin color	Pale
	Cyanotic (blue)
	Red (flushed, cherry)
	Yellow (jaundiced)
	Chalk white
Skin texture	Moist
	Dry (loss of turgor)
	Hot
	Cold
Symmetry	Face or mouth sagging
	Eyelid drooping
	Arm(s) and/or leg(s) hanging limp
Eyes	Lackluster
	Roving
	Deviated
Pupils	Dilated
	Constricted
	Unreactive
	Unequal
Speech	Slurred
	Garbled
	Absent
	Rapid
	Short phrases
State of mind	Disoriented
Level of consciousness	Responds only to verbal stimuli
	Responds only to painful stimuli
	Unresponsive
Initial vital signs	
Respiration	rapid (>30/min)
	slow (<10/min)
	absent
	labored
	noisy
	irregular with periods of apnea
Pulse	rapid (>120/min)
	slow (<55/min)
	absent
	thready
	irregular
Blood pressure	<90 mm Hg systolic
	>180 mm Hg systolic
	postural hypotension

Table 1–2. EMT TEAM CONCEPT: DIVISION OF RESPONSIBILITIES FOR PATIENT

EMT in Charge of Patient	EMT Partner	Additional EMT/First Aiders
Assess ABCs	Vital signs (every 5–10 min)	CPR team
Level of consciousness		Management of ABC
Interrogation	Blood pressure	Assist with treatment
Physical examination	Pulse	Runner for equipment
Assessment	Respiratory rate	Second patient
Determine course of treatment	Attach EKG monitor (if available)	
Report (written/verbal)	Interrogate family/witness	
Determine method of transportation	Patient's medicine (obtain list)	
Triage	Perform treatment as directed	

TEAM CONCEPT

A team of two EMTs per patient provides optimal care with a minimum of confusion. Additional manpower may be called upon, if necessary. One of the two EMTs in the team is in charge to provide leadership and avoid confusion. An understanding of who will assume the position of EMT in charge must be established before the team arrives at the scene. Table 1–2 outlines the division of responsibilities and the use of additional manpower.

The EMT in charge is also responsible for overall management at the scene. Management includes establishment of a manpower pool, traffic control, extrication, additional equipment, support of EMTs, and incoming transportation. These duties are to be assumed until a more senior responsible person arrives at the scene. In situations involving several patients, the EMT in charge of treatment becomes the triage officer (see Chapter 2) and assigns teams of EMTs as required. The EMT in charge is the last person to assume responsibility for treating a particular patient when sufficient manpower is available. It is essential that the EMT in charge maintain close communication with the senior officer at the scene.

The EMT in charge is responsible for the patient write-up. He/she must *never* leave writing the report to an EMT not involved in the actual interrogation and physical examination of the patient.

2

PATIENT ASSESSMENT

An understanding of the patient's mental and physical condition requires the EMT to use the senses of sight, smell, hearing, touch and (possibly) taste. These senses are used to accumulate a history and to understand the patient's symptoms (what the patient, family, witnesses told you in their own words about the patient's current problem) and signs (what you find out about the patient through examination).

The EMT must consider four methods of assessment: inspection, interrogation, palpation, and auscultation.

PATIENT EXAMINATION

INSPECTION

1. Make a rapid visual inspection of the patient's surroundings, general posture, and physical state.
   a. Does the patient look and act sick (pale, diaphoretic, anxious)?
   b. Is the patient's mental state appropriate considering the circumstances?
   c. Are there any obvious abnormal signs, particularly signs of respiratory distress?
2. Observe the reactions of the friends and family members to the patient's condition.

INTERROGATION

1. Trauma questions: Trauma patients sustain injury from accidents that are unexpected, and these patients can be approached in a straightforward manner. It is particularly appropriate to inquire directly about areas of pain with a trauma patient.
   a. Do you have any difficulty breathing?
   b. Do you hurt anywhere? (Have patient point to affected area.)
   c. What happened? (Include questions about seat belts, helmets, etc.)
   d. Do you have any current medical problems?
   e. Are you taking any medications? Any taken today?

   f. Are you allergic to any medications?

2. Medical questions: Patients should be made to describe these problems in their own words without much prompting or leading questions.
   a. What is the problem? (Interrupt only to keep patient discussing the current problem.)
   b. When did it begin?
   c. What were you doing when it began? How did it begin?
   d. Did this ever happen to you before? If so, what was done?
   e. Does anything make it better or worse?
   f. Do you take medications for this problem? Have you taken any today?
   g. Do you have any other current medical problems?
   h. Do you take any other medications?
   i. If complaint is about pain, have patient point to affected area and describe the nature of the pain, i.e., sharp, dull, cramping, pressure, steady, intermittent.

PALPATION

1. Determine general skin conditions (temperature, moisture); check capillary refilling by compressing fingernail.
2. Use gentle but firm pressure, starting at areas distant from reported pain and moving slowly toward the painful area.
3. In the trauma patient, touch every accessible bone and every joint.
4. Use your stethoscope as an additional device for palpating to confirm questionable areas of tenderness. The patient's reaction to the pressure of the stethoscope should be the same as to the pressure of your hand.

AUSCULTATION

The stethoscope should become the primary tool for listening to various parts of the trunk. Practice on healthy persons develops skills for recognizing abnormal airway, lung, and heart sounds. The stethoscope may be useful in confirming fractures by hearing crepitus (sound of grating bone).

PRIMARY SURVEY

The primary, basic function of all persons involved in emergency medical care is the rapid assessment, management, and reassessment of a patient's ABCs: Airway, Breathing, and Circulation.

The EMT has the added responsibility to perform a rapid assessment of the scene to determine (a) environmental dangers, (b) the number of patients to be treated, (c) the mechanism of injury, and (d) the problems of immediate extrication. In serious illness or trauma, aggressive management of major ABC problems is vital. The patient will die if these primary functions are neglected or managed carelessly.

A = AIRWAY

1. *Is it open?*
   Check for movement of air, look to see the chest rise, listen for air flow, feel chest wall for movement and crepitus, check for stoma.

2. *Is patient positioned properly?*
   Head tilt, neck or chin lift; jaw thrust for face or neck trauma (maintaining in-line cervical traction).

3. *Are respirations noisy, gurgling, or labored?*
   Check for partial obstruction, fluids, excess salivation.

4. *Look for inspiratory retractions at supraclavicular and intercostal space, diaphragmatic movement only without airflow.*
   Check for complete obstruction.

B = BREATHING

1. *Is patient breathing?*
   Mouth-to-mouth, mouth-to-mask, send for bag mask.

2. *Depth of respirations?*
   Inspect chest movement.

3. *Gasping respirations?*
   Palpate for flail, sucking chest wounds.

4. *Rate?*
   Rates <10/min should be assisted.

5. *Unusual patterns?*
   Cerebral insults produce specific patterns to record.

C = CIRCULATION

1. *Is there a palpable pulse?*
   Check carotid pulses; if none, do cardiopulmonary resuscitation (CPR). Use femoral pulse to confirm circulation with CPR.

2. *Is pulse rate <55 or >180/minute?*

Check for signs of inadequate perfusion.

3. *Is pulse irregular?*
   Compare apical and radial pulses for discrepancy, then check irregularities with electrocardiogram (EKG) monitor, if one is available (and EMT is so trained).

4. *Is there visible external hemorrhage?*
   Control external bleeding.

5. *Is there suspected internal bleeding?*
   Begin treatment for shock.

LEVEL OF CONSCIOUSNESS

In addition to the assessment of the ABCs, it is necessary to make initial assessment of the patient's level of consciousness.
1. State of mind.
   a. Is the patient oriented? Knows who he/she is, where he/she is, approximate time of day, circumstances of the event.
2. Level of consciousness.
   a. Alert: completely awake and acting appropriately.
   b. Lethargic: sleepy, but aware of surroundings.
   c. Stuporous: will awaken to vocal stimuli, prefers to remain asleep.
   d. Obtunded: will awaken to painful stimuli only.
   e. Comatose: nothing will awaken patient.
   Note: Medical terms such as "stuporous" or "obtunded" can be imprecise, meaning different things to different people, even within the medical community. An alternative approach characterizes levels of consciousness on the basis of response, as follows:
   a. Alert.
   b. Responsive to verbal stimuli: awakens only when spoken to.
   c. Responsive to painful stimuli: awakens only when ears are pinched.
   d. Unresponsive.
3. What is pupillary response to bright light? Do pupils constrict? Check for deviated gaze. Check pupillary size.
4. If the patient is conscious, inquire about chronic illness, current medications, allergies. If the patient is unconscious, check for medical alert wallet card, bracelet, or necklace.
5. Repeat assessment of ABCs during the secondary exam and treatment phase to make sure that the patient's condition is not worsening. Evaluation of pulse rate, respiratory rate, and blood pressure should be repeated at 10-minute intervals.

SECONDARY SURVEY

The head-to-toe exam is called the secondary survey and provides additional and specific information about the patient's condition. As it is being done, ask the patient about the chief complaint and associated symptoms. The secondary survey is divided into medical and trauma sections. This helps refine the approach to the special problems in each specific category. The equipment required includes a stethoscope, blood pressure cuff, and pen light.

MEDICAL SURVEY

Head, Eyes, Ears, Nose, Throat/Neck (HEENT)

1. *Look* for skin discoloration, moisture, drooling, blood, nasal flaring, frothy or bloody sputum, bloody emesis, facial sagging, drooping eyelid(s), deviated gaze, unequal pupils, eyelids held closed by patient, color of conjunctiva, distention of neck veins, retractions of accessory muscles at base of neck, presence of stoma, deviated trachea.
2. *Listen* for stridorous speech, whispered speech, snoring, gurgling, coughing.
3. *Feel* for tenderness, stiffened neck, bulging fontanel (infants).
4. *Smell* ketones, vomit, alcohol, fecal-like odor.

Chest

1. *Look* for respiratory rates and patterns: rapid (tachypnea), slow (bradypnea), shallow, irregular, painful (splinted), periodic (Cheyne-Stokes). Chest wall movement: intercostal retractions, barrel chest, obvious malformations.
2. *Listen* for absence of lung sounds, presence of rales or wheezes in either lung field.
   a. Patients who can sit: use stethoscope to listen to posterior thorax at apex, mid-scapula, and base, starting at the base and moving toward the head to compare both sides (Fig. 2–1). Have the patient breathe with mouth open while stethoscope is being used.
   b. Patients who are unable to sit: listen to anterior part of chest at second intercostal space lateral to sternum.

Abdomen

1. *Look* for changes in general contour, distention, presence of pulsatile mass lateral to midline; note scars, location.
2. *Feel*. With the patient lying down, start at the point furthest from area stated to be painful by patient. Patient may flinch or

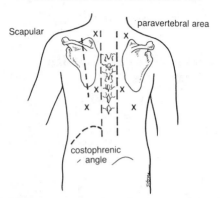

Figure 2–1. Surface anatomy of the back. The Xs indicate six places where lung sounds are auscultated on the back.

tense the muscles because of ticklishness or the examiner's cold hands. Confirm all reactions with patient verbally.

a. Begin with gentle palpation: Move fingers of one hand over the entire abdominal area, noting areas of tenderness, increased muscle resistance (spasm), or solid masses.

b. Deep palpation: With second hand pressing on top of the fingers of the first hand, slowly compress to a depth of 4–5 cm. Palpate the complete abdomen, noting tenderness or solid masses.

c. If there is a pulsating mass along midline between epigastrium and umbilicus, identify and mark the extent of the pulsatile mass, and check femoral pulses bilaterally for equal strength.

Extremities

1. *Look* for skin discoloration, moisture, texture, obvious deformities, symmetry, inflammation, edema of ankles and lower leg (note and mark extent), scars, needle marks, cyanosis of nail beds.

2. *Feel* for bilateral radial and/or pedal pulses, skin turgor of hands and arms, pitting edema (ankles, lower legs), equal bilateral grip strength, foot extension strength, equal movement, range of motion; touch for sensation.

TRAUMA SURVEY

The physical examination in patients with medical problems depends upon a careful interrogation and elicitation of past history. This directs the examiner to specific problem areas. The trauma patient must have a head-to-toe systematic examination. Knowing the mechanism of injury is important in understanding the extent of injury to the trauma patient. The EMT in charge, or his/her partner, must assess the accident scene for possible causes of injury. Remove or rearrange enough clothing to examine all parts of the body and to avoid missing hidden injuries.

Head, Eyes, Ears, Nose, Throat/Neck (HEENT)

Scalp
1. *Look* for areas of hemorrhage, hematoma, depressions, punctures.
2. *Feel* for deformity, blood. Neck must remain stable during exam; maintain in-line cervical traction.

Eyes
1. *Look* for constriction/dilation, unequal pupil size, deviated gaze, contact lenses, foreign objects, conjunctival discoloration, ecchymosis around eyes (raccoon eyes), other gross injuries. With pen light, check pupillary response to light, ability to follow an object through the full range of motion.
2. *Feel* for resistance by patient to opening eyelids, if behavioral disorder is suspected.

Ears
1. *Look* at outer ear and inside canal. *Look* for hemorrhage, drainage of clear or pink fluid, discoloration behind ear (mastoid area).

Nose
1. *Look* for hemorrhage, drainage of clear or pink fluid, deformity, nasal flaring.

Face
1. *Look* for wounds, discoloration.
2. *Feel* for deformity of cheekbones, instability of upper and lower jaw.

Mouth
1. *Look* for wounds, hemorrhage, discoloration (cyanosis, ecchymosis around lips), foreign objects, loose or missing teeth.
2. *Listen* for stridor, gurgling.

Neck (Anterior and Posterior)
1. *Look* for wounds, distended neck veins, stoma, deviated trachea, suprasternal retractions.
2. *Feel* for bony deformities, tenderness, muscle spasm, subcutaneous air.

Chest

1. *Look* for supraclavicular or intercostal retractions, wounds, discoloration, paradoxical respiratory movement (flail, diaphragmatic breathing), deformity.
2. *Listen* for sucking wounds, altered breath sounds (diminished or absent), wheezes or rales (anterior at second intercostal space and posteriorly above scapula), muffled or distant heart sounds (at apex, under left nipple).
3. *Feel* for deformity, tenderness, crepitus, muscle spasm; compress mid-sternum, gently, then firmly.

Abdomen

1. *Look* for wounds, discoloration, distention.
2. *Feel* for tenderness, muscle spasm (voluntary and involuntary). Palpate all four quadrants, gently, then deeply.

Lumbar Spine

1. *Feel* for tenderness, deformity, muscle spasm; minimize movement.

Pelvis

1. *Look* for wounds, discoloration, deformity.
2. *Feel* for deformity, tenderness, stability. Gently, then firmly, compress iliac crests toward midline, then downward. Palpate femoral pulses bilaterally for equality.

Buttocks/Genitalia

1. *Look* for wounds, discoloration.
2. *Feel* for tenderness.

Extremities

General

1. *Look* for wounds, deformity (swelling, angulation), discoloration (especially check skin color distal to an injury); ability to move spontaneously and on command.
2. *Feel* for tenderness, deformity.
   a. *Sensation:* check response to gentle touch (with patient looking away); then to painful stimuli.
   b. *Movement:* pain on movement, ability to move spontaneously and against resistance.
   c. *Pulses:* check distal circulation.

Legs
1. *Look* for ability to wiggle toes.
2. *Feel* for ability of foot to push against resistance.

Arms
1. *Look* for ability to wiggle fingers.
2. *Feel* for strength and equality of grasp.

RECORD VITAL SIGNS

1. Respiratory rate.
2. Pulse rate.
3. Blood pressure.
4. Skin: temperature, color, moistness.
5. State of consciousness.
6. Calculate Severity Index Score, if indicated (see Appendix 6 for Apgar and other scales).

REPORTING METHODS

Just as important as the ability to perform rapid and concise assessment and treatment is the ability to report these findings and treatment in an organized manner to persons giving the next level of medical care. The most practical and professional method is a written form, which is sent with the patient (e.g., fire department releasing the patient to an ambulance for transport) or left with the patient at the hospital by the treating EMT, if transported (Figs. 2–2, 2–3, 2–4, and 2–5). Written professionally, this report will be important for the physician. Hospitals make this report part of the patient's permanent medical record. It is a legal record and provides documentation of the pre-hospitalization findings and the care given. This report must be written by the EMT in charge of the patient; it cannot be left to another EMT, who may have only a partial idea of the details concerning the patient's condition and treatment.

NARRATIVE FORMAT

The most widely accepted format—S.O.A.P.—is patterned after the method used by much of the medical profession. It is a simple format that follows the same logic used in the patient interrogation and examination (Fig. 2–6).
1. S = *Subjective* (patient's symptoms). Include chief complaint(s),
Text continued on page 20

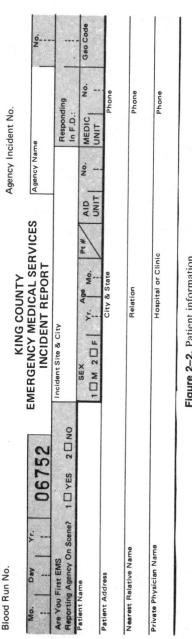

Figure 2–2. Patient information.

ACTION TAKEN

1 ☐ Examine Only
2 ☐ Examine & Assist
3 ☐ No Exam (Unneeded)
4 ☐ Exam/Treatment Refused

INCIDENT CODE

Mechanism
Type

SEVERITY

1 ☐ Non urgent
2 ☐ Urgent
3 ☐ Immediate Life Threat
4 ☐ Not Applicable

PROCEDURES

1 ☐ O_2
2 ☐ Wound Care
3 ☐ Extrication/Rescue
4 ☐ Splinting
5 ☐ Oral Airway/Bag Mask
6 ☐ ECG Monitor
7 ☐ Shock Trouser
8 ☐ CPR
9 ☐ Plan A–1
10 ☐ Plan A–2
11 ☐ Plan B
12 ☐ Endotracheal Intubation
13 ☐ IV–Central Line
14 ☐ IV–Peripheral
15 ☐ DC Shock By EMT
16 ☐ Intracardiac Injection
17 ☐ Flutter Valve
18 ☐ Pericardiocentesis
19 ☐ Cricothyrotomy
20 ☐ Esophageal Obturator
21 ☐ Other ______

PROCED NUMBER 12-20 ONLY | EMS NUMBER

ECG RHYTHM

1 ☐ Sinus
2 ☐ V Fib
3 ☐ V Tach
4 ☐ Asystole
5 ☐ Idioventricular
6 ☐ Other
7 ☐ Unknown

DR. CONTACTED 1 ☐ YES 2 ☐ NO

Name of Doctor and Hospital Contacted:

1. ______ 2. ______

Figure 2–3. Procedures.

Time Of Call (24 Hr.)	Response Time (Min.)		Out Of Service Time (Min.)		Source Of Alarm:	Responding From Quarters?	Transported To:
- - - - - - - - -	AID	- -	AID	- -	1 ☐ Citizen 2 ☐ Police 3 ☐ MD/RN 4 ☐ F.D. 5 ☐ Ambulance 6 ☐ Other	1 ☐ Yes 2 ☐ No	- -
	MEDIC	- -	MEDIC	- -			Transported By: - -
							Ambulance Response Time (Min.) - -

Figure 2–4. Dispatch information.

VITAL SIGNS	POSITION	BLOOD PRESSURE	PULSE RATE	RESPIRATORY RATE	CONSCIOUSNESS	PUPILS	
	←→	/		30 / Min.		☑ Conjugate	☑ Reactive
	↑__↓	200 / 140	120	Est. Air Exchange	☑ Alert		☐ Unreactive
				☐ Normal	☐ Semi-Conscious	☐ Dysconjugate	☐ Dilated
TIME 0430	↕	/		☑ Increased	☐ Comatose		☑ Mid
				☐ Decreased			☐ Constricted

FLOW CHART

TIME →	0435	0442	0447
Blood Pressure	200/130	186/126	184/124
Pulse Rate	120	110	110
Respiratory Rate	30	26	24
Consciousness	A/O →		
Pupils	M=R →		
Rhythm (ECG)	A-fib ē PVC's		
Morphine			
Oxygen	5 liters nasal → bag mask assist		
DC Shock			

Figure 2–5. Flow chart includes the initial set of vital signs, subsequent vital signs, and time taken, with space for other procedures as required.

Medications Taken By Patient At Home: NTG, Digitalis

Narrative (Subjective, Objective, Assessment, Plan)

S: 65 y/o ♂ c̄ sudden onset of aching, substernal chest pain. Rad. to Ⓛ arm, c̄ sweating, nausea. SOB. Pt. stated pain awoke him from sleep ≈ 0400 hrs today → took 2 NTG → no relief. Pt. recently req'd 2 pillows to avoid SOB @ night when sleeping. PHx-MI x 2, HypoI-T, Angina. Meds-NTG, Digitalis, all taken as prescribed.

O: Upon my arrival pt. sitting, A/O, grossly diaphoretic, pale, anxious, speaking in short phrases.
HEENT-Pupils PERL, neck veins distended c̄, pale, diaphoretic.
Chest-Rales bilat. from bases to apex.
Abdom-Distended c̄ ascities, palp. tender RUQ.
Ext- Pitting edema bilat. legs/ankles

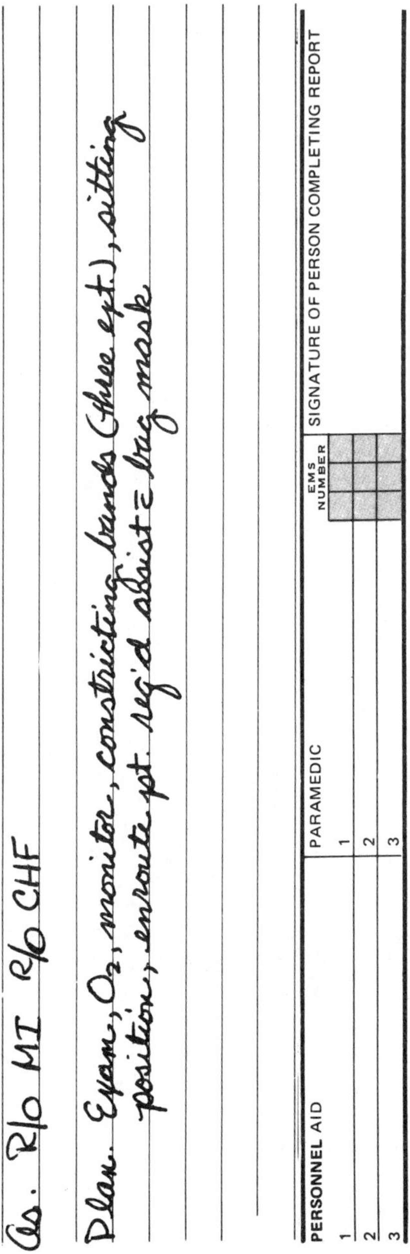

As. R/o MI R/o CHF

Plan. Exam, O₂, monitor, constricting bands (three ext.), sitting position, enroute pt. req'd assist c̄ bag mask

PERSONNEL AID	PARAMEDIC	EMS NUMBER	SIGNATURE OF PERSON COMPLETING REPORT
1	1		
2	2		
3	3		

Figure 2–6. Open narrative section for S.O.A.P. format.

associated symptoms, and time of onset as described by the patient, family, and witnesses. Include brief past history, current medications and when taken, and allergies. Condense to brief format, but use patient's language.

2. O = *Objective* (signs examiner sees, feels, etc.). General conditions of patient including age, sex, level of consciousness, emotional state, position or location as actually seen by examiner.
   a. HEENT: head, eyes, ears, nose, throat/neck, cervical spine. Include all signs in each area that are abnormal.
   b. Chest: thorax, front and back.
   c. Abdomen: list lumbar spine and pelvis separately when applicable.
   d. Extremities: arms/legs, hands/feet, including pulses.

3. A = *Assessment* (conclusion/impression). Using the term "rule out" (R/O) only suggests a diagnostic impression, not a firm diagnosis. More than one R/O may be listed, if applicable. Preface the conclusion with the term "possible" unless injury is obvious.

4. P = *Plan* (actual treatment). Include all methods of treatment and equipment used to treat patient, even when obvious. Record equipment left at the hospital with patient.

TRIAGE

A challenge facing the EMT is a setting with multiple casualties, especially at the outset when there are more patients then rescuers. Because of the numerous variations possible in any situation involving multiple victims, only a general outline of priorities is presented here. Common sense is the best rule to go by. For example, when there are not enough personnel to perform triage, the EMT in ch. ·ge must not stop and become involved in care of any one patient. Conversely, when the ratio of rescuers to patients is high, this rule can be modified. The EMT in charge becomes the triage officer. Each patient at triage should be tagged and given a treatment and transport priority.

TRIAGE CATEGORIES

1. Highest priority for treatment and transport:
   a. Airway and breathing difficulties.
   b. Severe hemorrhage.
   c. Severe chest injuries.
   d. Open abdominal wounds.
   e. Severe head injuries.

   f. Chronic medical problems; i.e., cardiac disease, diabetes, chronic obstructive pulmonary disease (COPD), if patients are severely symptomatic.
   g. Cardiac arrest—becomes third priority unless sufficient manpower is available.
   h. Severe shock.
2. Second priority to be treated and transported after highest priority patients:
   a. Burns without airway difficulty or severe hypotension.
   b. Major or multiple fractures.
   c. Back injuries, with or without spinal damage.
3. Third priority—last to be treated and transported:
   a. Minor fractures.
   b. Minor injuries.
   c. Obviously dead (gross injuries, decapitation).
   d. Obviously mortal wounds; decision not to treat is based upon available manpower, skill level of manpower, distance to hospital.

TRIAGE CARDS

Specially designed cards are available to attach to each patient after initial assessment to indicate which patients have been seen and the priority for treatment and transportation.

II

SIGNS AND SYMPTOMS

INTRODUCTION

The purpose of Part II is to provide an organized list of signs and symptoms in order to help guide the EMT through the steps of assessment, diagnosis (most likely condition, impression), and treatment (management). Signs and symptoms are included here only if they either (1) may be present in more than one condition and lead to the search for further signs and symptoms or (2) indicate the immediate need for some action by the EMT, such as treatment, stabilization, or rapid transport to advanced life support (ALS) services. It is often thought that the EMT needs to go through the following steps in sequence:

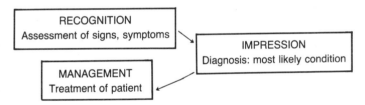

However, we believe that in many cases the patient is best served if the EMT progresses directly from recognition of signs and symptoms to immediate action (management).

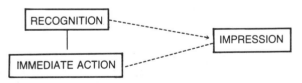

In these cases, the need for immediate action by the EMT, such as provision of oxygen therapy, is greater than the need for a detailed or prolonged search for an exact diagnosis.

Entries for each condition thus have two parts: *characteristics* and *immediate action.*

Characteristics are the guide to recognition of the condition—specific indications to look for in assessing the patient. The list does not include every possible sign or symptom of a condition, only those helpful in differentiating one cause of a symptom from another. Not all patients with a particular condition will show all of the characteristics listed. In fact, many will have only one or two, but the presence of these hallmarks will suggest that the particular condition is the most likely. In this way, the EMT forms an impression. This impression of the most likely condition can direct the EMT in management of the patient.

Immediate action is the basics only—specific indications for stabilization or rapid transport. All patient management is guided by severity of the patient's condition. The most severely injured or ill patients need the most rapid and aggressive therapy. Nevertheless, these immediate actions do not imply a halt in the thorough head-to-toe survey of the patient. A thorough search for other conditions (medical or trauma) is essential for good patient assessment. For the most severely ill or injured patient, "rapid transport" means that much of that search will continue while en route to ALS.

The listing of the causes for a particular symptom is in rough order of the importance for immediate action. This order is modified by the frequency of occurrence of the conditions. For the most part, traumatic conditions are not included in this section. Although they have been included here where they are useful, recognition of the most likely condition is usually based upon the history of the mechanism of injury. Furthermore, even (or perhaps especially) when the impression is not obvious, all patients with significant head or chest trauma need rapid transport to ALS, not a detailed, prolonged search for an exact diagnosis.

RAPID TRANSPORT

The term "rapid transport" is used throughout Part II to mean rapid provision of, or transport to, advanced life support services. In some urban and suburban communities, these services are provided in the field by paramedics in a "tiered response" system. In these systems, the EMS communication center dispatches the closest Basic Life Support (BLS) unit and the closest ALS unit simultaneously when a life-threatening emergency is suspected. Since there are fewer ALS units than BLS units, the ALS response time is greater, and the EMT at a BLS unit must manage the patient until the paramedics arrive. When a life-threatening emergency was not suspected by the dispatcher but is found to be present by the EMT, appropriate patient management requires a radio request for the ALS unit to respond.

In some communities, the ALS unit response will be delayed, usually because of the remote location of the emergency, causing prolonged travel times. In this circumstance, the EMT can request the dispatcher to arrange for ALS unit "intercept" (or "rendezvous"). This means that the ALS unit will start travelling toward the scene while the EMTs transport the patient in the BLS unit, and the two units will meet at some pre-arranged location in between.

In some other communities, no ALS services are available in the field. In this case, the EMT must recognize that rapid transport to the hospital may be the best management of the most severely ill or injured patient. The indications for "immediate action" in Part II attempt to put this need for rapid transport in the context of the patient's total needs. Naturally, the provision of airway control and ventilatory assistance, for example, must precede rapid transport. As stated above, for the most severely ill or injured patient, especially those with significant head or chest trauma, rapid transport has priority over the comprehensive patient examination. The term "rapid transport," then, is used in Part II when it is a critical part of the "immediate action."

ADRENALINE RESPONSE

The term "adrenaline response" is used in Part II and throughout the book to draw attention to the common response that many acutely ill or injured patients have, which makes many of the different medical conditions appear quite similar. The human body reacts to acute stress by the production of hormones, as if to prepare for what has been called "fight or flight." The preparation for "fight or flight" requires the body to increase the blood supply to vital areas and decrease it to non-essential areas. Thus, the heart rate speeds up, and blood is diverted from the skin (making it cool and pale) and diverted from the gastrointestinal tract (causing nausea). The pupils of the eyes dilate to improve vision, and circulation is increased to the brain (causing increased awareness but also anxiety) and to the skeletal muscles. The sweat glands on the hands also are activated (possibly this helped our prehistoric ancestors hold onto their clubs). The hormone principally causing these effects, epinephrine, is also known as adrenaline. Epinephrine is released when the body is trying to compensate for some acute insult. It does not matter whether the insult is a disease or an injury; the response is the same, and the signs and symptoms of that response only indicate that the body is attempting to compensate. Therefore, the observation by the EMT that a patient is exhibiting an adrenaline response is not enough for determining the underlying problem. The EMT must look further—beyond the rapid pulse; pale, cool, clammy skin; anxiety; thirst; and nausea—to the underlying cause. Instead of a separate list of all these signs and symptoms, in Part II the term "adrenaline response" is used to indicate this common compensatory action when it may be present.

3

RESPIRATORY DISTRESS

DYSPNEA (SHORTNESS OF BREATH)

Definition. Subjective difficulty in breathing. Sensation of not getting enough air. Respiratory rate increased. May speak in short phrases only.

Causes	Characteristics	Immediate Action
CHF/Pulmonary edema	Past cardiac history, rales, frothy cough, nocturnal onset, position dependence (orthopnea).	Oxygen. Assist ventilation if necessary. Sitting position. Rotating tourniquets if EMT is trained in use.
COPD	Past history, yellow-green sputum, pursed lip breathing.	Low flow oxygen if cyanotic. Obtain physician concurrence if possible. Monitor respirations closely.
Asthma	Past medical history, often rapid onset of acute attack, wheezes usually in all lung fields, prolonged expiration with quick inspiration.	Humidified oxygen, sitting position.
Airway obstruction (partial)	Present history of incident, stridor.	If air exchange is good, oxygen and transport. If air exchange is poor, back blows and manual thrusts.
Croup	Stridor, barking cough, common age six months to three years.	Cool, humidified oxygen; gentle handling.
Epiglottitis	Rapid onset; position: upright, leaning forward, chin thrust out; drooling, pain on swallowing, stridor; fever; common age two to seven years.	Humidified oxygen, sitting position, *avoid any stimulation of mouth or throat* (no airway, no suctioning), rapid transport.
Anaphylaxis	Past medical history of hypersensitivity; present history of exposure; skin: itching, swelling, rash, hives; hoarseness, stridor; hypotension; tachycardia.	Oxygen; venous tourniquet above site if stung; if hypotensive, position flat with legs raised; anti-shock trousers (MAST); rapid transport to ALS.
Pulmonary embolism	Sudden onset, history of recent inactivity (such as post-surgery), pregnancy, inflamed veins, heart valve surgery, birth control pill use, sharp chest pain, pink sputum, wheezes audible near pain source.	Oxygen, therapy for shock if hypotensive.

Causes	Characteristics	Immediate Action
Pneumothorax (spontaneous)	Sudden onset; sharp, unilateral chest pain; history of vigorous coughing; decreased sounds unilaterally; possible tracheal shift toward affected side.	Oxygen, avoid positive pressure ventilation if possible, position lying with affected side down.
Pneumonia	Fever, shaking chills, chest pain on inspiration, cough, dark sputum, rales or rhonchi usually involving one lung only.	Oxygen, position of comfort.

HYPOVENTILATION

Definition. Reduced rate and/or depth of breathing, resulting in decreased exchange of air. Rates less than 10 per minute usually do not exchange enough air. Depth of ventilation is inadequate when breath sounds are audible only at the top portion of the lungs.

Immediate Action. Oxygen therapy and ventilatory assistance. Rapid provision of (or transport to) advanced life support (ALS) services.

Causes	Characteristics	Immediate Action
Chest injury: pneumo- or hemothorax	Penetrating injury with sucking wound, blunt injury with multiple rib fractures or flail, paradoxical chest wall movement, unilateral reduced breath sounds.	Seal sucking wounds, oxygen therapy, airway control, ventilatory assistance, position with injured side down, observe for possible progression to tension pneumothorax.
Cerebral injury: trauma or CVA	Head injury, unilateral paralysis or sensory loss.	Oxygen, airway control, ventilatory assistance.
Drugs: depressants	History of opiate or sedative use, bradycardia.	Oxygen, airway control, ventilatory assistance.
Hypothermia	Cold skin	Oxygen, airway control, ventilatory assistance, rewarm the core before the extremities (heated oxygen or hot packs to chest and neck).

HYPERVENTILATION

Definition. Increased rate and/or depth of breathing. Rates of greater than 20 per minute are excessive.

Causes	Characteristics	Immediate Action
Shock	Hypotension from hypovolemia, cardiac pump failure, or vasodilation; signs of adrenaline response: fast pulse, pallor, diaphoresis, nausea.	Oxygen, maintain body heat, anti-shock trousers (MAST), rapid transport

Causes	Characteristics	Immediate Action
COPD	Past history, yellow-green sputum, pursed lip breathing.	Low flow oxygen if cyanotic. Obtain physician concurrence if possible. Monitor respirations closely.
CHF/Pulmonary edema	Past cardiac history, rales, frothy cough.	Oxygen. Assist ventilation if necessary. Sitting position. Rotating tourniquets if EMT is trained in use.
Airway obstruction (partial)	Present history of incident, stridor, dyspnea.	If air exchange is good, oxygen and transport. If air exchange is poor, back blows and manual thrusts.
Pain	Injury or illness.	Treat cause.
Anxiety	Peripheral numbness and tingling.	Paper bag or rebreather mask.
Drugs: stimulants	History of stimulant use, tachycardia.	Call local Poison Control Center for assistance.

DIAPHRAGMATIC BREATHING

Definition. Breathing efforts performed by the contraction of the diaphragm alone, without the assistance of the intercostal muscles. Upper abdomen bulges with inspiration.

Causes	Characteristics	Immediate Action
Airway obstruction (complete)	Present history of incident, intercostal and supraclavicular retractions.	Back blows, manual thrusts.
Spinal cord injury	Present history of incident, injury above C6.	Stabilization of cervical spine, oxygen.

ABNORMAL BREATH SOUNDS

Stridor

Definition. Shrill, high-pitched sound heard on inhalation, originating in narrowing of the upper airway.

Causes	Characteristics	Immediate Action
Anaphylaxis	Past medical history of hypersensitivity; present history of exposure; skin: itching, swelling, rash, hives; hoarseness, dyspnea, hypotension, tachycardia.	Oxygen, venous tourniquet above site if stung; if hypotensive: position flat with legs raised, anti-shock trousers (MAST); rapid transport to ALS.
Croup	Dyspnea, barking cough, common age six months to three years.	Cool humidified oxygen, gentle handling.

Causes	Characteristics	Immediate Action
Epiglottitis	Rapid onset; position: upright, leaning forward, chin thrust out; drooling; pain on swallowing; dyspnea; fever; common age two to seven years.	Humidified oxygen; sitting position; *avoid any stimulation of mouth or throat* (*no* airway, *no* suctioning); rapid transport.
Airway obstruction (partial)	Present history of incident, rapid respiratory rate, dyspnea.	If air exchange is good, oxygen and transport. If air exhange is poor, back blows, manual thrusts.
Trauma to the neck	Present history of incident, blunt trauma, superheated air, bruises, deformity, loss of voice, swelling, subcutaneous emphysema.	Suspect spinal cord injury, stabilize neck; oxygen, coach to breathe slowly, monitor closely for progression to total obstruction.

Wheezes

Definition. High-pitched, whistling noises produced by air flowing through narrowed airways. Just as pursing the lips produces a whistle, wheezes can sound musical. Often audible without a stethoscope, wheezing is usually louder during the expiratory phase.

Causes	Characteristics	Immediate Action
Airway obstruction (partial)	Present history of incident, rapid respiratory rate, dyspnea.	If air exchange is good, oxygen and transport. If air exchange is poor, back blows, manual thrusts.
Asthma	Past medical history, often rapid onset of acute attack, dyspnea, prolonged expiration with quick inspiration.	Humidified oxygen, sitting position.
CHF/Pulmonary edema	Past cardiac history, dyspnea, frothy cough, rales. Nocturnal onset, position dependence (orthopnea). Lung bases may be silent in severe cases.	Oxygen. Assist ventilation if necessary. Sitting position. Rotating tourniquets, if EMT is trained in use.
Pulmonary embolism	Sudden onset, history of recent inactivity (such as post-surgery), pregnancy, inflamed veins, heart valve surgery, birth control pill use, dyspnea, sharp chest pain, tachycardia, pink sputum, wheezes audible near the pain source.	Oxygen, therapy for shock if hypotensive.

Causes	Characteristics	Immediate Action
Anaphylaxis	Past medical history of hypersensitivity, present history of exposure; skin: itching, swelling, rash, hives; hoarseness, dyspnea, hypotension, tachycardia.	Oxygen; venous tourniquet above site if stung; if hypotensive, position flat with legs raised, anti-shock trousers (MAST); rapid transport to ALS.

Rales and Rhonchi

Definition. *Rales* are fine crackling sounds much like the sound produced by rolling strands of hair between the fingers, next to your ear. They originate from fluid in the alveoli. The greater the amount of fluid, the louder and more bubbly the sound. *Rhonchi* originate from fluid or mucus in the bronchioles or bronchi, and are louder, coarser, and wetter than rales.

Causes	Characteristics	Immediate Action
CHF/Pulmonary edema	Past cardiac history, dyspnea, frothy cough. Nocturnal onset, position dependence (orthopnea). Lung bases may be silent in severe cases.	Oxygen. Assist ventilation if necessary. Sitting position. Rotating tourniquet if EMT is trained in use.
COPD	Past history, dyspnea; yellow-green sputum, pursed lip breathing. Lung bases may be silent in severe cases.	Low flow oxygen if cyanotic. Obtain physician concurrence if possible. Monitor respirations closely.
Pneumonia	Fever, shaking chills, dyspnea, chest pain on inspiration, cough, dark sputum, usually involves one lung only.	Oxygen, position of comfort.

4

CIRCULATORY/CARDIOVASCULAR DISTRESS

CHEST PAIN

Definition. Subjective sensation, can be described as "heavy," "squeezing," "crushing," "tight," etc. Ask patient about: pain quality, intensity, onset, duration, location, radiation, aggravation, alleviation, nausea, dyspnea, and past medical history.

Causes	Characteristics	Immediate Action
CARDIAC		
Myocardial infarction (heart attack)	Substantial chest pain, radiation to arms, neck, jaw; weakness; dizziness; irregular pulse; palpitations; dyspnea; signs of adrenaline response: fast pulse, pallor, diaphoresis, nausea.	Oxygen; gentle handling; semi-reclining position; monitor closely for possible onset of cardiogenic shock, pulmonary edema, cardiac arrest.
Angina	Past history; substernal pressure; radiation; onset with exertion, cold, emotional stress; relieved by rest, nitroglycerin; duration less than 10 minutes.	Oxygen.
Pericarditis	Substernal or pre-cordial pain.	Oxygen.
PULMONARY		
Dyspnea	See previous chapter, page 26.	
Pulmonary embolism	Sharp pain, sudden onset; history of recent inactivity (such as post-surgery), pregnancy, inflamed veins, heart valve surgery, birth control pill use, pink sputum, wheezes audible near the pain source, dyspnea, hyperventilation.	Oxygen, therapy for shock if hypotensive.
Pneumothorax (spontaneous)	Sharp unilateral pain; sudden onset; present history of incident; coughing; decreased breath sounds unilaterally; possible tracheal shift toward affected side; dyspnea.	Oxygen, avoid positive pressure ventilation if possible, position with affected side down.

Causes	*Characteristics*	*Immediate Action*
Pleurisy (pleuritis)	Localized pain, increased with deep inspiration, coughing; may be associated with pulmonary embolism or infection.	Oxygen, position of comfort.
CHEST WALL MUSCLES	Unilateral pain, aggravated by movement (twisting, bending) or palpation.	Examine to rule out traumatic injury such as pneumothorax, cardiac tamponade, or lacerated liver or spleen.
AORTIC ANEURYSM	Pain radiating to abdomen, back; history of hypertension.	Oxygen, shock therapy if hypotensive, rapid transport.
ESOPHAGITIS	Substernal pain, "burning" relieved by antacids.	Sitting position.
GALL BLADDER INFLAMMATION (CHOLECYSTITIS)	Pain in right lower chest, abdominal pain in right upper quadrant (RUQ), radiation to right scapula.	None.
ANXIETY	Hyperventilation, peripheral numbness or tingling, high systolic pressure with normal diastolic pressure.	Paper bag or rebreather mask.

TACHYCARDIA

Definition. Increased heart rate. Adults: over 100 beats per minute; infants: over 140 beats per minute.

Causes	*Characteristics*	*Immediate Action*
Shock	Hypotension from hypovolemia, cardiac pump failure, or vasodilation; signs of adrenaline response: fast pulse, pallor, diaphoresis, nausea.	Oxygen, maintain body heat, anti-shock trousers (MAST) at direction of physician, rapid transport.
Myocardial infarction (heart attack)	Substernal chest pain, radiation to arms, neck, jaw; weakness, dizziness; palpitations, irregular pulse, dyspnea; signs of adrenaline response: fast pulse, pallor, diaphoresis, nausea.	Oxygen; gentle handling; semi-reclining position; monitor closely for possible onset of cardiogenic shock, pulmonary edema, cardiac arrest.
Pain or fear	Injury or illness.	Treat cause.
Anxiety	Hyperventilation, peripheral numbness or tingling, high systolic blood pressure with normal diastolic pressure.	Paper bag or rebreather mask.

Causes	Characteristics	Immediate Action
Drugs (stimulants)	History of stimulant use, hyperventilation.	Call local Poison Control Center for assistance.

BRADYCARDIA

Definition. Decreased heart rate. Adults: less than 60 beats per minute. Well-trained athletes may have resting rates as low as 40 beats per minute without adverse effects.
Immediate Action. Oxygen therapy.

Causes	Characteristics	Immediate Action
Head injury	Trauma, hypoventilation, hypertension.	Oxygen, airway control, ventilatory assistance.
Pacemaker failure	Past cardiac history, palpable pacemaker under skin.	Oxygen.
Drugs (depressants)	History of opiate or sedative use, hypoventilation.	Oxygen, call Poison Control Center.
Shock (terminal stage)	Hypotension from hypovolemia, cardiac pump failure or vasodilation.	Oxygen, maintain body heat, anti-shock trousers (MAST), rapid transport.
Hypoxemia (terminal stage)	Massive injury or severe illness.	Oxygen, rapid transport.

HYPOTENSION

Definition. Systolic blood pressure less than 90 mm Hg. Postural hypotension exists when there is an increase in pulse rate of 20 beats per minute or more, or a decrease in systolic pressure of 20 mm Hg or more, when the patient is moved from a supine to a sitting position.

Causes	Characteristics	Immediate Action
Hypovolemia	Fluid loss from external hemorrhage, internal hemorrhage (dissecting aortic aneurysm, ruptured ectopic pregnancy, gastrointestinal bleeding), or plasma volume loss (burns, ascites, dehydration, hyperglycemia). Signs and symptoms are specific to the cause. Signs of adrenaline response: fast pulse, pallor, diaphoresis, nausea.	Oxygen, maintain body heat, anti-shock trousers (MAST), rapid transport.

Causes	Characteristics	Immediate Action
Cardiogenic shock	Cardiac pump failure from heart attack or trauma (cardiac tamponade, tension pneumothorax). Signs and symptoms are specific to the cause. Signs of right heart failure: distended neck veins, peripheral edema. Signs of left heart failure: pulmonary edema. Signs of adrenaline response: fast pulse, pallor, diaphoresis, nausea.	Oxygen, rapid transport. Anti-shock trousers (MAST) only at direction of physician.
Vasodilation	Peripheral pooling of blood from sepsis, anaphylaxis, or neurogenesis (central nervous system injury, overdose). Signs and symptoms are specific to the cause. Signs of adrenaline response: fast pulse, diaphoresis, nausea; skin is not pale or cool, but warm and of good color.	Oxygen, maintain body heat, anti-shock trousers (MAST), rapid transport.

HYPERTENSION

Definition. Systolic blood pressure of over 140 mm Hg or diastolic pressure of over 90 mm Hg. Malignant hypertension exists when the blood pressure is dangerously high, often 200/140 mm Hg or higher. Hypertension can be associated with (although it is not caused by) cerebral vascular accident, aortic aneurysm, congestive heart failure/pulmonary edema, or angina.

Causes	Characteristics	Immediate Action
Head injury	Trauma; bradycardia; hypoventilation.	Oxygen, airway control, ventilatory assistance.
Essential hypertension (cause unknown)	Past medical history.	Oxygen.
Toxemia of pregnancy	First pregnancy, edema, headache, seizures.	Oxygen, minimize external stimulation.
Anxiety	Hyperventilation, peripheral numbness or tingling, high systolic pressure with normal diastolic pressure.	Paper bag or rebreather mask.

5

CENTRAL NERVOUS SYSTEM

HEADACHE

Definition. Subjective sensation of pain in the head. Headache can be seen in a wide variety of medical conditions. Its onset can be gradual or very sudden. This section is only concerned with the headache of sudden, acute onset.

Causes	Characteristics	Immediate Action
Cerebrovascular accident (CVA): hemorrhage	Subarachnoid rupture: severe headache, rapid progression to coma, history of hypertension, stiff neck.	Oxygen, airway control, exam.
Toxemia of pregnancy (eclampsia)	Primigravida, edema, hypertension, seizures.	Oxygen, exam.
Chemical agent: carbon monoxide	Toxic environment.	100% oxygen, airway control, ventilatory assistance as needed.
Hypertension	Past medical history, nosebleed, diastolic pressure > 120 mm Hg.	Oxygen.
Meningitis	Stiff neck, onset may be over hours rather than sudden; fever.	Communicable disease precautions (masks, etc.).

PARALYSIS

Definition. Reduction or complete loss of the ability to move. Partial paralysis may appear as subtle weakness or lack of coordination.

Causes	Characteristics	Immediate Action
CVA	Unilateral paralysis, throat muscle paralysis affecting swallowing or speech, history of atherosclerosis, hypertension, headache.	Oxygen, airway control.
Head injury: trauma	Bradycardia, hypertension, hypoventilation.	Oxygen, airway control, ventilatory assistance, spinal immobilization, rapid transport.
Cervical spine injury: trauma	Paralysis below the neck, diaphragmatic breathing.	Stabilization of cervical spine, oxygen.
Lumbar spine injury: trauma	Paralysis below the waist.	Stabilization of lumbar spine.
Chemical agent: poisoning, snakebite, insect bite	Full bilateral paralysis.	Treat cause, isolate exposure site.

COMA

Definition. Unresponsiveness to both verbal and painful stimuli. Because injury or illness in any of the body's systems may lead to coma, it is important not to rely on one major clue and ignore other important findings. For example, the injured patient may have a medical problem that led to the injury. Likewise, the comatose patient who smells of alcohol may have a head injury or a diabetic emergency.

Immediate Action. Oxygen, airway control, thorough exam, careful monitoring, position on side.

Causes	Characteristics	Immediate Action
ANATOMIC/ STRUCTURAL		
Trauma: head injury	Bradycardia, hypertension, hypoventilation.	Oxygen, airway control, ventilatory assistance, spinal immobilization, rapid transport.
CVA-ischemia/hemorrhage	History of atherosclerosis, hypertension, headache; unilateral paralysis; facial asymmetry.	Oxygen, airway control.
Shock: insufficient cerebral circulation	Hypotension from hypovolemia, cardiac pump failure, or vasodilation. Signs of adrenaline response: fast pulse, pallor, diaphoresis.	Oxygen, airway control, maintain body heat, anti-shock trousers (MAST), rapid transport.
Seizure: post-ictal (see also Seizures [Convulsions])	History of convulsion.	Oxygen, airway control.
METABOLIC		
Hypoglycemia (low blood sugar)	History of diabetes, sudden onset; drooling; adrenaline response: fast pulse, pallor, diaphoresis.	Oxygen, airway control, suction, exam. Sugar: 40% dextrose, oral liquid preparation, placed inside the cheek in small amounts, repeatedly.
Hyperglycemia (high blood sugar)	History of diabetes, gradual onset; infection, hyperventilation, ketone breath, fever, dehydration.	Oxygen, airway control. If in doubt whether patient has low or high blood sugar, give 40% dextrose as above.
Oxygen deficit: hypoxia	Environmental (asphyxia, toxic gas), respiratory distress (see Chapter 3).	Oxygen, airway control.
Drug/alcohol overdose	History of incident.	Oxygen, airway control, exam, identify the drug, save vomitus.
Infection (septicemia, meningitis, etc.)	History of illness, fever, stiff neck, febrile seizures.	Oxygen, airway control, exam. Communicable disease precautions (masks, etc.).

METABOLIC *(Continued)*

Heat stroke	Hot, red skin (see Chapter 7).	Oxygen, airway control, rapid cooling.
Other	Imbalance of the body chemistry (electrolytes, calcium, water); failure of organ systems (kidney, liver, thyroid, adrenal); CO_2 narcosis (COPD). Signs and symptoms are specific to the cause; e.g., jaundice and distended abdomen (ascites) in a known alcoholic suggest hepatic coma.	Oxygen, airway control.
Psychogenic ("pseudocoma")	History of incident; fluttering eyelids, especially when touched lightly.	Cautious handling.

SYNCOPE (Fainting)

Definition. Transient state of unconsciousness from which the victim has recovered. Unresponsiveness for longer than 3 minutes in the supine position is considered to be coma (see previous section).

Causes	Characteristics	Immediate Action
Cardiac rhythm disturbance (Stokes-Adams)	Irregular pulse, elderly patient.	Position flat, lower legs raised; oxygen.
Postural hypotension	Hypotension from hypovolemia, cardiac pump failure, or vasodilation.	Oxygen, airway control, position flat, lower legs raised.
Venous pooling (orthostatic)	History of prolonged standing motionless, especially in the heat, or sudden standing after prolonged sitting or lying.	Position flat, lower legs raised.
Vasovagal (vasodepressor)	History consistent with stimulation of the vagus nerve: neck manipulation (such as sudden turning or tight collar), straining to urinate or defecate, coughing; can occur while sitting or lying; bradycardia.	Position flat, lower legs raised, loosen tight clothing.
Psychogenic (anxiety, fear, pain)	Vagal stimulation from pain or fear, respiratory alkalosis from hyperventilation, staged faint (hysterical "pseudo-syncope").	Position flat, lower legs raised.
Cerebrovascular insufficiency (TIA)	History of atherosclerosis, hypertension, headache; unilateral weakness or numbness, temporary loss of speech or vision.	Reassurance, monitor progression of symptoms or return to function.

Causes	*Characteristics*	*Immediate Action*
Drug overdose (common prescription medicines)	Medication history can include Inderal (propanolol), insulin, diuretics, nitroglycerin, narcotics.	Position flat, lower legs raised.

SEIZURES (Convulsions)

Definition. Sudden episode of involuntary muscular contraction and relaxation; may involve generalized tonic-clonic activity (grand mal), followed by post-ictal unconsciousness and then confusion, or may be focal, with localized twitching or jerking. Status epilepticus exists when there is a rapid succession of repeated seizures without regaining of consciousness during the intervals.

Immediate Action: Protect from injury, oxygen, suction, position on side after seizure is complete.

Causes	*Characteristics*	*Immediate Action*
Epilepsy	Generalized fits, history, aura, incontinence, post-ictal drooling, hyperventilation, tachycardia.	Protect from injury, oxygen, position on side.
Head injury: trauma	Bradycardia, hypertension, hypoventilation.	Oxygen, airway control, ventilatory assistance, spinal immobilization, rapid transport.
CVA: ischemia, hemorrhage	History of atherosclerosis, hypertension, headache; unilateral paralysis.	Oxygen, airway control.
Drug/alcohol overdose or withdrawal	History.	Oxygen, airway control, identify the drug, save vomitus.
Oxygen deficit: hypoxia	Environmental (asphyxia, toxic gas); respiratory distress (see Chapter 3); hypotension, cardiac arrhythmias (see Chapter 4).	Oxygen, airway control.
Hypoglycemia (low blood sugar)	Diabetic history, sudden onset, drooling, signs of adrenaline response: fast pulse, pallor, diaphoresis.	Oxygen, airway control, suction, exam. When seizure stops, give sugar: 40% dextrose, oral preparation, placed inside the cheek in small amounts, repeatedly.
Infection: childhood febrile seizures	History of illness, fever, stiff neck. Check for stiff neck while patient is in post-ictal state by flexing head forward: chest to chin.	Oxygen, airway control; exam. Cool with tepid sponging. If neck stiff: communicable disease precautions (masks, etc.).
Heat exhaustion: sodium depletion	History; heat cramps; pale, moist skin; orthostatic syncope.	Position flat, lower legs raised; oxygen; airway control; cool with ice packs to armpits, neck, groin if available.
Toxemia of pregnancy (eclampsia)	Primigravida, edema, headache, hypertension.	Oxygen, airway control.

Causes	Characteristics	Immediate Action
Psychogenic: "hysterical seizures"	Bizarre random thrashing.	Cautious handling.

PUPILS

Definition. The pupil is the opening in the colored iris, which contracts when exposed to bright light. Both pupils should react equally even if the light source is focused into only one pupil. Nystagmus—rapid, repetitive eye movements—can occur with overdoses of sedatives, Dilantin, or alcohol.

Table 5–1. PUPILLARY STATUS CHART

Pupil	Equal		Unequal	
	Reactive	*Unreactive*	*Reactive*	*Unreactive*
Dilated	Hypoxia Pain Drugs alcohol stimulants Dim light (normal)	Anoxia Seizures Drugs glutethimide (Doriden) belladonna (atropine) psychodelics		CVA Head injury Eye trauma
Mid	Normal	Hypothermia Methanol	Normal in 4% of popu- lation	Glass eye
Constricted to Pinpoint	Bright light (normal)	Drugs opiates barbiturates Brainstem injury		

ABDOMINAL PAIN

Definition. The term "acute abdomen" refers to conditions in which the abdominal lining is inflamed and painful. The pain can be characterized by location, radiation, onset/duration, constancy, and associated symptoms or signs. Related signs include abdominal distention, vomiting bloody or "coffee-ground" material (hematemesis), or bloody or tarry black stools. Physical exam may reveal abdominal rigidity, tenderness, or a pulsating belly mass (aortic aneurysm).

Causes	Characteristics	Immediate Action
In the field, it is often difficult to assess the specific cause of abdominal pain, such as from blood, acids, or feces from diseased or damaged organs.	Inflamed abdominal lining (peritonitis) can often be rapidly diagnosed by performing palpation and quickly removing the palpating hand from the abdominal surface (rebound tenderness).	Position of comfort, oxygen, monitor closely for signs of impending shock, transport.

Abdominal and gastrointestinal disorders are discussed more fully in Chapter 12.

Definitions. Assessment of the most likely condition through exam of the skin focuses on three aspects: color, temperature, and moistness. *Color:* normal skin is pink (mucous membranes in non-Caucasians) because of oxygenated blood in capillaries of normal size. Dilated skin vessels cause red skin; constricted skin vessels, pale skin. *Temperature:* normal skin is warm because of warm blood in capillaries. *Moistness:* normal skin is dry. Some medical conditions are notable for other skin findings: *Edema* (swelling) can be seen in injury, heart failure, or anaphylaxis. *Subcutaneous emphysema* (air crackling beneath the skin) can be seen in tracheal injury or pneumothorax.

PALE, COOL SKIN

Causes	Characteristics	Immediate Action
MOIST PALE, COOL SKIN		
Adrenaline response	Compensatory response to acute illness or injury, fast pulse, pallor, diaphoresis, nausea.	Treat cause if possible.
Fear/fright	Psychogenic adrenaline response.	Reassurance.
Hypovolemia	Hypotension; adrenaline response.	Therapy for shock: oxygen, maintain body heat, anti-shock trousers (MAST), rapid transport.
Heat exhaustion: sodium and water depletion	History, heat cramps, orthostatic syncope.	Position flat, lower legs raised; cool packs to armpits, neck, groin; fluids to drink.
DRY PALE, COOL SKIN		
Normal reaction to cold exposure	Normal compensatory response.	No action.
Hypothermia	If mild to moderate: conscious, CNS dysfunction (motor, sensory, judgment). If severe: may be unresponsive.	If mild to moderate: protect from environment, remove wet clothing, insulate; rewarm the core before the extremities (heated oxygen or hot packs to chest and neck); carbohydrate intake; exam. If severe: gentle handling; oxygen, rapid transport.

RED, HOT SKIN

Causes	Characteristics	Immediate Action
MOIST RED, HOT SKIN		
Normal reaction to heat exposure	Normal compensatory response.	No action.
Exertional heat stroke	Hot, humid environment; athletic exertion; hypotension; psychological changes, coma; temperature over 41°C (106°F).	Rapid cooling, oxygen, airway control.
DRY RED, HOT SKIN		
Infection (fever)	History of illness, stiff neck, febrile seizures, coma.	Oxygen, airway control, exam. Cool with tepid sponging. If neck stiff: communicable disease precautions (masks, etc.).
Classic heat stroke	Hot, humid environment; elderly; chronic disease; hypotension; dehydration; vasodilation; coma; temperature over 41°C (106°F).	Rapid cooling, oxygen, airway control.
Dehydration	Poor skin turgor, "tenting," sunken eyes, dry mucous membranes.	Examine for cause (diabetic ketoacidosis/hyperglycemia, childhood diarrhea, vomiting, ascites).

NORMAL TEMPERATURE

Causes	Characteristics	Immediate Action
PALE, DRY SKIN		
Anemia	Internal or external bleeding, often chronic.	Oxygen.
RED, DRY SKIN		
Anaphylaxis (with rash)	Past medical history of hypersensitivity, present history of exposure; itching, swelling, hives; hoarseness; dyspnea; hypotension; tachycardia.	Oxygen; venous tourniquet above site if stung; if hypotensive: position flat with lower legs raised, anti-shock trousers (MAST); rapid transport to ALS.
Carbon monoxide poisoning	Toxic environment.	100% oxygen, airway control, ventilatory assistance.
BLUE SKIN (cyanosis)		
Hypoxemia	Inadequate oxygenation of the tissues from respiratory or cardiac failure.	Oxygen, airway control, ventilatory assistance.
YELLOW SKIN (jaundice)		
Liver disease	Distended abdomen (ascites), history of alcoholism.	None.
Gall bladder inflammation (cholecystitis)	Right lower chest pain, abdominal pain in RUQ, radiation to right scapula.	None.

Table 7-1. SKIN COLOR, TEMPERATURE, AND MOISTNESS

Temperature	Pale		Pink/Red		Blue (Cyanosis)	Yellow (Jaundice)
	Moist	Dry	Moist	Dry		
Cool	Adrenaline response Fear/fright Shock Low blood sugar Heat exhaustion	Normal reaction to cold exposure Hypothermia				
Normal		Anemia		Anaphylaxis (with rash) Carbon monoxide High blood sugar	Hypoxemia	Liver disease Gall bladder disease
Hot			Normal reaction to heat exposure Exertional heat stroke	Infection (fever) Classic heat stroke		

III

SPECIFIC EMERGENCIES

8

ARREST

AIRWAY OBSTRUCTION AND CHOKING

Foreign body obstruction of the airway commonly occurs during eating. Meat is the most common cause of obstruction in adults. Various other foods and foreign bodies cause choking in children. Factors associated with choking on food include large, poorly chewed pieces of food; elevated blood alcohol; and upper and lower dentures. Choking emergencies occurring in restaurants have been mistaken for a heart attack, giving rise to the name "cafe coronary."

When the airway is obstructed, the EMT must open it as rapidly as possible. The following figures show the methods for opening an obstructed airway suggested by the American Heart Association. Advanced life support assistance should also be requested if available.

EMT Treatment of Conscious Patient, Sitting or Standing

1. Establish presence of complete obstruction. Identify complete airway obstruction by asking patient, "Can you speak?" Look, listen, and feel for breathing.
2. Encourage the victim to cough. If the victim is still able to move some air past the obstruction, his efforts will be more effective than the EMT's.
3. If there is no air moving past the obstruction, administer four back blows (Figure 8–1). Deliver four sharp blows rapidly and forcibly to the patient's back between the shoulder blades; support the patient's chest with the other hand.
4. If the above procedure fails, give four abdominal thrusts (Figure 8–2). Stand behind the patient and wrap your arms around his waist. Grasp one fist with your other hand and place the thumb side of your fist between breastbone and navel. Press fist into the abdomen with quick upward thrusts.
   a. The sequence of back blows and abdominal or chest thrusts may be more effective than either maneuver used alone.
5. An alternative to abdominal thrusts is four chest thrusts (Figure 8–3). Stand behind the patient and place your arms under the patient's armpits to encircle the chest. Grasp one fist with the other hand and place the thumb side of your fist on the breastbone. Press with quick backward thrusts.
   a. Chest thrusts are more easily delivered than abdominal

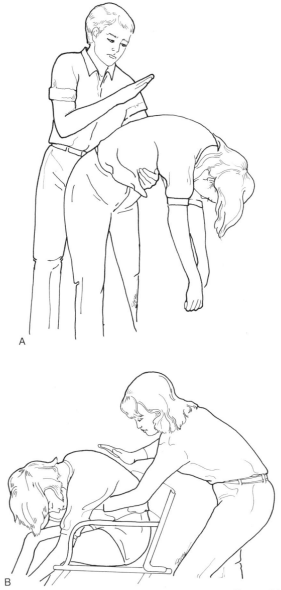

A

B

Figure 8–1. Back blows. *A*, Conscious patient in standing position. *B*, Conscious patient in sitting position.

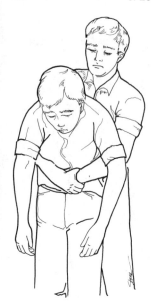

Figure 8–2. Abdominal thrusts. Patient in standing position.

Figure 8–3. Chest thrusts. Conscious patient in standing position.

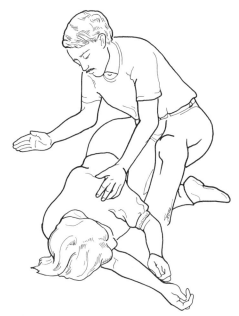

Figure 8–4. Back blows. Unconscious patient lying down.

thrusts when the abdominal girth is large, as in gross obesity or advanced pregnancy.
6. If obstruction remains, repeat the above sequence as often as necessary until the obstruction is relieved or the victim becomes unconscious.

EMT Treatment of Unconscious Victim, Supine

1. Establish unresponsiveness. Shake shoulder and shout, "Are you okay?" Call for help as required.
2. Open airway. Establish breathlessness. Look, listen, and feel with patient lying on back, face up.
   a. Use head tilt with one hand on patient's forehead and neck or chin lift with other hand.
3. Attempt ventilation. If airway remains obstructed, reposition the patient's head and reattempt ventilation.
4. If airway remains obstructed, give four back blows (Figure 8–4). Roll patient toward you, using your thigh for support. Give four forceful and rapidly delivered blows to the back between the shoulder blades.
5. If back blows fail to open airway, give abdominal thrusts (Figure 8–5). Position yourself with your knees close to the patient's hips. Place the heel of one hand between the lower breastbone

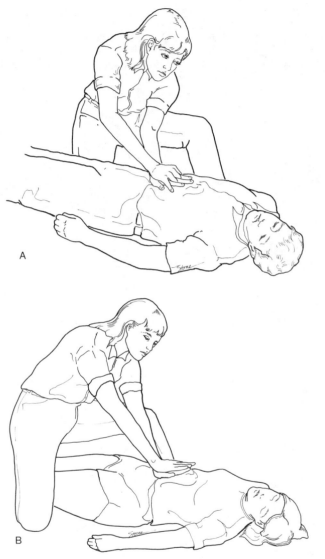

Figure 8–5. Abdominal thrusts. *A,* Unconscious patient in prone position. *B,* Alternate position for rescuer.

and the navel, and the second hand on top of the first. Press into the abdomen with quick upward thrusts.

6. An alternative to abdominal thrusts is chest thrusts. Use the same hand position as that for applying closed chest cardiac compressions. Exert quick downward thrusts.
   a. Chest thrusts are preferred when the abdominal girth is large (advanced pregnancy, obesity).

7. Check for foreign body. Turn the patient's head to the side, open the mouth with the jaw-lift technique, and probe deeply into the mouth along the cheek with a hooked finger.
   a. A dislodged foreign body may now be manually accessible if it has not been expelled.

8. Attempt to ventilate. Reposition the patient's head and ventilate the patient if possible.

9. If obstruction remains, repeat the above sequence as often as necessary until obstruction is relieved.
   a. The longer the patient remains comatose, the more relaxed the muscles become; this may make it easier to remove the obstruction.
   b. Continue to ventilate the patient with 100% oxygen even after the obstruction has been removed, until the patient has been seen by advanced medical care providers.

CARDIORESPIRATORY ARREST

Cardiac arrest is the sudden cessation of an effective cardiac output that will result in permanent organ damage or death if not treated. Respiratory arrest is the equally sudden inability to oxygenate blood and thereby maintain tissue metabolism. Although cardiac and respiratory arrest may have independent causes, they produce the same result and are often difficult to tell apart. Therefore, the combined term "cardiorespiratory" or "cardiopulmonary" arrest is frequently preferable. Cardiorespiratory arrest is the most common mode of death in American adults, representing the final catastrophic manifestations of many underlying disorders. The most common of these disorders is ischemic heart disease, which is also known as atherosclerotic cardiovascular disease or coronary artery disease. Some 650,000 Americans die each year of ischemic heart disease; half of these deaths take place outside the hospital and within two hours of the onset of symptoms.

Cardiopulmonary resuscitation (CPR) is the initial treatment for cardiorespiratory arrest. Although this term implies that the heart and lungs are resuscitated, CPR should be called cardiopulmonary cerebral resuscitation to remind us that the brain is the organ most vulnerable to hypoxia and therefore should be the focus of CPR. Cerebral function is impaired if the brain is deprived of oxygenated blood for more than 4 to 6 minutes, so CPR must be performed immediately to be effective. In Seattle, where basic life support has been taught to about one third of the residents, 43% of patients who received bystander-initiated CPR survived an episode of ventricular fibrillation and ultimately left the hospital, compared with 21% for whom resuscitation was delayed until the arrival of paramedical personnel. Patients receiving CPR from bystanders also had a lesser incidence of subsequent shock, coma, and dysrhythmias. Both groups of patients did better than similar patients in cities lacking both basic life support training and community-wide rapid response systems. The superior outcome of patients in Seattle suggests that all adults should understand the pathophysiology of cardiorespiratory arrest, the mechanism of CPR, and its application.

As defined by the American Heart Association, basic life support is a technique that externally supports the circulation and respiration of a victim of cardiac or respiratory arrest through cardiopulmonary resuscitation. It uses the three ABCs of CPR: *A*irway, *B*reathing, and *C*irculation. This sequence is chosen because even an adequate cardiac output cannot nourish the brain if blood is unoxygenated. The following protocol is based on American Heart Association recommendations for treating unwitnessed cardiorespiratory arrest outside the hospital that can be adapted to most circumstances. The steps designed to aid respiration can be omitted in patients with spontaneous ventilation, just as the steps designed to aid the circulation can be omitted if circulation is adequate. However, if the situation is unclear, the protocol should be followed precisely as described.

1. *Establish unresponsiveness* by tapping or gently shaking the patient or by shouting at him. Avoid cervical spine injury by sudden movement or displacement of the neck.

2. *Position the patient*, preferably on his back, to perform artificial ventilation and closed chest compression. Take care to avoid cervical spinal cord injury; use log-rolling technique if moving the patient.

3. *Open the airway.* The tongue is the most common cause of upper airway obstruction in unconscious persons because it falls posteriorly when its muscles are relaxed. To overcome this obstruction, the head should be tilted by placing one hand on the patient's forehead and applying firm backward pressure with the palm. This head tilt can be combined with a neck lift by placing the other hand beneath the neck and lifting it upward, care being taken to avoid excess movement of the cervical spine. If these two maneuvers do not open the airway, use the chin lift. This is accomplished by placing the tips of the fingers of one hand under the lower jaw on the bony part near the chin and pulling upward. The other hand continues to press on the patient's forehead to tilt the head back. The chin should be lifted so the teeth are nearly brought together, but the rescuer should avoid closing the mouth entirely. Loose dentures should be held in position to facilitate creation of

a mouth-to-mouth seal. If the dentures cannot be managed in place, they should be removed.

4. *Establish breathlessness* by positioning the ear over the patient's nose and mouth, looking toward his chest, and observing its rise and fall while listening and feeling for airflow during exhalation. If the patient is breathing, make sure the airway is not obstructed. If it is, or if he is not breathing, breathe for him.

5. *Rescue breathing* is performed with the patient's nostrils pinched shut by the thumb and fingers of the rescuer's hand, with the palm on the forehead. Initially, the rescuer blows deeply four times into the patient's mouth without allowing for complete deflations between breaths. The rescuer should watch out of the corner of his eyes to see if the chest is rising and falling. Some resistance should be encountered during inhalation, and air should be felt and seen to leave the lungs during exhalation. Artificial ventilation may be facilitated by mouth-to-nose or mouth-to-stoma breaths in some patients. An artificial airway may be inserted at this point, but artificial ventilation should not be delayed to obtain or apply adjunctive devices.

6. *Recognize upper airway obstruction* by the signs and symptoms just discussed. Patients with partial obstruction should be encouraged to breathe on their own as long as gas exchange appears to be adequate. However, if severe stridor, cyanosis, or depressed consciousness are initially present or develop, steps given under Airway Obstruction and Choking must be taken to overcome obstruction.

7. *Establish circulatory inadequacy* by palpating the carotid pulse in adults, or the brachial pulse in infants.

8. *Begin closed chest compression* if indicated. Even during properly performed CPR, blood flow to the brain is prevented or reduced by gravity if the head is elevated above the level of the heart. Thus, the patient should be placed in a supine position, with the legs up to enhance venous return. The rescuer should position himself close to the side of the patient's chest and locate the lower margin of the rib cage on the side nearest to him. He moves his fingers across the rib cage until they reach the xyphoid process, selects a site two fingerbreadths up the sternum toward the head, and places the heel of the hand that previously had been used to maintain the head tilt on the lower half of the sternum above the fingers of the other hand. He then extends his fingers to prevent their tips from lying on the chest, locks his elbows, and delivers closed chest compression from his shoulders. This should be done with enough force to depress the sternum 4 to 5 cm (1 ½ to 2 in) in the adult. In infants and young children, the rescuer should depress the sternum 2 cm (½ to 1 in) with two fingertips or with the heel of the hand placed over the middle of the sternum. Pressure should be released after each compression to let the sternum return to its original position. As noted previously, 15 compressions are delivered for every two ventilations in one-rescuer

CPR and five compressions for each one ventilation in two-rescuer CPR. To maintain an artificial heart rate of 60 beats per minute, 80 compressions must be delivered each minute in an adult. One hundred compressions per minute are required to maintain a rate of 80 heart beats per minute in an infant or young child. If two rescuers are performing CPR, they should independently perform compressions and ventilations and switch positions periodically. The patient should not be moved until he improves or until other arrangements have been made. Basic life support should not be discontinued until advanced cardiac life support can be initiated, a physician or other responsible health professional calls a halt, or the rescuers are too tired to do more.

Table 8–1. CPR CHEST COMPRESSIONS

	Infants	Children	Adults
Depth	1.5 to 2.5 cm (½ to 1 in)	2.5 to 4 cm (1 to 1½ in)	4 to 5 cm (1½ to 2 in)
Use	Fingertips	One hand	Both hands
Rate	100/min	80/min	1 rescuer: 80/min
			2 rescuers: 60/min
Ratio	5:1	5:1	1 rescuer: 15:2
			2 rescuers: 5:1

9

SHOCK

Shock refers to a lack of adequate tissue perfusion because of insufficient blood flow to vital organs. It can be caused by hypovolemia, inadequate cardiac function, or vasodilation (relative hypovolemia).

HYPOVOLEMIC SHOCK

Definition
A loss of circulating blood volume resulting in inadequate tissue perfusion.

Causes
1. External fluid loss.
   a. Hemorrhage (any obvious source).
   b. Abdominal tract (vomiting, diarrhea).
   c. Kidney (diabetes, diuretics).
   d. Skin (burns, sweating).
2. Internal fluid loss.
   a. Fracture.
   b. Ascites (peritonitis, pancreatitis, cirrhosis).
   c. Intestinal obstruction.
   d. Internal bleeding (hemothorax [chest], rupture of organ or great vessels into abdomen, rupture of ectopic pregnancy).

History: Subjective Reports
External hemorrhage or fluid loss is usually obvious. Internal losses may be more difficult to determine. A history of abdominal pain or complaints with postural hypotension, fainting, and/or lightheadedness in an upright posture suggests acute abdominal hemorrhage. Alcoholics are particularly prone to gastrointestinal bleeding.

Examination: Objective Physical Findings
Determine the postural blood pressure (not necessary when the patient has a supine systolic blood pressure of 80 mm Hg or less). Return patient to supine position immediately if patient becomes faint in upright position.
1. Shock is often classified into mild, moderate, or severe:
   a. Mild shock.
      i. Postural pulse increase of 10 to 20 beats per minute.
      ii. Postural systolic blood pressure drop of 10 mm Hg.

       iii. Flat neck veins while patient is supine.
    b. Moderate shock.
       i. Postural pulse increase of 20 beats per minute.
       ii. Postural systolic blood pressure drop of 20 mm Hg.
       iii. Pale, sweaty, anxious, agitated.
       iv. Confused mental state.
    c. Severe shock.
       i. Nonrecordable blood pressure in any position.
       ii. Pale, cyanotic, sweating, tachycardia.
       iii. Confusion or coma.
       iv. Apparently absent neck veins while patient is supine.
2. A convenient way to categorize shock due to acute hemorrhage is that proposed by the American College of Surgeons. Acute hemorrhagic shock is divided into four classes (Table 9–1). The classification is valid only for acute hemorrhage and is intended only as a guide. Tachycardia may not be seen in the elderly. Alcohol intoxication may alter the anticipated clinical signs of acute blood loss.
3. Continue to monitor patient with frequent reassessment.

EMT Management

1. Positive pressure to external hemorrhage sites.
2. Oxygen, positive pressure ventilation as needed.
3. Apply anti-shock trousers (MAST) (if trained in use).
4. Supine position, elevated lower extremities (if patient is on a backboard, raise foot of board).

EMT Special Considerations

Patients require volume replacement with whole blood or other fluids. Often, surgical intervention is required. Rapid recognition of shock condition, control of external hemorrhage, and delivery to the hospital are the key ingredients in patient survival.

CARDIOGENIC SHOCK

Definition

Inadequate tissue perfusion resulting from circulatory failure secondary to inability of the heart to pump blood adequately.

Causes

1. Myocardial infarction is the most common cause of cardiogenic shock.
2. Other causes include arrhythmias, severe congestive heart failure, acute valvular damage (trauma or infection), pulmonary embolism, dissecting aortic aneurysm, acute pericardial tamponade (bleeding into the sac around the heart, causing a squeezing effect on the heart), tension pneumothorax.

Table 9–1. CLASSES OF ACUTE HEMORRHAGE*

	Class I	Class II	Class III	Class IV
Blood loss in ml	up to 750 ml	1000 to 1250 ml	1500 to 1800 ml	2000 to 2500 ml
Blood loss in %†	up to 15%	20 to 25%	30 to 35%	40 to 50%
Pulse rate‡	72 to 84 beats/min	100 beats/min	120 beats/min	140 beats/min, or greater
Blood pressure§	118/82 mm Hg	110/80 mm Hg	70–90/50–60 mm Hg	50–60 mm Hg
Pulse pressure (mm Hg) ‖	36 mm Hg	30 mm Hg	20 to 30 mm Hg	10 to 20 mm Hg
Capillary blanch test	Normal	Positive	Positive	Positive
Respiratory rate	14 to 20	20 to 30	30 to 40	35
CNS mental status	Slightly anxious	Mildly anxious	Anxious and confused	Confused, lethargic

*Adapted from Committee on Trauma, American College of Surgeons: *Advanced Trauma Life Support Course*, 1981, p. 45.
†% of blood volume in an average 70-kg male.
‡Assume normal of 72 beats/min.
§Assume normal of 120/80 mm Hg.
‖Difference between systolic and diastolic.

History: Subjective Reports

The most common complaint is chest pain, suggesting myocardial infarction. Often the patient has had pain for many hours without seeking assistance.

Examination: Objective Physical Findings

1. Low or absent blood pressure, particularly with the patient upright.
2. Other findings that may be present include agitation, confusion, anxiety, and unconsciousness.
3. Evidence of cardiac failure, distended neck veins, pulmonary edema.

EMT Management

1. Oxygen with positive pressure ventilation, if needed.
2. Supine position if blood pressure is absent. Anti-shock trousers (MAST) only at direction of physician.
3. Rotating constricting bands with evidence of pulmonary edema.
4. Cardiac monitor, if available and EMT is so trained.

EMT Special Considerations

This is a life-threatening emergency. The patient requires definitive medical care as rapidly as possible. The mortality rate is 80 to 90%.

ANAPHYLACTIC SHOCK

Definition

Circulatory failure resulting from an allergic reaction that occurs after exposure to a foreign substance (antigen).

Causes

Causes include drugs; i.e., penicillin; diagnostic agents, i.e., x-ray contrast agents; insect stings or bites; foreign serum; desensitizing antigens (extracts of pollen).

Examination: Objective Physical Findings

1. Respiratory, cardiovascular, soft tissue, and gastrointestinal systems may all be involved (Table 9–2).
2. Generalized warmth with flushing red skin.
3. Lower airway obstruction is characterized by wheezing as a result of pulmonary edema.
4. Convulsions may be seen in severe cases.

Table 9–2. CLINICAL FEATURES OF ANAPHYLACTIC SHOCK

System	Reaction	Symptoms	Signs
Respiratory	Laryngeal edema, bronchospasm	Dyspnea, wheezing, cough	Stridor, respiratory distress
Cardiovascular	Vascular pooling, arrhythmias	Faintness, apprehension	Hypotension, loss of consciousness
Skin	Hives, facial swelling	Itching	Raised, red rash; edema of soft tissue, lips, tongue, posterior pharynx, eyelids, hands
Gastrointestinal	Smooth muscle contractions	Nausea, abdominal cramps	Vomiting, diarrhea

EMT Treatment

1. Isolate the antigen, if possible, by applying a tourniquet to the extremity that received the injection, diagnostic agent or insect sting.
2. Oxygen by mask or nasal prongs, positive pressure, if necessary.
3. With vascular collapse, place patient in supine position. Apply anti-shock trousers (MAST) (if trained in use).
4. Cardiac monitor if available.

EMT Special Considerations

In severe cases, death may occur in minutes, usually from respiratory obstruction and vascular collapse. All patients, regardless of response to treatment, should be transported to the hospital.

SEPTIC SHOCK

Definition

Vascular collapse brought about by severe systemic infection. Usually seen in elderly, debilitated, or alcoholic patients.

Causes

Severe infection from any source, such as ruptured appendix, ruptured bowel with peritonitis, severe pneumonia, or pyelonephritis.

History: Subjective Reports

Recent acute localized infection, which becomes generalized to involve the whole body. Usual sites of infection are lung and urinary tract (kidney).

Examination: Objective Physical Findings

Some of the following findings may be present:
1. Low blood pressure, rapid pulse.

2. Pale, sweaty, cyanotic.
3. Delirium, confusion.
4. Fever.
5. Source of infection may or may not be obvious.

EMT Treatment
1. Oxygen by mask or nasal prongs, positive pressure if needed.
2. Supine position with lower extremities elevated as needed to support blood pressure. Apply anti-shock trousers (MAST) (if trained in use).
3. Cardiac monitor if available.
4. Rapid transport or call for paramedic help, if available.

10

TRAUMA MANAGEMENT

This section on trauma is a continuation of that part of Chapter 2 dealing with examination of the trauma patient. Specific field management of injuries found during the secondary examination is outlined.

Emphasis must be placed on the management of Airway, Breathing, and Circulation (ABC). Never become involved with obvious but non–life-threatening injuries and neglect a more serious problem of management of the ABCs. All necessary manpower and effort must be focused on treating disorders in Airway, Breathing, and Circulation. In caring for the trauma victim, time becomes the fourth factor to consider. At present, the only oxygen-carrying substance is whole blood, available only at major treatment facilities. Therefore, it is imperative that trauma patients be extricated and moved to those facilities as rapidly as is practical. Picture-perfect extrications can be counter-productive if they become too lengthy and the patient progresses into hypovolemic shock.

Whenever possible, the EMT charged with management of a patient should handle treatment of all ABC problems during periods of extrication. He must keep a check on the patient's vital signs and become the natural "time-keeper." In areas with paramedic services, it is important to contact paramedics as soon as possible so that IV fluids and advanced airway controls can be supplied.

The EMT in charge should also assess the circumstances surrounding the trauma scene to determine the mechanism involved. These circumstances include deceleration force applied to the patient, speed of vehicle, use of seat belts, helmets, and amount and location of damage to vehicle(s). When a weapon is involved, it is important to know the caliber, type (length of knife, for example), and position of patient relative to assailant, if possible.

Other important facts to determine include loss of consciousness and significant medical history. Determine whether the patient has been drinking alcohol or taking prescription or street drugs.

In the trauma setting, one EMT must become the leader and maintain control of the overall scene.

INITIAL MANAGEMENT

All efforts must be made to support airway/breathing/circulation and to control bleeding before continuing with a more detailed patient examination.

1. Airway/breathing: Immediately, determine the quality and volume of respirations as well as patient's ability to breath adequately. Check for obvious obstructions. Then, with the stethoscope, just below the clavicles, check for presence and symmetry of breath sounds.
   a. Pay special attention to the comatose patient's ability to avoid choking on blood, secretions, and vomit.
   b. Check gag reflex on all patients with reduced level of consciousness.
   c. Be alert for stridor (raspy, noisy respirations) secondary to trauma to the trachea.
   d. Apply bag mask if patient's respiration is slow, labored, or absent.
2. Circulation: Assess the presence, rate, and quality of the pulse. CPR is of little value if the patient is in upright position. Rapid extrication of pulseless patients is therefore essential.
3. Bleeding: Check for obvious gross hemorrhage and treat as required if severe. As quickly as possible, determine blood pressure and note initial time it was taken. The second blood pressure should be taken 5 minutes thereafter or less.
4. The partners of the EMT examining the patient should have the first complete set of vital signs (blood pressure, pulse, respiratory rate) by the time the initial assessment is completed and should be assisting with treatment of immediate life-threatening problems.
5. A natural by-product of the primary survey is an understanding of the patient's state and level of consciousness.
6. Patients found unconscious or with injury to the face and head, or who have been involved with a mechanism that could have caused trauma to the head or neck, should have a firm cervical collar in support of their neck before extrication. Head is to be stabilized by an EMT holding head and neck in normal anatomical position until mechanical stabilization (sandbags, etc.) is established.

SECONDARY MANAGEMENT

Once the primary systems have been stabilized, and after patient has been extricated from any dangerous location, a more thorough secondary assessment of the less potentially life-threatening injuries is performed.

1. Continue frequent checks of patient's vital signs, especially if there is multiple-system trauma, as internal hemorrhage may not be apparent.
2. Reassess lung sounds, respiratory volume, and rate, and apply oxygen as required.
3. If time permits, treat lesser injuries, beginning with those injuries which have the greatest potential to further affect the patient's ABCs.

4. Be aware that the patient may have chronic illnesses that are not readily apparent. If the patient is conscious, question him/her about medical history, medicines, alcohol, street drugs. Alcohol or sedatives can mask severe injury.

HEAD

See Figures 10–1 and 10–2 for anatomy of the head.
1. Always assume that patients who have sustained serious head trauma may have injuries to the cervical spine. Stabilize the head and neck with a firm cervical collar while examining the spine.

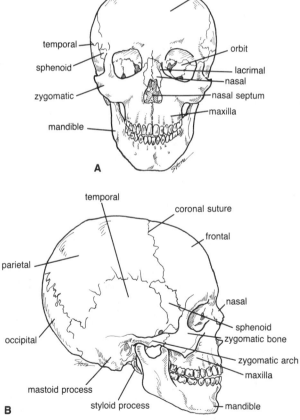

Figure 10–1. Skull. *A*, Frontal view. *B*, Side view.

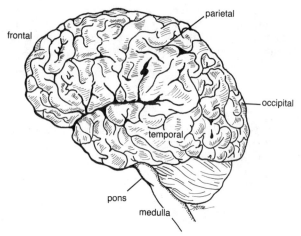

Figure 10–2. Areas of the brain and brain stem.

2. Administer oxygen as required, using bag mask ventilation if there is any doubt of patient's ability to oxygenate adequately on his/her own.
3. Suction blood or secretions. Caution: Application of suction should not exceed 15–second intervals.
4. Scalp lacerations, even with arterial bleeding, can be controlled with direct pressure and direct pressure bandages.
5. Injuried areas of the skull should be palpated carefully, as hematomas can hide underlying fragmented skull fractures.
6. Open skull fractures with exposed brain tissue should be covered with a sterile dressing. Do not push tissue back into the skull.
7. Head trauma alone does not cause shock unless it is serious enough to cause death. Look for other sources, such as bleeding or injury, if shock is present.
8. Patients with head injuries should be transported with head and upper body elevated.
9. See Table 10–1 for characteristics of lateral hematoma, of superior (supratentorial) hematoma (Figs. 10–3 and 10–4), basilar skull fracture, and concussion.
10. Maintain a neurological check sheet on all head injured patients (Appendix 7).

Vital Signs	Shock	Increasing Intracranial Pressure
Pulse	Fast	Slow
Blood pressure	Low	High

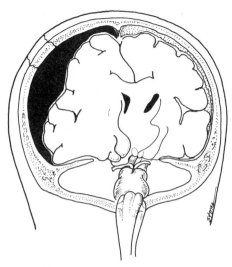

Figure 10–3. Lateral hematoma.

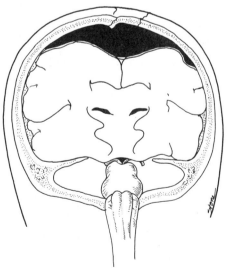

Figure 10–4. Superior hematoma.

Table 10–1. CHARACTERISTICS OF LATERAL HEMATOMA, SUPERIOR HEMATOMA, BASILAR SKULL FRACTURE, AND CONCUSSION

Cause	Pupillary Size	Respiratory Pattern	Remarks
Lateral hematoma: injury to temporal area of skull with bleeding into temporal area of brain. Bleeding causes brain to shift to one side and down, affecting basic brain functions.	Dilated unreactive pupil on same side as injury. Drooping eyelid.	Sustained hyperventilation.	1. Patient is often conscious in early stages. 2. Becomes stuporous to comatose in late stages. 3. Patient paralyzed on same side as injury to skull. 4. Important to recognize this condition early, as bleeding may stop, patient may apparently return to normal, and a second, fatal bleeding may occur, usually within 30 minutes. 5. Problem can be resolved only in hospital by twist drilling of skull to relieve pressure. 6. Patient may have projectile vomiting, yawning, hiccups.
Superior hematoma: injury to top (parietal) area of skull with bleeding across top of brain. Bleeding causes both sides of brain to be compressed downward.	Pupils are small with sluggish reaction to light initially; become fixed in mid-position as bleeding progresses and compression of brain stem causes different levels of brain to stop functioning.	Cheyne-Stokes respiration early in injury, to sustained hyperventilation, to slow, irregular, and finally respiratory arrest as medulla (respiratory center) is affected.	1. Patient is often conscious in early stages. 2. Becomes stuporous to comatose in late stages. 3. Patient will display decorticate* rigidity early with noxious stimulus. 4. Progresses to decerebrate‡ rigidity when brain stem is affected. 5. Becomes flaccid without response to noxious stimuli in late stages (medulla affected). 6. May have projectile vomiting, yawning, hiccups.

Basilar skull fracture: severe trauma causing skull to fracture along the base. Fracture can be only on one side.	Pupillary response is same as in superior hematoma, depending on area of brain affected. Discoloration of soft tissue around the eyes (periorbital ecchymosis, or "raccoon eyes").	Respiratory patterns will depend on the level of brain damage, as in superior hematoma.	1. Patient usually has decreased level of consciousness. 2. Blood or cerebrospinal fluid from ear(s), nose is common sign. 3. Discoloration of mastoid behind ear(s) (Battle sign). 4. May have projectile vomiting, yawning, hiccups.
Concussion: period of being "knocked out" or unconscious with related period of amnesia, lasting from seconds to several minutes. Can be thought of as bruise, as opposed to severe bleeding. Injury may be at impact site or on opposite side of brain, because of rebound force.	Not specific.	Not specific.	1. Patient unconscious because of interruption of the portion of the brain that maintains wakefulness (reticular activating system, or RAS). Unconsciousness is not caused by bleeding inside the skull. 2. The longer the patient is unconscious, the more severe the damage. 3. Normal side effects: headache, dizziness, fatigue. 4. Patient must be carefully monitored to determine whether injury is more serious (e.g., subdural bleeding).

*Patient is supine with one or both arms bent at elbows, fists clenched, hands on chest, and toes pointed down. Extremities rigid.
‡Patient is supine with one or both arms extended down along chest, fists clenched, and toes point down. Extremities rigid.

FACE

1. Upper face.
   a. Control bleeding with direct pressure.
   b. Blunt trauma to the forehead may produce significant trauma to the frontal lobes of the brain. Such an injury may cause behavioral changes, agitation (patient yelling, attempting to refuse treatment, or combative), or occasionally seizures. Note all changes in behavior, and state levels of consciousness.
2. Eyes.
   a. Note pupillary changes. Dilated, slowly reactive pupils in alert patients may indicate trauma to the eye(s) and may not necessarily indicate brain damage.
   b. Note position of eyes. A fixed eye that cannot be moved laterally or down, with an orbit sunken into the skull or a globe bulging outward, implies orbit fracture. Cover both eyes to prevent undue movement.
   c. Test visual acuity. Have patient identify the number of fingers held before him/her. Test each eye individually. Do not do this when globe is lacerated or has been impaled by a foreign object. Stabilize the object—never remove it—cover the uninjured eye, and transport immediately.
   d. Lacerations of the lid may be controlled with gentle direct pressure. Lacerations preventing lid closure should be treated with moistened eye patches to protect the cornea from damage.
   e. Hemorrhagic discoloration of soft tissue around the eyes, or raccoon's eyes, in the presence of head trauma implies basilar skull fracture. Be alert for changes in patient's neurological status.
   f. When a small foreign body is lodged under the eyelid, attempt to rinse it out with sterile saline. If it cannot be rinsed free, bandage the eyes and transport the patient.
   g. Stabilize an impaling object in place, bandage both eyes, and transport the patient.
   h. The eyeball avulsed from it socket should be protected in the same fashion as one impaled by an object.
   i. Chemical burns to the eyes should be rinsed for 20 minutes with sterile water (irrigating fluid). Thermal burns are dressed and bandaged. Ultraviolet (UV) light burns, from welding arc or snow blindness, feel like sand in the eye. Treat with cool compresses over closed eyelids.
   j. Contact lenses should be left in place until the patient reaches the emergency department.
3. Midface: nose.
   a. Nose
      i. Clear fluid from the nose is a sign of serious trauma to skull. The fluid should be allowed to drain freely.

ii. Bleeding from the nostril(s) without obvious deformity or swelling of the nose may be a sign of basilar skull fracture.

b. Unstable zygomatic or maxillary bones with soft tissue swelling of the face (pumpkin face) may progress to complete airway obstruction. The patient requires immediate airway control.

c. Foreign bodies in the nose, if they have not been removed by the child or parent, will not be removable by the EMT.

4. Lower face: mouth, jaw
   a. Lacerations of the tongue or oral soft tissue may require direct pressure to stop bleeding. Use suction as necessary.
   b. Severe trauma to area around mouth may cause soft tissue swelling and can progress to complete airway obstruction.
   c. Fracture of both sides of the jaw (known as "bucket handle" fractures) may allow the tongue to fall downward and occlude the airway.
   d. Because bleeding from an object impaled in the cheek can present airway problems, the object may be removed. Suction as necessary. Pack the inside of the cheek with dressings, and monitor the airway carefully.

5. Ear
   a. Bloody or clear fluid leaking from the ear(s) indicates basilar skull fracture.
   b. Complete or partial avulsions of the ear should be packed in sterile dressings. Unattached portions should be placed in solution and brought to the hospital with the patient.
   c. Ruptured or punctured eardrums require no special treatment. Cover the ear lightly with a sterile dressing.
   d. Foreign bodies in the ear should be left in place.

NECK/SPINE

See Figure 10–5 for anatomy of the spine.

1. Perform rapid neurological evaluation whenever practical after life-threatening problems are under control. Stabilize the neck manually prior to assessment.
   a. Assess gross movement and sensation of extremities.
      i. Have patient wiggle feet and toes; lightly pinch top of each foot.
      ii. Have patient lift each leg 3 to 4 inches; lightly pinch each leg
      iii. Have patient grasp examiner's fingers and squeeze; lightly pinch top of each hand or forearm.
   b. If patient displays a lack of movement or sensation during gross neurological evaluation, perform a more specific sensation evaluation by pinching various surface body areas, starting with the feet, until pain is noted by patient. Note

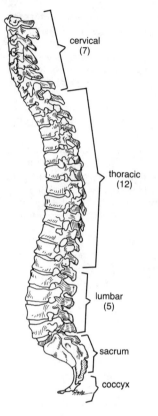

cervical
(7)

thoracic
(12)

Figure 10–5. Spine.

lumbar
(5)

sacrum

coccyx

the level at which pain was experienced, and record and convey this information to the next level of medical care.

c. Check abdomen for paradoxical movement with respirations. This indicates that the patient may require ventilatory assistance.

2. Suspected or actual neck injuries require immediate stabilization. Head and neck should always be placed in normal anatomical position by means of gentle manual traction. Place a firm cervical collar, and secure head/shoulders on backboard. Be sure that cervical collar is the proper size.

a. To apply traction, grasp jaw lines on both sides of head, holding the palms of each hand flat against the head at the ears. Pull with just enough force to maintain the head and neck in a straight line.

b. Even when the cervical collar is in place, someone should maintain stabilization of the head and neck during periods of extrication, assisted ventilation with bag mask, and so on.

    c. When patients with suspected neck injuries are being transported, sand bags should be placed on both sides of the head and held with cravats or tape attached across patient's forehead to the backboard. Other major portions of patient should be tied to backboard securely.

3. Patients with neck injuries requiring assisted ventilation with a bag mask should not have neck hyperextended to open airway. Use alternate methods: jaw thrust or chin lift.

4. Blunt trauma to the neck can collapse the trachea (windpipe). The victim may not be able to talk, and signs include bruising, deformity, subcutaneous emphysema (air bubbles under the skin), and respiratory distress. The patient needs high-concentration oxygen, calming reassurance, and rapid transport to hospital.

5. Penetrating trauma to the neck can put the victim at risk for air embolism, when a neck vein is severed. Treat with an occlusive dressing and head-down position.

6. Rescue procedures are tailored to the specific situation. The neck is always stabilized manually until the spine is fully immobilized.

    a. After a diving accident the neck is stabilized and artificial respiration begun (if necessary) while the victim is still in the water. A wooden backboard is floated under the victim and sand bags placed alongside the head. If there is no pulse the victim must be removed from the water to begin chest compressions. Otherwise, the victim is immobilized on the board in the water.

    b. The procedure for removal of a motorcycle helmet (or other helmet) is outlined in Appendix 8.

CHEST

1. The first step in the management of chest trauma is the assessment of air movement by use of a stethoscope to evaluate breath sounds.

    a. The examiner should listen to both anterior and posterior as well as upper and lower portions of the chest.

    b. Examination of the trauma patient should include listening below each clavicle and comparing presence and symmetry of breath sounds.

    c. The primary consideration is to establish an accurate baseline for later comparisons.

2. Significant trauma to the clavicle(s) and the body region under the clavicle(s), the first rib, is correlated with major vessel injury. The aortic arch, subclavian arteries, and veins are located in this region.

    a. Blood pressures should be determined in both arms. Look for significant differences (systolic difference greater than 10 mm Hg).

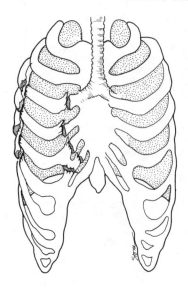

Figure 10–6. Flail chest.

b. Assess the equality of both radial pulses for unequal palpable pressure.
c. Observe neck veins for distention indicating obstructed venous return.
3. Presence of a flail sternum (sternum moving inward with inspiration and outward with expiration) may require ventilatory assistance with bag mask. There is a high correlation of cardiac damage with a flail sternum.
4. Blunt trauma, without obvious chest wall injury, may cause cardiac damage.
5. A simple rib fracture is recognized by point tenderness, and localized pain aggravated by deep breathing. EMT treatment consists of manual stabilization with a pillow, sitting position, and administration of oxygen.
6. Damage to the aorta or large vessels or to the heart may cause cardiac tamponade.
   a. Signs of cardiac tamponade:
      i. Hypotension (especially with narrow pulse pressure— the gap between systolic and diastolic pressures).
      ii. Distended neck veins.
      iii. Muffled heart sounds.
   b. This is an emergency and requires rapid definitive treatment.
7. A flail chest (a portion of the chest wall moving inward with inspiration and outward with expiration) may require ventilatory assistance with bag mask (Figs. 10–6 and 10–7).
8. A penetrating injury to the chest may result in a sucking chest

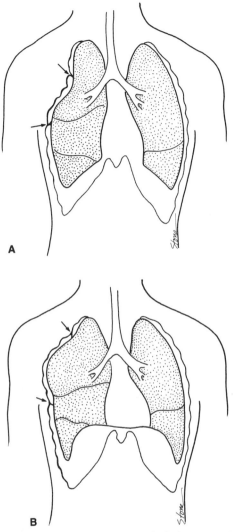

Figure 10–7. Flail chest. Notice the paradoxical movement of the flail segment. *A*, Inspiration. *B*, Expiration.

wound. EMT treatment consists of an occlusive dressing, high concentration oxygen, very careful monitoring of respiratory status, and rapid transport to hospital (call for paramedics if available). Transport with injured side down.

9. Anticipate the possibility of the development of tension pneumothorax (Fig. 10–8). Check lung sounds on the injured side frequently. Signs of tension pneumothorax include

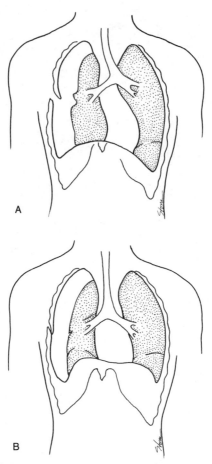

A

B

Figure 10–8. Tension pneumothorax. *A,* Inspiration. Notice the shift of the trachea. *B,* Expiration.

a. Absence of breath sounds on affected side.
b. Subcutaneous air or blood (tissue swelling, feels like break-fast cereal under the skin if air, or spongy if blood).
c. Hypotension that worsens with loss of breath sounds.
d. Distended neck veins.
e. Deviation of trachea away from injured side. Grasp fingers around trachea just above suprasternal notch to locate position relative to midline of neck.

This is a life-threatening emergency and requires rapid treat-ment. An occlusive dressing should be opened briefly to see if air under pressure escapes. Provide high-concentration oxygen and rapid transport with injured side down. Call for paramedics if available.

10. Blunt or penetrating trauma to the lower chest may also cause damage to the contents of the upper abdomen: liver, spleen, kidney(s).
    a. All three organs are susceptible to deceleration type injuries without obvious gross injury to the surface of the thorax.
       i. When possible, postural blood pressure should be determined to check for hypovolemia.
       ii. Distention of the abdomen may be a clue to internal hemorrhage.
       iii. Treat for hypovolemia as required with elevation of extremities. Patient requires volume replacement as soon as possible.
    b. Penetrating injuries are usually obvious—treat with occlusive dressing.
    c. Do not remove objects impaled in the chest, even if in or near the heart. Stabilize with gauze packing prior to transport.

ABDOMEN

As with chest trauma, the two factors dictating management of blunt or penetrating injury are the mechanism and the signs and symptoms of hypovolemic shock.
1. Repeat vital signs at a minimum of every 10 minutes.
2. Re-examine abdomen frequently, noting distention, tenderness, guarding.
3. Do not return bowels or viscera back to abdomen. Cover with sterile, moist (if sterile solution is available) dressings, then cover completely with occlusive dressing.
4. Do not remove objects impaled in the abdomen. Stabilize with gauze packing.
5. Elevate extremities as required to maintain BP.
6. Hypotension may be treated with anti-shock trousers. With pregnant patients, do not inflate the abdominal segment.

BACK/SPINE

1. Patient should be placed on backboard. Secure patient for minimal movement after padding space at lower back and behind the knees and ankles. A folded blanket is also placed between the legs from groin to ankles, and at the sides from armpit to heels.
2. Motor and sensory neurological checks should be performed before and after patient is placed on backboard. Make note of any changes.
3. Spinal (neurogenic) shock may be present in association with low cervical or high thoracic injury. Treat by elevating the

extremities, and administer oxygen. Apply anti-shock trousers (MAST) if indicated.
4. Try to understand the mechanism of injury. The spine may be fractured even if the patient does not have signs/symptoms of injury initially.

PELVIS

1. Pelvic fractures and penetrating wounds in the pelvic area may injure large blood vessels, bladder, bowel, or uterus, causing severe hemorrhage without obvious external signs.
2. Take vital signs frequently during treatment phase to assess for hypovolemia.
3. Patient should be placed on backboard in the position of greatest comfort and secured firmly.
4. Hypotension may be managed with anti-shock trousers. Use care with pregnant patients.
5. Pad both sides of pelvis with rolled blankets prior to securing to backboard.
6. It is often difficult to distinguish between fractures of the pelvis and fractures of the head or neck of the femur(s). If in doubt, do not use traction splint on leg; use anti-shock trousers (MAST).
7. Assess femoral pulses for equal strength.

GENITALIA

1. Maintain privacy during treatment and examinations. Explain to patients what you are doing at all times, as they often will be unable to see the examination or treatment procedures.
2. Control bleeding with direct pressure. Vaginal bleeding can be treated by packing vaginal opening with 4″ × 4″ sponges. Never perform a direct internal examination of the vagina.
3. Injuries to the testicles should be stabilized and the testes supported during transport.
4. Take vital signs frequently and treat shock as required.

EXTREMITIES

See Figures 10–9, 10–10, and 10–11 for the bones of the extremities.
1. If the patient does not have severe life-threatening injuries, take time to assess the full extent of injury and to determine precise location of injury on the extremity.
   a. Check distal motor and sensory neurological functions.
      i. Sensory: lightly pinch surface skin after asking patient not to observe test. Support limb.

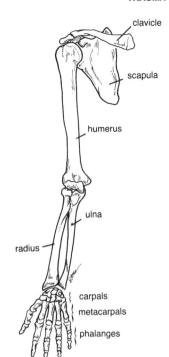

clavicle

scapula

humerus

ulna

radius

carpals

metacarpals

phalanges

Figure 10–9. Bones of the shoulder, arm, and hand.

  ii. Motor: have patient wiggle fingers or toes distal to injury.
  iii. Test should be performed before and after treatment.
 b. Check for distal pulses before and after treatment.
2. Use direct pressure to control bleeding; supplement with pressure dressings once major bleeding is controlled.
3. Fractured limbs should be realigned as nearly as possible to an anatomical position. Types of fractures are shown in Figure 10–12.
 a. Apply traction in the direction limb is originally found, and gently move limb to correct anatomical position.
 b. Support joints and the limb below fracture site during realignment and splinting.
 c. Bones protruding from open fractures may be pulled back into the skin once gross impurities are removed.
 d. Do not attempt to realign bones end to end. It is only necessary to place them near their normal position to relieve pain and allow nerves and vessels to return to normal positions.
 e. Maintain traction until splinting is completed with a minimum of movement once limb is aligned.

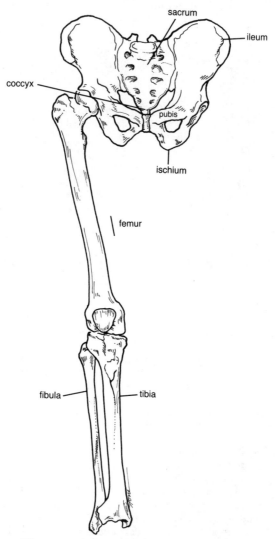

Figure 10–10. Bones of the pelvis, hip, and leg.

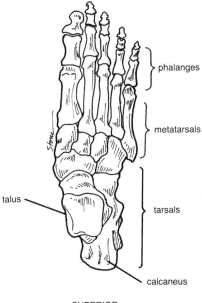

SUPERIOR

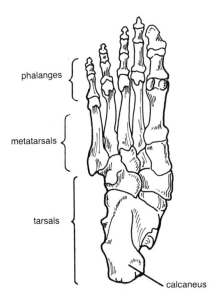

PLANTAR

Figure 10–11. Bones of the feet.

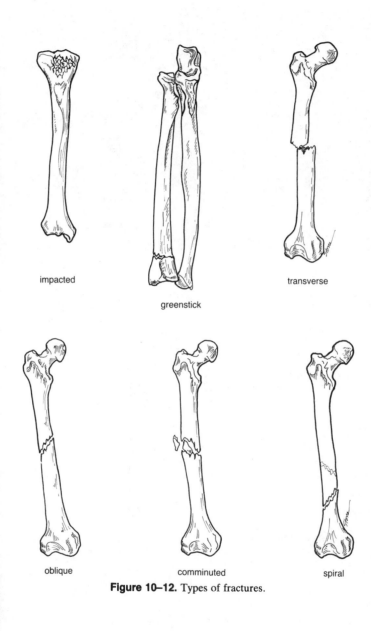

impacted

greenstick

transverse

oblique

comminuted

spiral

Figure 10–12. Types of fractures.

f. Use sterile dressing to cover open wounds at fracture site.

g. When possible, elevate extremity after splinting. Place cold pack near fracture site.

4. Splint all injured joints as found. Do not attempt to realign the limb.

5. Save bone fragments and pack in sterile dressing. Moisten with sterile solution when available.

6. It is possible to damage or sever major blood vessels, especially in thigh or groin areas and the knee, causing significant hemorrhage. Watch for shock signs/symptoms.

Table 10–2. INJURIES TO THE EXTREMITIES

Characteristics	Dislocation	Sprain	Strain	Fracture
Location	Joint	Joint	Between joints	Either
Symptoms				
Pain	Yes	Yes	Yes	Yes
Loss of function	Yes	No	No	Usually
Signs				
Deformity	Yes	No	No	Usually
Swelling	Yes	Yes	No	Yes
Bruising	Occasionally	Usually	No	Yes

HIP

1. Fractures and/or dislocations of the hip may be associated with pelvic fractures.

2. Check distal pulses and perform simple motor and sensory examination.

   a. Motor: have patient wiggle toes and flex foot.

   b. Sensory: lightly pinch skin or lower extremity and top of foot.

3. If in doubt whether injury is the femoral neck or pelvis, do not use traction splint.

   a. Place patient on backboard using position that is most comfortable. A patient with a posterior dislocation may prefer the affected leg to remain toward the uninjured side.

   b. Use plenty of heavy padding; i.e., blankets, to stabilize extremity and pelvic area.

   c. Check for distal pulses after splinting or moving.

AMPUTATION

1. Direct pressure at the amputation site will normally control bleeding. Use tourniquets only as a last resort.

2. Partial amputations should be put in normal anatomical alignment.
   a. Wrap with bulky pressure dressing to control bleeding.
   b. When possible, elevate extremity after bleeding is controlled.
3. Completely amputated portions should be wrapped in sterile dressings, soaked with sterile solution, and placed in a closed, plastic bag, which is placed on ice and sent with the patient in same transporting vehicle. (Use caution to avoid frostbite of the severed part.)
4. Treat for shock as required. Amputations of toes and fingers do not normally required paramedical assistance unless the patient has lost a large volume of blood.

TRAUMA TO PREGNANT PATIENTS

1. All pregnant patients involved with trauma are to be evaluated by a physician in a hospital.
2. Give O_2 to all pregnant patients involved with trauma.
3. Check for fetal heart sounds and continue to monitor during treatment. *Note:* The EMT may not be able to hear fetal heart sounds with a regular stethoscope. Use fetal stethoscope, if available.
4. Penetrating abdominal trauma, vaginal bleeding, or fetal heart rate of less than 100 beats per minute should be considered critical. Use paramedical assistance if available or rapid transport to facility with emergency obstetric personnel.

BURNS

DEFINITION

1. Burns are divided into three categories.
   a. Thermal: burns from contact with flame, hot gases, or hot objects.
   b. Electrical: burns from electrical charge passing through tissue and bone.
   c. Chemical: burns caused by caustic substances that have made direct contact with the skin.
2. Classification by severity (see Table 11–1).
   a. First degree: superficial, mild, requiring little or no medical attention. Treatment is usually to relieve pain.
   b. Second degree: blisters with possible moderate damage to the skin. Will usually heal over a period of days or weeks.
   c. Third degree: full thickness of skin through the dermis. Will require skin grafting unless only a small area is affected.
   d. Fourth degree: through muscle and/or bone. The extent of this type of burn may not be obvious, as the most common source is accidental electrocution. All that may be visible is the damaged areas at entrance and exit of the electrical source.
3. Burn classifications.
   MAJOR
   a. Second-degree burns involving more than 25% of adult's body surface or more than 20% of child's body surface.
   b. Third-degree burns involving 10% or more of body surface.
   c. Burns involving hands, face, eyes, ears, feet, and perineum.
   d. All inhalation injuries.
   e. Electrical burns.
   f. Burns complicated by fractures and other trauma.
   g. Burns in poor-risk patients, i.e., infants, elderly with severe chronic illness.
   MODERATE
   a. Second-degree burns involving between 15 and 25% of adult's body surface or 10–20% of child's body surface.
   b. Third-degree burns of 2–10% of body surface, not involving eyes, ears, face, hands, feet, perineum.
   MINOR
   a. Lesser burns.

Table 11–1. BURN CHARACTERISTICS

Classification	Damage	Examples	Appearance	Sensation
First	Superficial	Sunburn	Redness	Moderately painful
Second	Partial thickness (mostly epidermal damage)	Heat/flame	Blisters	Very painful
Third	Full thickness (epidermis and dermis)	Heat/flame	White, leathery, charred	No pain at site
Fourth	Full thickness (includes muscle and/ or bone)	Electricity	Exposed muscle, bone, charred surface	No pain at site

HISTORY

1. Obtain as much information as possible concerning mechanism or source of burns.
2. Determine if additional mechanism that could cause other trauma is suspected.
3. Determine if patient has chronic illness that could be complicated by burns or that may complicate recovery from them.

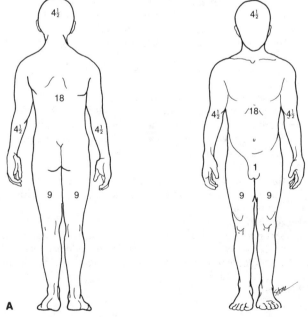

Illustration continued on opposite page

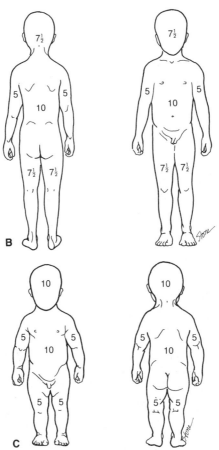

Figure 11–1. Relative percentages of body area. *A,* Adult. *B,* Child. *C,* Infant.

EXAMINATION

1. Determine the approximate total percentage of skin area involved by burns (Fig. 11–1). Use rule of nines for adults. It is sometimes more accurate to approximate the unburned percentage of skin and subtract that percentage from 100% to determine the percentage of the skin area involved. Estimate percentage of each classification of burn. If in doubt whether it is second or third degree, consider it third degree.
2. Inspect patient's mouth and nasal hairs for charring, soot residue, redness, or swelling as indication of early signs of possible upper airway edema/swelling.

    a. Listen for upper airway respiratory stridor, raspy speech.
    b. Check for charcoal-flaked sputum.
3. Complete full body exam, checking for trauma secondary to the incident.
4. Blood pressure can be taken on burned extremity when necessary. First place gauze over area to be covered by blood pressure cuff.

EMT TREATMENT

1. Remove patient from source of burns.
    a. Douse and remove smoldering clothes from patient.
    b. Remove patient from electrical source. DO NOT ENDANGER RESCUERS. USE EXTREME CAUTION.
    c. Wash chemicals off patient with copious amounts of water.
    d. Brush solid substances, i.e., lime, off patient.
2. Treat as any other injured patient.
    a. Observe for airway obstruction secondary to inhalation of hot gases. If airway problem is suspected, administer high-flow oxygen.
       i. If respiratory distress is progressively worsening (hoarseness, wheezing, cough), patient requires paramedical assistance or rapid transport to medical facility.
    b. Control hemorrhage with direct pressure and pressure bandage.
    c. Treat shock and hypotension as with any trauma patient. Initial hypotension should not be due to burns.
    d. Treat any medical emergencies according to regular approach.
3. Cover burns with dry dressings or sheets. Dressing/sheets should be sterile when possible, but that is not essential.
    a. Same burns may be cooled with cold towels if this is done immediately after burn, but moist towels have a wick effect, drawing bacteria into burned area. Moist towels should therefore be replaced with dry dressings.
    b. Do not apply ointments, sprays, or creams to burns, as the hospital burn staff will have to remove them, causing more discomfort to the patient.
    c. Do not apply ice to burn surface.
4. Conserve body heat. Once treatment is complete, cover the patient with warming blankets. Burns covering large surface areas lose great amounts of moisture from evaporation, as protective skin layer is destroyed, thus making burn patients prime candidates for hypothermia.
5. To avoid the problems with swelling that can occur after a burn, remove all rings, bracelets, and so on, and elevate the burned extremity.

12

MEDICAL EMERGENCIES

RESPIRATORY DISTRESS

INTRODUCTION

As indicated in Chapter 3, there several different aspects of respiratory distress. Some are objective signs, observable by the EMT: changes in respiratory rate, diaphragmatic breathing, or abnormal breath sounds. The subjective symptom shortness of breath is called dyspnea. What is common to all forms of respiratory distress is some interference with gas exchange. The result is either too little oxygen or too much carbon dioxide in the blood.

This chapter discusses the medical causes of acute respiratory distress. Other causes are covered elsewhere in this book: obstruction of the upper airway in Chapter 8; trauma to the chest in Chapter 10; respiratory burns in Chapter 11, inhaled poisons in Chapter 13, asphyxia from drowning in Chapter 14, pediatric respiratory distress in Chapter 16, and hyperventilation syndrome in Chapter 17.

ASTHMA

Definition

Asthma is an episodic disease manifested by bronchial constriction from smooth muscle contraction and/or excessive mucus secretions. The patient with asthma has often had similar attacks in the past and may be receiving prescribed medications such as steroids. Between attacks the person is usually free of symptoms.

The term "status asthmaticus" refers to a particularly severe ongoing asthmatic attack that does not respond to the usual medications and may be fatal.

Acute Cause

An attack is usually provoked by an outside source such as pollutants, smoke, dust, stress, exercise, pollens and other allergens, or infection. The bronchi trend to increase in diameter with inhalation but collapse on exhalation, causing pronounced wheezing and an extended, forced expiratory phase. Many asthmatic patients use aerosol inhalers or bronchodilator pills when they feel an oncoming attack and may only call the EMS when that treatment has failed to give relief.

History: Subjective Reports

The chief complaint will be shortness of breath (dyspnea). The patient in status asthmaticus may relate a history of the present incident lasting for several hours, possibly days. These patients may also complain of fatigue and drowsiness.

Usually, the patient is known to be asthmatic. The past medical history may include similar attacks and treatment in an emergency department. It is important to obtain a medication history.

Examination: Objective Physical Findings

The patient is usually found in sitting forward and is often wheezing audibly. The patient often appears pale, diaphoretic, and tachypnic, with cyanosis at lips and nail beds, tachycardia, and prolonged expiratory phase, speaking in short phrases and coughing. Most asthmatic persons in acute distress are tired from the effort required to breathe and are very frightened.

1. Determine how long patient has been in acute distress.
2. Check lips and nail beds for cyanosis.
3. Check neck veins for distention while patient is in sitting position.
4. Check for retractions at the base of the neck with inspiration.
5. Listen to lung sounds (posterior thorax). Wheezes may be heard over all lung fields with inspiration and expiration.
6. Absence of lung sounds in all or part of lung fields ("quiet chest") is a serious indication of severe life-threatening asthma. The patient with a severe asthma attack may also appear very drowsy and have an extremely distended (hyperinflated) chest.

EMT Treatment

1. Provide immediate oxygen at 2–4 liters per minute or 28% Ventimask. Oxygen should be humidified if possible.
2. Place the patient in a sitting position.
3. Often the patient can be comforted with a calm approach and reassurance.
4. Assist the patient in taking any prescribed medications.
5. Be prepared to ventilate with a bag mask should respiratory arrest occur.
6. Call for paramedic assistance, if available.
7. Patients with severe asthma attacks need rapid provision of, or transport to, advanced life support services.

EMT Special Considerations

1. Acute asthmatic attacks can be a common problem with asth-

matic children. Parents usually won't call for help unless attack is severe.
2. Keep everyone at the scene calm and avoid obvious hurry.
3. Asthma patients many times will tolerate oxygen at a higher rate of flow per minute. Be alert for respiratory arrest, however.

CHRONIC OBSTRUCTIVE PULMONARY DISEASE (COPD)

Definition

COPD is divided into two basic categories: chronic bronchitis and emphysema. Both diseases involve progressively destructive changes in the lungs, and patients will give a history of long-standing disease. Most of these patients have been heavy smokers for years. Other factors are exposure to allergens, chemicals, or pollutants or repeated infections. The result of the destruction of alveoli, airways, and pulmonary blood vessels is poorly functioning gas exchange. This results in high levels of CO_2 and low levels of O_2 in the blood. Unlike healthy persons, whose automatic impulse to breathe is regulated by the level of CO_2 in the blood, breathing in the person with COPD (who has been living with high levels of CO_2 for years) is regulated by the level of oxygen in the blood.

Chronic Bronchitis is defined as a productive cough for three months of a year for at least two consecutive years. In chronic bronchitis, the lungs produce an excess of mucus and have difficulty expelling mucus from the bronchioles. The CO_2 retained in the lungs creates pulmonary hypertension, which can lead to right heart failure.

Emphysema is characterized by a decreased elasticity of the lung tissue, resulting in distention of the alveoli, which are filled with trapped air.

Acute Cause

The patient with COPD has little respiratory reserve to compensate for even minor demands on the respiratory system. The stress of an otherwise minor respiratory illness, such as an infection like the flu, can push this patient into acute respiratory distress.

History: Subjective Reports

The chief complaint of the COPD patient who is experiencing difficulty will be shortness of breath (dyspnea). The history of the present episode may reveal a recent "chest cold," fever, increasing dyspnea on exertion, and a change from a persistent (but often unproductive) cough to an increasing cough productive of thick yellow/green sputum. Usually, the patient has a known past medical history of COPD.

Examination: Objective Physical Findings

The COPD patient typically will be anxious-looking, older person with a barrel-shaped chest, sitting upright and leaning forward. Speech will come in short phrases, as the patient will be breathing rapidly through pursed lips, using the accessory muscles of the neck and chest to aid respiration. (The very acutely ill patient may actually have a decreased respiratory rate because of the very high level of CO_2 in the blood. This is called "CO_2 narcosis.") A prolonged expiratory phase will be noted. The patient may cough up yellow-green sputum. Auscultation of the chest may reveal rales, rhonchi, wheezes, or squeaks. These sounds may be faint and only present high up on the posterior chest.

Although it may be difficult (and unimportant) to distinguish between the two, chronic bronchitis and emphysema may present somewhat differently. The patient with *chronic bronchitis* may be markedly cyanotic and obese, and medical personnel often call these patients "blue bloaters." The COPD patient with chronic bronchitis who has some degree of right heart failure will have swelling of the ankles (peripheral edema) and distended neck veins. The patient with *emphysema* may be thin and not cyanotic and may be "puffing" through pursed lips. Medical personnel often call these patients "pink puffers." In practice, it may be difficult to tell them apart, especially when an emphysema patient's respiratory distress is acute and cyanosis is present. The EMT treatment for both types of COPD patient is the same.
1. Determine how long the patient has been in acute distress.
2. Listen to lung sounds. Wheezes may be heard in upper portions of the lungs. Rhonchi (coarse moist sounds) are the most likely sound to be heard. Rales (fine popping sounds) could be present.
3. Check lips and nail beds for cyanosis.
4. Check neck veins for distention while sitting.
5. Check for retractions at base of neck and between ribs.
6. Check for barrel chest.
7. Check for peripheral edema and pitting in lower extremities.
8. Check for tobacco stains on fingers.

EMT Treatment

1. Immediate oxygen at 2 liters per minute (or 24% Ventimask), if shortness of breath is present. Obtain physician concurrence, if possible.
2. Rule out other possible causes of symptoms, such as congestive heart failure with pulmonary edema.
3. Patient should be in a sitting position.
4. Loosen garments, but keep patient warm.

5. Give reassurance and reduce stress.
6. Encourage the patient to cough.
7. Monitor closely the effectiveness of breathing—its rate and depth. Coach the patient when to breathe and to breathe deeply. Be prepared to ventilate patient with bag mask should respiratory arrest occur.

Special Considerations

It is particularly important to emphasize that the COPD patient in acute respiratory distress needs oxygen, despite the possibility that raising the blood oxygen level could reduce the impulse to breathe. *Never* withhold oxygen from the COPD patient in respiratory distress.

PULMONARY EDEMA

Definition

Pulmonary edema is the accumulation of fluids in the lungs. The most common cause of pulmonary edema is cardiac dysfunction: failure of the left side of the heart to efficiently pump out the blood that is returning from the lungs. This cardiac dysfunction is caused by acute myocardial infarction (MI) or congestive heart failure (CHF). The capillaries in the lungs and other pulmonary vessels lose fluid into the alveoli, interfering with the exchange of oxygen and carbon dioxide.

Other less common causes of pulmonary edema include conditions in which the alveoli are directly damaged: smoke inhalation or other toxic inhalation, near drowning, aspiration, pneumonia, or infection. More rarely, pulmonary edema is seen in some other conditions: narcotic overdose; high altitude (HAPE); central nervous system damage, such as head injury or spinal injury; or chronic conditions such as cancer or liver disease. Occasionally, the patient who is receiving IV fluids can have circulatory overload if the flow rate is not carefully monitored ("runaway IV").

Acute Cause

Pulmonary edema can result suddenly following a myocardial infarction (heart attack). However, pulmonary edema generally does not have a sudden onset. Usually, it takes several hours to develop. As a result, patients often minimize the seriousness of the problem (hoping it will go away if they ignore it) until the dyspnea becomes impossible to ignore. Therefore, the EMT is likely to encounter the patient with pulmonary edema in an advanced state of acute respiratory distress.

History: Subjective Reports

The chief complaint of the pulmonary edema patient will be shortness of breath (dyspnea). This history of the present episode will reveal dyspnea that is worse while the patient is lying flat (orthopnea) and often wakes the patient from sleep during the night with the sensation of needing air (paroxysmal noctural dyspnea or PND). These patients often sleep with two or three pillows, in a semi-sitting position. Their dyspnea is often worse on exertion (DOE). Chest pain may be present. Often the patient has a past medical history of heart disease or high blood pressure (hypertension).

Examination: Objective Physical Findings

The patient will be an anxious-looking person, sitting bolt upright, possibly agitated or combative. The patient may cough up frothy, pink (blood-tinged) sputum. Cyanosis may be present. Respirations are rapid and shallow, tachycardia is usually present, and blood pressure is generally elevated. Auscultation of the chest may reveal rales, rhonchi, or wheezes. Lung bases may be silent in severe cases, and lung sounds may only be heard high up on the posterior chest.

The patient in CHF may have both left heart failure (leading to pulmonary edema) and right heart failure. If significant right heart failure is present, the patient will have swelling of the ankles (peripheral edema) and distended neck veins.

It can be difficult to distinguish cardiac pulmonary edema from COPD with acute respiratory failure. Because the treatment is different, Table 12–1 may help.

EMT Treatment

The following therapeutic measures should be performed in the sequence listed below and only as necessary.
1. Oxygenation: use condition of patient as guide to method and amount, ranging from nasal prongs with low flow (2 liters per minute) to immediate bag mask assist with 100% O_2. Start with 2 liters per minute if patient has COPD.
2. Ventilation: patients with cardiac pulmonary edema can usually ventilate adequately on their own; mechanical ventilation with bag mask or demand valve may be necessary if the patient's condition is severe. Patient may resist initial attempt at bag mask assist but will stop resisting as breathing becomes easier.
3. Position: sitting upright with dangling feet to reduce venous return (most patients will already be doing this). Keep patient upright with feet dangling while enroute to the hospital.
4. Constricting bands to reduce venous return on three of the four extremities, rotating one every 15 minutes. This therapy (called

Table 12–1. DISTINGUISHING CHARACTERISTICS OF CARDIAC PULMONARY EDEMA AND COPD WITH ACUTE RESPIRATORY FAILURE

	Cardiac Pulmonary Edema	COPD with Acute Respiratory Failure
History	May have cardiac medications (nitroglycerin, digoxin, propranolol)	May have lung medications (theophylline, home oxygen)
	May have history of angina, MI	May have history of recent upper respiratory infection
Physical Signs		
"Barrel" chest	Rare	Often present
Clubbing of fingers	Rare	Often present
Cyanosis	Less prominent	More prominent
Mental confusion	Associated with hypotension	Associated with normal blood pressure
Wheezing	Less common	More common
Prolonged expiratory phase	Rare	Often present
Sputum	White or pink	Yellow-green

"rotating tourniquets") should only be used if the EMT is trained in its use. Start by applying the constricting bands around both legs at the mid-thigh and around one upper arm. Tie with a slip knot. Check for a pulse below the band; if no pulse is found, the band is too tight and needs to be loosened. Blood pressure cuffs can also be used, and they should be inflated to a value between the patient's diastolic pressure and the systolic pressure.

PULMONARY EMBOLISM

Definition

An *embolism* is a blood clot or foreign body lodged in a blood vessel, blocking the circulation of blood to areas beyond the site. When an embolism lodges in a pulmonary artery or arteriole, blocking the flow of blood to part of the lungs, it is called a *pulmonary embolism*. Blood clots generally come from other parts of the body, usually from the veins of the legs or pelvis, and occasionally from around an artificial heart valve. Blood clots are formed in a number of different medical conditions: inactivity (such as prolonged bed rest after surgery); inflamed veins (thrombophlebitis), or birth control pill use. Foreign body embolism can be a fat particle from a broken bone end, an air bubble from a neck wound, or amniotic fluid as a complication of childbirth.

Acute Cause

The sudden blockage of circulation to part of the lungs causes the sudden onset of respiratory distress, because the part of the lung deprived of circulation no longer participates in the exchange of gases.

History: Subjective Reports

The symptoms resulting from pulmonary embolism may vary depending upon the site and location of the embolism. The chief complaint will be the sudden onset of severe shortness of breath (dyspnea). Patients may also complain of chest pain. The history of the present illness may reveal the coughing up of blood (hemoptysis). The past medical history may include one of the predisposing conditions just discussed, such as thrombophlebitis.

Examination: Objective Physical Findings

Determination of vital signs will reveal rapid breathing, tachycardia, and possibly hypotension. Auscultation of the chest may reveal wheezes audible near the pain source. Check the lower extremities for evidence of inflammation of the veins.

EMT Treatment

1. 100% oxygen should be provided in high concentration, for example, with a non-rebreathing mask.
2. Therapy for shock may be indicated, if patient is hypotensive.
3. Acutely ill patients need rapid provision of, or transport to, advanced life support services.

PNEUMONIA

Definition

Pneumonia is an inflammation of the lungs, which occurs when a portion of the lung is filled with fluid or pus. The most common cause is infection, from bacteria or virus. It can also be caused by aspiration of vomitus, toxic inhalation, or cancer.

Acute Cause

Pneumonia causes acute respiratory distress when the inflammation interferes with the exchange of gas.

History: Subjective Reports

The symptoms resulting from pneumonia may vary depending upon the cause. When the pneumonia is from a lung infection, the chief complaint may be the sudden onset of shaking chills and fever. Shortness of breath (dyspnea) is usually present. Chest pain, especially on inspiration, may be present. The history of the present illness may reveal a cough productive of dark sputum.

Examination: Objective Physical Findings

The patient will often be an elderly, debilitated person. The skin will be hot and dry. Respirations will be rapid. Ausculation of the chest may reveal rhonchi, usually involving one lung only.

EMT Treatment

1. Provide oxygen.
2. Place the patient in a position of comfort.

PLEURISY (PLEURITIS)

Definition

Pleurisy (pleuritis) is an inflammation of the double-layered lining of the lung (pleura). Injury or disease can cause the loss of friction-free movement of the chest wall lining (parietal pleura) with the lung covering (visceral pleura). The most common cause is infection. Less common causes include pulmonary embolism or cancer.

Acute Cause

Severe pain can come from the friction of the inflamed lining surfaces rubbing against each other. The onset may be sudden.

History: Subjective Reports

The chief complaint will be localized pain associated with respiration, especially increased with deep inspiration. The patient may be short of breath if the pain is severe.

Examination: Objective Physical Findings

Examination may be unremarkable, except for a possibly increased respiratory rate and coughing.

EMT Treatment

1. Provide oxygen.
2. Place the patient in a position of comfort.

CARDIOVASCULAR DISORDERS

INTRODUCTION

As was indicated in Chapter 4, there are several different aspects to cardiovascular distress. Some are objective signs, observable by the EMT, such as changes in heart rate or blood pressure. Chest pain, on the other hand, is entirely subjective. The medical causes of these signs and symptoms are the subject of this section. Other illnesses or trauma can cause similar signs and symptoms, as listed in Chapter 4.

HEART ATTACK (MYOCARDIAL INFARCTION)

Definition

An acute myocardial infarction (MI) occurs when there is a sudden blockage of circulation through a coronary artery, which supplies blood to the heart muscle (myocardium). A portion of the myocardium dies after being deprived of oxygenated blood. An MI occurs as a result of a disease process called atheroslcerosis, which involves the narrowing and hardening of the blood vessels. Atheroslcerosis in the coronary arteries is called coronary artery disease (CAD). Atherosclerosis occurs in the blood vessel walls when cholesterol deposits, scarring, and calcium deposits gradually build up over the years. Coronary artery disease can start at a very early age. It takes years to progress. Thus, MI most occurs commonly in persons in their 50s, 60s, and 70s but can occur when they are in their 30s and 40s.

Acute Cause

A myocardial infarction is an acute medical emergency because the MI patient is at high risk for three very serious complications: sudden cardiac arrest, cardiogenic shock, and pulmonary edema. Cardiac rhythm disturbance (arrhythmias) occur with the greatest frequency in the first hour after MI, and arrhythmia can cause sudden cardiac arrest in the MI patient without warning.

History: Subjective Reports

The chief complaint of the MI patient will usually be intense, continuous chest pain, located under the sternum. The patient may report that the pain radiates down the left arm (in approximately 25% of patients) or to both arms, the jaw, neck, back, or stomach. Patients may use any of several words to describe the quality of the pain, such as crushing, squeezing, heavy, tight, or aching. The history may reveal that the pain has been present for 15 minutes or more. The onset may have occurred while the patient was at rest, sleeping or sitting quietly. The pain has not been relieved by nitroglycerin tablet, rest, or antacids.

Other associated symptoms may be present: weakness, nausea, vomiting, dizziness, or palpitations. Some patients may feel that if they could only belch, the pain would go away. If significant left heart failure has occurred and pulmonary edema is developing, dyspnea and cough may be present. The past medical history may reveal some of the risk factors for MI: diabetes, hypertension, or smoking.

The MI patient is usually extremely anxious and fearful, with a feeling of impending doom. People express fear in different ways. Some become demanding and may refuse the oxygen mask adamantly. Others may have *denial* and minimize the severity of the symptoms.

A small percentage of patients may experience a silent MI, also called "MI without tears." These patients are usually elderly and do not complain of chest pain. Their only complaint may be sudden shortness of breath, lightheadedness or confusion, weakness, or mild epigastric distress.

Examination: Objective Physical Findings

The MI patient will be anxious-looking person, usually with pale, cold, clammy skin, which may appear gray in Caucasians. A rapid, irregular pulse will be present, although occasionally patients may have a very slow pulse rate. The blood pressure will have fallen, but it may only be down to "normal" if the past medical history included hypertension. If significant pulmonary edema has occurred, the respiratory rate may be rapid, and ausculation of the chest may reveal rales.

1. Have the patient take a deep inspiration. The pain should not change with chest wall movement.
2. Listen to the lungs.
3. Monitor vital signs closely. Take special note of irregular pulse. Pulse can be categorized as regularly irregular (such as a dropped beat every three or four beats) or irregularly irregular (random, with no regular pattern).
4. Look for ankle swelling (peripheral edema). Press with the thumb to see if indentation persists (pitting edema).
5. Check neck veins for distention.

EMT Treatment

1. If patient is unconscious, treatment consists of assessment and management of ABCs: airway, breathing, circulation. Once these priorities are managed, provide oxygen in high concentra-

tion. Assure rapid provision of, or transport to advanced life support services.

2. Keep the patient calm, if conscious, and provide reassurance. Do not have patient walk or exert himself. Lift, move, or carry the patient as necessary to avoid additional demands on the heart.

3. Provide oxygen in high concentration, as with a non-rebreathing mask. Extremely anxious and fearful patients may refuse the mask, and a nasal cannula may be better tolerated, but that is a second choice.

4. Place patient in semi-reclining position.

5. Monitor vital signs closely.

6. Avoid the use of sirens unless absolutely necessary.

7. Assure rapid provision of, or transport to, advanced life support services.

ANGINA PECTORIS

Definition

Angina pectoris refers to pain in the chest (literally, "choking in the chest"). Angina is a symptom of coronary artery disease and is caused by an insufficient blood supply to the heart muscle. The pain occurs when the need of the myocardium for oxygen exceeds the available supply of oxygenated blood. It is usually triggered by physical exertion or emotional stress and is relieved by rest. It is of short duration, usually less than 10 minutes. Angina differs from MI in that the flow of oxygenated blood is only reduced rather than completely blocked.

Acute Cause

Angina occurs as a symptom of coronary artery disease, which is a chronic disease most patients learn to live with. These patients may call for the ambulance when they are having increasing angina or when they are getting less relief from rest or the heart medication nitroglycerin. Increasing angina can be a sign of worsening coronary artery disease, which can lead to acute myocardial infarction (MI).

History: Subjective Reports

The chief complaint of the angina patient will usually be mild to moderate chest pain, located under the sternum. The patient may report that the pain radiates down the left arm or to both arms, the jaw, or the epigastrium. Rarely the pain only occurs at a remote site such as the left arm or jaw. Patients may use any of several words to describe the quality of the pain, such as squeezing, pressure, aching, tight, or discomfort. The history of the present

Table 12–2. DISTINGUISHING CHARACTERISTICS OF ANGINA PECTORIS AND MYOCARDIAL INFARCTION

Characteristic	Angina	Myocardial Infarction
Pain		
Intensity	Mild to moderate	Severe, frightening
Duration	3–5 minutes (rarely over 10 minutes)	Over 15 minutes
Setting of onset	Physical exertion Emotional stress Cold weather	May occur at rest
Alleviation of pain	Rest, nitroglycerin	Not by rest or nitroglycerin
Associated symptoms	May be none	Often nausea, weakness, anxiety, sweating
Pulse	Usually regular	Often irregular
Blood Pressure	Usually unchanged	Often low

illness may reveal that the pain has a short duration, usually 3 to 5 minutes and rarely more than 10 minutes. The onset may have occurred with physical exertion, emotional stress, cold weather, or a large meal. The pain will usually be relieved by rest or nitroglycerin tablets. The pain will not change with respiration or change of position.

Other associated symptoms may be present: weakness, nausea, or anxiety. Patients will often have a past medical history of cardiac disease and may be taking prescribed cardiac medications, such as nitroglycerin or amyl nitrite.

It can be difficult to distinguish angina pectoris from acute myocardial infarction (MI) (Table 12–2). When there is any doubt, treat the patient as if an MI were occurring.

Examination: Objective Physical Findings

1. During episode of pain, the patient may look quite ill but will take on normal appearance rapidly when the pain subsides.
2. Conduct the same physical examination as for MI.
3. Determine if patient required normal number of nitroglycerin tablets to relieve pain and if the nitroglycerin produced a "bite" when used. This indicates that the medicine is still good. Moisture decreases the effectiveness of nitroglycerin, and patients who require frequent doses of their nitroglycerin will find it loses effectiveness sooner. Do not rely on the issue date on the bottle.
4. Determine if the episode is the same as previous episodes as regards the onset, intensity, and duration of pain. If the patient describes the current episode as different from previous experiences, treat as if for an MI.

EMT Treatment

1. If current episode is normal, based upon previous episodes, assist with oxygen (2–4 liters per minute) until pain subsides.
2. Keep the scene calm and quiet.
3. Assist the patient with prescribed medications, if any.
4. Transport, even if the pains go away.

CONGESTIVE HEART FAILURE

Definition

Congestive heart failure (CHF) occurs when failure in a heart muscle causes fluid accumulation in the tissue spaces. When the left side of the heart fails, fluid accumulates in the lungs (pulmonary edema). When the right side of the heart fails, fluid accumulates in the extremities (peripheral edema). If right heart failure exists for a long period, fluid eventually also accumulates in the abdominal organs, resulting in abdominal distention from fluid accumulation (ascites).

The most common cause of CHF is myocardial infarction (MI). The onset of CHF may be three to seven days or more after the occurrence of the MI. Other causes of CHF include cardiac rhythm disturbance; high blood pressure (hypertension); blood volume (fluid) overload from various sources, such as excess salt in the diet; or heart valve disease.

CHF may be mild or severe and life-threatening. Pulmonary edema is the most extreme form of CHF. Full description of the signs, symptoms, and treatment of pulmonary edema is given in the previous section on respiratory distress.

Acute Cause

The patient with right heart failure rarely calls an ambulance for that problem alone. Generally, right heart failure is seen in patients who are calling for some other, more urgent reason, such as COPD (chronic bronchitis) with respiratory decompensation or MI. Similarly, left heart failure can be mild, as in chronic CHF, or acute, as in acute MI with pulmonary edema.

History: Subjective Reports

Since the patient with right heart failure will usually be seen by the EMT when there is some more pressing emergency condition, the chief complaint will not be related to the right heart failure.

The chief complaint of the patient with left heart failure will be shortness of breath (dyspnea). The patient may also complain of progressive fatigue. If the left heart failure is advanced, the patient may complain of all the symptoms of pulmonary edema (see p. 91).

Examination: Objective Physical Findings

The patient with right heart failure will have swelling of the extremities (peripheral edema). Press with the thumb to see if indentation persists (pitting edema). Pitting edema can occur when the peripheral edema has persisted for a long time (chronic CHF). Abdominal fluid accumulation (ascites) and distended neck veins may also be seen.

The patient with left heart failure may have all or only a few of the signs of pulmonary edema: frothy, pink sputum; cyanosis; rapid, shallow respirations; tachycardia; high blood pressure; and rales or rhonchi (see p. 30). The patient with CHF may have both left and right heart failure at the same time and thus have signs of both.

EMT Treatment

1. Right heart failure requires no specific treatment by the EMT.
2. CHF with left heart failure is treated the same as pulmonary edema (see p. 92): oxygenation, ventilation, position upright with feet dangling, and rotating tourniquets if the EMT trained in their use and if the situation is severe.

Special Considerations

Be aware that sudden worsening of chronic CHF is often caused by myocardial infarction (MI).

PACEMAKER FAILURE

Definition

A *cardiac pacemaker* is a device that artificially delivers an electrical impulse to the heart to control its rate and rhythm. Implanted during an operation, it has two parts: the generating unit, placed under the skin near the surface; and the wires, which are sewn into the myocardium. *Pacemaker failure* occurs when something goes wrong with the device and it fails to deliver the electrical impulse to the heart. Failure is a rare event, and it is usually caused by battery failure or mechanical malfunction, not by loose wires.

Acute Cause

The pacemaker failure may cause the heart to be unable to maintain a rate adequate for normal blood pressure. The patient is then at risk for heart failure or cardiogenic shock.

History: Subjective Reports

The chief complaint of the patient with pacemaker failure is likely to be sudden weakness or dizziness. The past medical history will indicate heart disease, pacemaker implant surgery, and cardiac medications.

Examination: Objective Physical Findings

The heart rate in pacemaker failure will be slow: usually less than 50 beats per minute, often 35 to 45 beats per minute. However, it may increase initially. The rate is usually fixed and regular, although occasionally it may be irregular. Some patients may have syncopal episodes.

The pacemaker generating unit should be palpable under the skin, usually on the chest just below the collarbone (clavicle).

EMT Treatment

1. Provide oxygen.
2. Transport.

Special Considerations

The artificial cardiac pacemaker does not prevent heart disease, such as atherosclerosis or coronary artery disease. Thus, it is possible for a patient with an implanted pacemaker to have angina pectoris, congestive heart failure (CHF), or even myocardial infarction (MI). Any patient with signs and symptoms of angina, CHF, or MI who also has a pacemaker is treated the same as any other patient with those signs and symptoms.

STOKES-ADAMS ATTACKS

Definition

Stokes-Adams attacks are cardiac rhythm disturbances in which the heart rate becomes very fast or very slow, causing a temporary reduction in cardiac output. The reduction in cardiac output results in transient hypotension, a reduction in cerebral blood flow, and often fainting.

Acute Cause

Stokes-Adams attacks can cause fainting (syncope), during which the patient can sustain injury while falling. Stokes-Adams attacks can recur and may last long enought to cause cardiac arrest.

History: Subjective Reports

Usually, patients do not have any warning that Stokes-Adams attacks are about to occur. The chief complaint may be related to injury sustained from a fall during the syncopal episode. Patients may complain of palpitations or lightheadedness.

Examination: Objective Physical Findings

The Stokes-Adams patient is often an elderly person and is usually found by the EMT after the pulse has returned to normal. Patients typically return to consciousness spontaneously. Injury may be found if the patient fell during a syncopal episode.

EMT Treatment

1. Keep the patient flat, with the lower legs raised.
2. Administer oxygen.
3. Monitor pulse rate closely. Document irregularities by recording time of occurrence, duration of irregularity, and pattern (regularly irregular or irregularly irregular). Record findings.
4. Examine for possible injuries.

Special Considerations

Stokes-Adams attack is only one of many possible causes of fainting (syncope). A list of others can be found in Chapter 5.

PERICARDITIS

Definition

Pericarditis is inflammation of the pericardial sac surrounding the heart. It is most commonly caused by a viral infection. It may also appear in post-myocardial infarction patients at three to six weeks after the MI, which may be after the patient has been discharged to go home.

Acute Cause

Severe pain can come from the friction of the inflamed lining surfaces rubbing against each other. The patient is at risk for the complications of cardiac rhythm disturbance (arrhythmia) or cardiac tamponade.

History: Subjective Reports

The chief complaint will be substernal or precordial chest pain, of variable intensity. The pain may radiate to the shoulders. The quality of the pain is also variable, from a deep, dull ache to a sharp, burning pain. The patient may report that the onset of the pain was not sudden, but rather developed over hours or days. The pain may be affected by a change in position to a leaning-forward posture. The pain is often not relieved by nitroglycerin. It may be aggravated by deep breathing, swallowing, or coughing. Shortness of breath (dyspnea) may be present, as the patient attempts to avoid the pain of deep breathing. Past medical history may include cardiac disease and a recent myocardial infarction (MI).

Examination: Objective Physical Findings

The pericarditis patient will be an anxious-looking person, who may be breathing rapidly to avoid the pain of deep breathing. A slight fever may be present.

EMT Treatment

1. It may be difficult to distinguish pericarditis from acute myocardial infarction. When in doubt, treat the patient as if an MI were occurring.
2. Provide oxygen.
3. Transport.

HYPERTENSION

Definition

Hypertension simply means high blood pressure. It is defined as a systolic pressure of over 140 mm Hg or a diastolic pressure of over 90 mm Hg. The causes of hypertension, which are listed in Chapter 4, include head injury, essential hypertension (cause unknown), toxemia of pregnancy, and anxiety. Hypertension can be associated with (although it is not caused by) CVA, aortic aneurysm, CHF, pulmonary edema, or angina.

Acute Cause

"Malignant hypertension" exists when the blood pressure is dangerously high, often 200/140 mm Hg or higher. This can cause severe vascular damage (such as CVA or dissecting aortic aneurysm), congestive heart failure with pulmonary edema, acute kidney failure, and death. In patients with known hypertension who abruptly stop therapy, hypertensive emergencies may develop.

History: Subjective Reports

The chief complaint may be headache or blurred vision. Associated symptoms include severe nosebleeds, nausea, or dyspnea.

The past medical history may include hypertension, cardiac disease, vascular disease, or alcoholism.

Examination: Objective Physical Findings

High blood pressure is the hallmark finding. Other findings may depend upon the cause of the hypertension (such as toxemia in the pregnant patient) or may be the result of chronic hypertension (such as CHF). Similarly, the signs of a CVA or a dissecting aortic aneurysm will be specific to those medical conditions.

Occasionally, a severe nosebleed that does not stop after the usual treatment is associated with high blood pressure.

EMT Treatment

1. Treatment may be specific to the other medical conditions found.
2. If no other medical condition is found, place the patient in a sitting position, provide oxygen, and transport.

AORTIC ANEURYSM

Definition

Outpouching from weakening of an arterial wall is called an aneurysm. The term *dissecting aneurysm* refers to bleeding through a tear of the arterial wall between the inner and outer linings. This creates a false channel in the arterial wall, which may result in occlusion of arteries branching off the injured artery. *Rupture of an aneurysm* is the worst complication, as the rupture will lead to massive hemmorhage. Aortic aneurysm can occur in either the thorax or the abdomen (Figs. 12–1 and 12–2).

Acute Cause

There are no symptoms associated with the formation and development of an aneurysm. However, when an abdominal aortic aneurysm dissects, blood can leak into the abdominal cavity. Signs and symptoms of an "acute abdomen" then occur, because blood is an irritant to the abdominal lining (peritoneum). Likewise, if blood from a thoracic aortic aneurysm leaks into the thoracic cavity, chest pain occurs.

When an aortic aneurysm ruptures, the rapid hemorrhage causes hypovolemic shock.

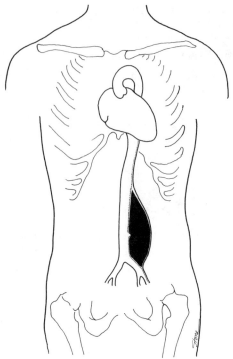

Figure 12–1. Abdominal aortic aneurysm involving a portion of the femoral artery.

History: Subjective Reports

Thoracic

1. Patients often have a history of hypertension.
2. Pain may begin in the chest and progress toward the legs or into the back.
3. Pain often described as tearing or "hot poker" through the chest.
4. Patient may have fainting spell, with or without associated pain, which can include all the symptoms of shock.
5. Pain is steady and unchanged with position.

Abdominal

1. Patients often have history of arteriosclerosis.
2. May report previously diagnosed aneurysm.
3. Pain often described as tearing through to lower back.
4. Patient may have fainting with or without associated pain, which can include all the symptoms of shock.
5. Pain is steady and unchanged with position.
6. One or both extremities may be said to be extremely cold.

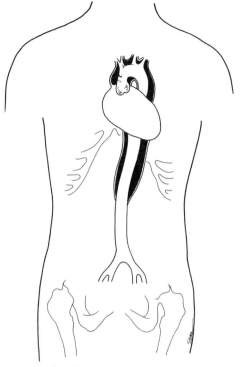

Figure 12–2. Thoracic aortic aneurysm.

Examination: Objective Physical Findings

Thoracic

1. Take and compare radial pulses in both arms and for gross difference in amplitude.
2. Take and compare blood pressure in both arms for gross difference in pressure readings.
3. Check carotid pulses for difference in amplitude. Do not check both sides at the same time.
4. Check for neurological symptoms as result of occluded carotid artery or arteries.

Abdominal

1. Gently palpate midline of abdomen for pulsatile mass extending to one side of mid-line (aorta).
2. Compare amplitude of femoral pulses.
3. Palpate abdomen for fluid and increasing abdominal size.
4. Take vital signs frequently to monitor for shock.
5. Determine postural blood pressure if patient's systolic blood pressure is above 80 mm Hg.

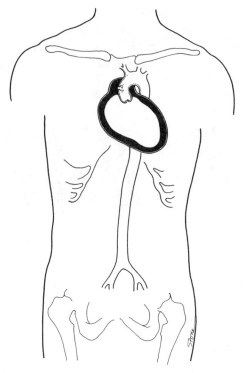

Figure 12–3. Dissecting thoracic aortic aneurysm causing cardiac tamponade.

Thoracic

5. Check for symptoms of *cardiac tamponade* (Fig. 12–3).
   a. Distended neck veins.
   b. Distant heart sounds.
   c. Falling blood pressure.
6. Determine postural blood pressure if patient's systolic blood pressure is above 80 mm Hg.

Abdominal

6. Compare warmth and color of legs.

EMT Treatment

1. Use oxygen, 4–6 liters per minute, or bag mask as required.
2. Place patient with lower extremities elevated to combat low blood pressure.
3. Anti-shock trousers should be applied if available. Use only sufficient pressure to maintain blood pressure at 60 mm Hg.
4. Request paramedical assistance if available, otherwise provide rapid transport to hospital.

NEUROLOGICAL DISORDERS

INTRODUCTION

As indicated in Chapter 5, there are several different aspects of problems originating in the central nervous system. Neurological problems include impairments in consciousness (coma, syncope) and in voluntary control over movement (seizures, paralysis). These signs can occur as a result of problems that do not originate in the central nervous system, and those other medical or traumatic conditions (listed in Chapter 5) are discussed in other sections of this book. The subject of this section is neurological disorder.

STROKE (CEREBROVASCULAR ACCIDENT)

Definition

A cerebrovascular accident (CVA) is interruption in blood supply to a portion of the brain. The effects depend upon which part of the brain is involved, such as the part controlling speech or the parts controlling movement of one side of the body. Three distinctly different mechanisms can cause CVA. The most common is a clot (thrombus) that progressively blocks a cerebral artery, usually as a result of atherosclerosis. Another cause is a wandering blood clot (embolus) that lodges in a cerebral artery, blocking blood flow. This can result from heart valve disease, cardiac rhythm disturbance (atrial fibrillation), sickle cell disease, or rarely birth control pill use. The third possible cause of CVA is hemorrhage into brain tissue from rupture of a cerebral aneurysm, usually associated with high blood pressure (hypertension).

Acute Cause

Strokes can vary in severity from mild, in which only a small area of the brain is affected and little difficulty is experienced by the patient, to severe, with coma, seizures, or respiratory difficulty.

History: Subjective Reports

What the patient relates as present problems may indicate whether the CVA is thrombotic, embolic or hemorrhagic, as Table 12–3 demonstrates.

Examination: Objective Physical Findings

Findings will depend upon the portion of the brain involved. Signs of CVA include facial asymmetry, speech disturbance, lack

Table 12–3. TYPES OF CEREBROVASCULAR ACCIDENT

Symptom	Thrombus	Embolus	Rupture
Headache	Mild	Moderate	Severe
Onset of symptoms	Can evolve over several hours	Sudden	Sudden
History of TIAs	Often	Occasional	None
Past medical history	Atherosclerosis	Heart valve disease/atrial fibrillation/sickle cell disease	Hypertension
Associated symptoms	One-sided weakness; dizziness	One-sided weakness; dizziness	Stiff neck

of coordination, unequal pupils, unequal grip strength, unilateral paralysis, decreased level of consciousness, or seizures. It is useful to conduct a neurological exam in order to document the level and type of dysfunction present. The observations made in the field serve as useful reference observations should the dysfunction change. Record (with time taken), the following observations:

1. Vital signs.
    a. Respiratory rate.
    b. Pulse rate and regularity.
    c. Blood pressure.
2. Orientation to surroundings.
3. Speech.
4. Response to stimulus.
5. Pupils.
6. Ability to move.
    See Appendix 7 for a neurological checklist.

EMT Treatment

1. Low-flow oxygen should be administered to all patients.
2. Monitor vital signs closely. Be alert for respiratory difficulty that may require ventilatory assistance. Be especially alert for a rising blood pressure with a falling pulse rate; this indicates a need for rapid transport to a hospital.
3. Emotional support to the patient is very important, especially if he/she is conscious and understands what is happening. Explain to the patient that he/she may be having a stroke and it is impossible to say what the final outcome will be, but there is hope that the problem is temporary and that much function will return. Always try to be reassuring to the patient, but do not make exaggerated claims that everything will be all right.
4. Protect paralyzed extremities from injury.
5. Give nothing by mouth.

EMT Special Considerations

Be aware that inability to speak can occur in a patient otherwise quite capable of hearing, thinking, and feeling. The EMT may be able to communicate *to* the patient, even when the CVA patient is not able to communicate back to the EMT. Avoid thoughtless comments that an apparently unconscious patient could misinterpret and find upsetting. Remember that these patients may be able to follow simple commands, such as "squeeze my hand."

TRANSIENT ISCHEMIC ATTACK (TIA)

Definition

Transient ischemic attacks (TIAs) refer to symptoms of stroke that subside completely within 24 hours and usually within 6 hours. TIAs (also called "little strokes") are caused by temporary reduction in blood supply to a portion of the brain. The relationship between TIA and CVA is very similar to the relationship between angina and MI. In fact, the underlying disease is the same: atherosclerosis. TIAs vary in frequency, and affected persons are normal between attacks.The diagnosis can be made only after rapid recovery has occurred; it cannot be made prior to complete recovery from the symptoms.

Acute Cause

The sudden changes in behavior, speech, or motor function result from cerebral vascular insufficiency. A TIA can present as a syncopal episode.

History: Subjective Reports

The symptoms experienced by the patient will depend upon the portion of the brain affected. Common symptoms include headache, dizziness, unilateral weakness or numbness, and loss of speech or vision. The past medical history will often reveal recurrent episodes of similar symptoms.

Examination: Objective Physical Findings

The most common presentation is a syncopal episode. Other signs of TIA depend upon the portion of the brain involved: speech disturbance, lack of coordination, unilateral paralysis, and so on. Because it may not be possible in the field to tell a TIA from a CVA, a thorough neurological examination is indicated. The same responses as listed in the previous section are recorded (p. 110).

EMT Treatment

1. If the signs and symptoms are not completely resolved, treat as if a CVA were occurring.

2. If the signs and symptoms have completely resolved, monitor the progression of symptoms or return of function. Transport to the hospital, even if the symptoms have cleared.

EPILEPSY

Definition

Epilepsy is a chronic disease characterized by seizures. It can be caused by an old brain injury with scarring, a birth injury, or genetic predisposition. Epilepsy is usually easily controlled by medication. *Seizures* are sudden episodes of involuntary muscle contraction and relaxation, caused by excessive brain cell electrical activity. Seizures have many other causes in addition to epilepsy, as listed in Chapter 5. Seizures can involve generalized tonic-clonic activity ("grand mal") followed by unconsciousness and then confusion (post-ictal state), or seizures may be partial (focal) and limited. Partial seizures include such activity as localized muscle jerking, fleeting localized painful sensations, or involuntary repetitive behavior. Some partial seizures progress to generalized muscular activity. Generalized seizures include full body convulsions or brief lapses of awareness ("petit mal"). *Status epilepticus* exists when there is a rapid succession of repeated seizures without regaining of consciousness during the intervals.

Acute Cause

Seizures are the acute manifestation of epilepsy. Medications keep the disease under control, but occasionally patients forget to take them or the dose is not sufficient. Status epilepticus is an acute medical emergency because the patient could die of hypoxia or aspiration during the episode.

History: Subjective Reports

The patient may report an aura—a sensation of light, color, or smell—before a seizure occurs.

The post-ictal patient may complain of a headache. Post-seizure confusion and amnesia for the seizure and preceding events may occur.

Examination: Objective Physical Findings

In some patients, a generalized seizure begins with focal signs or deviation of the eyes. The actual beginning of a generalized seizure is sudden unconsciousness with a short (30-second) period of tonic stiffening. This leads into the thrashing tonic-clonic activity, which generally lasts about two minutes. During this period, three things can occur. First, loss of control over the bowels and bladder is common, resulting in staining of clothing. Second, contraction of the chest muscles interferes with respiration, resulting in temporary cyanosis, which usually resolves rapidly after the seizure is over. Third, contraction of the jaw muscles can occasionally cause biting of the tongue or lips.

During the post-ictal period, seizure patients need to be examined for injuries of the extremities caused by the thrashing. Other signs in the post-ictal period include slow return to consciousness, disorientation, drooling, rapid pulse, or rapid respirations. The patient should be searched for a medical ID tag.

EMT Treatment

1. Protect the patient from injury during the seizure. Do not attempt rigid restraint of the patient.
2. If the jaws have not yet clenched, a padded tongue blade (bite block) should be placed between the patient's back teeth. Do not force into place during active seizure. Do not use front teeth. Do not insert fingers. Avoid allowing the bite block to slip into the mouth and obstruct the airway.
3. Provide oxygen and suction, as necessary. During transportation, low-flow oxygen (2 liters per minute) should be administered.
4. In the post-ictal period, examine the patient and turn on side to facilitate drainage and prevent aspiration.
5. Provide emotional support and reassurance to the confused post-ictal patient.
6. Transport all seizure patients to the hospital. Bring the patient's medications.
7. For *status epilepticus*, provide
   a. Oxygen in high concentration.
   b. Ventilatory assistance.
   c. Rapid transport. Call for paramedics if available.

DIABETES

LOW BLOOD GLUCOSE (HYPOGLYCEMIA)

Definition

Diabetes mellitus is a disease in which the body is unable to efficiently utilize glucose (sugar) for energy. It is caused by a decrease in insulin, a hormone produced by the pancreas. There are two types of diabetes: a milder form, usually appearing in adults, and a more severe form, usually appearing in childhood, in which the diabetic is dependent upon insulin injections. Diabetes is controllable through diet, oral pills that stimulate insulin production, or insulin injections. Diabetic persons need to balance their food intake with the amount of insulin used. *Low blood glucose* (hypoglycemia) occurs when a diabetic has taken too much insulin, has not eaten enough food, has had too much exercise, or has some combination of these factors. This condition is also called "insulin shock."

Acute Cause

In hypoglycemia, the glucose is taken up by the body cells faster than it appears in the blood stream. The brain is the most quickly affected organ.

History: Subjective Reports

The onset of hypoglycemia is generally rapid, although it may be gradual if a long-acting insulin is used. The patient will be a known diabetic, usually with a medical ID tag. If conscious, the patient will often relate a history of taking the regular amount of insulin, but exercising particularly strenuously or not eating. Common symptoms are headache, dizziness, confusion, weakness, and hunger. If the patient is alert and oriented, ask these questions:

1. Did you eat today?
2. Did you take your insulin today?

If the patient did not eat adequately and took insulin, the patient probably has low blood glucose. If the patient ate and did not take the insulin, the patient probably has high blood glucose (discussed in the next part of this section).

Examination: Objective Physical Findings

If conscious, the patient may exhibit various disturbances in behavior: disorientation, lack of coordination, confusion, irritability, or hostility.

If the patient is unconscious, the history may be difficult to obtain. Usually the only information from bystanders that is reliable is whether the onset of symptoms was sudden (over minutes) or gradual (over hours or days). Assessment of the patient then depends upon physical findings. Signs of low blood sugar include drooling; pale, cool, moist skin; full, rapid pulse; normal blood pressure and respirations; and seizures in late stages.

It can be difficult to distinguish low blood glucose from high blood glucose (Table 12–4). When there is any doubt, treat the patient as if low blood glucose were present.

Table 12–4. DISTINGUISHING CHARACTERISTICS OF LOW BLOOD GLUCOSE (HYPOGLYCEMIA) FROM HIGH BLOOD GLUCOSE (HYPERGLYCEMIA)

	Low Blood Glucose	High Blood Glucose
The Three Most Reliable Signs:		
Onset	Rapid—minutes	Gradual—hours to days
Skin moistness	Wet, drooling	Dry
Respirations	Normal or shallow	Rapid, deep
History:		
Food intake adequate	No	Yes
Insulin	Excessive	Insufficient
Strenuous exercise	Often	Rare
Associated symptoms	Hunger	Thirst
	Headache	Abdominal pain
	Dizziness	Nausea, vomiting
		Infection, fever
Physical Findings:		
Blood pressure		May be decreased, with postural signs
Breath odor (acetone)	None	Sweet, fruity
Skin: temperature, color	Cool, pale	Warm, flushed
Behavior	May be uncoordinated, confused, combative	Restlessness
Seizures	In late stages	Rare
Improvement with sugar	Rapid: 1–2 minutes	No response

EMT Treatment

1. If patient is conscious, administer sugar by mouth in the form of candy, sweetened fruit juice, or sugar cubes.
2. If patient is unconscious, first attend to the ABCs: airway, breathing, circulation. Provide oxygen and suction, as necessary.
3. Assure rapid provision of, or transport to advanced life support services.
4. If, for any reason, transport (or arrival of paramedics) will be delayed, sugar can be administered to the unconscious diabetic with *extreme caution* to avoid aspiration. A commercially available oral preparation of 40% dextrose, or some other thick, sweet substance, such as honey or jelly, can be smeared on the membranes inside the patient's cheeks. It should be applied in small amounts, repeatedly. Neither liquids nor solids such as sugar cubes should be used with an unconscious patient.

EMT Special Considerations

Alcoholism presents two special problems in the management of diabetic emergencies. The first is the problem of misidentification: police and others have been known to assume that a person acting oddly who has a breath odor is drunk, when in fact the person is a diabetic. When that person needs treatment for hypoglycemia and receives a jail cell instead, death is the probable result. When there is reasonable doubt, treat as if diabetic.

The second problem alcoholism presents is in the patient who simultaneously is acutely intoxicated and has a diabetic emergency. It is too easy to assume that an inebriated person (or an unconscious person smelling strongly of alcohol) has only one problem. Physical examination of every patient needs to be thorough enough to uncover *all* likely conditions. Medical ID tags can be very useful, but only if they are looked for and looked at. Again, when in doubt, opt in favor of the patient and treat as if diabetic.

HIGH BLOOD GLUCOSE (HYPERGLYCEMIA)

Definition

High blood glucose (hyperglycemia) occurs when glucose accumulates in the body because it is not being efficiently utilized. This occurs when the amount of insulin in the body is not adequate. When the body cells are not able to utilize glucose for energy, fat is broken down, and waste products of ketones (such as acetone) and acids are produced. For that reason, this condition is also called *ketoacidosis*. It can occur when a diabetic person fails to take insulin or when the body is challenged by some unusual stress, such as infection.

Acute Cause

The body produces extra urine in an attempt to eliminate the extra sugar circulating in the blood. This fluid loss, combined with the acidosis, causes coma (also called "diabetic coma"). The dehydration can also cause hypovolemia and hypotension. In an attempt to correct the acidosis, hyperventilation occurs.

History: Subjective Reports

The onset of hyperglycemia is generally gradual, over 12 to 48 hours. The chief complaint will often be abdominal pain, with nausea and vomiting. The history of the present illness may reveal intense thirst, increased urination, a recent infection, or fever.

If the patient is alert and oriented, ask these questions:
1. Did you eat today?
2. Did you take your insulin today?

If the patient ate and did not take the insulin, the problem is probably high blood glucose. If the patient did not eat adequately and took insulin, the problem is probably low blood glucose.

Examination: Objective Physical Findings

If the patient is unconscious, the history may be difficult to obtain. Assessment of the patient then depends upon physical findings. Signs of high blood sugar include warm, dry skin; rapid, deep respirations (Kussmaul); rapid, weak pulse; possibly lowered blood pressure with postural hypotension; and possibly a sweet, fruity breath odor (acetone), which smells like nail polish remover.

It can sometimes be difficult to distinguish high blood glucose from low blood glucose (Table 12–4). When there is any doubt, treat as if low blood glucose were present.

EMT Treatment

1. If patient is conscious, transport to hospital. If the patient is in serious condition and if any doubt exists whether the condition is hyperglycemia or hypoglycemia, administer sugar by mouth in the form of candy, sweetened fruit juice, or sugar cubes.
2. Treat hypotension, if present, with oxygen, position flat with lower legs raised, and give other therapy for hypovolemic shock as necessary.
3. If patient is unconscious, assure an open airway, administer oxygen, and assist ventilation as necessary.
4. Assure rapid provision of, or transport to, advanced life support services.

ABDOMINAL AND GASTROINTESTINAL DISORDERS

ACUTE ABDOMEN

Definition

The term "acute abdomen" refers to a wide variety of medical conditions that result in irritation or inflammation of the abdominal lining (peritoneum), causing abdominal pain. An acute abdomen can originate from problems in the gastrointestinal system, cardiovascular system, or genitourinary system.

The major reasons for abdominal pain are listed by usual location (Fig. 12–4).

RUQ	EPIGASTRIC	LUQ
Acute cholecystitis	Myocardial infarction	Ruptured spleen
Duodenal ulcer	Duodenal ulcer	Duodenal ulcer
Pancreatitis	Esophagitis	Pancreatitis
Pyelonephritis		Pneumonia with
(inflamed kidney)		pleural reaction
Hepatitis		Pyelonephritis

RLQ	PERIUMBILICAL	LLQ
Appendicitis	Intestinal obstruction	Ectopic pregnancy
Ectopic pregnancy	Appendicitis	Ovarian cyst
Ovarian cyst	Pancreatitis	Incarcerated hernia
Incarcerated hernia	Aortic aneurysm	Diverticulitis
Diverticulitis	Diverticulitis	Kidney stone
Kidney stone		

Additional causes, generally with no unique localization, include the following:

1. Intestinal obstruction
2. Mononucleosis
3. Uremia
4. Sickle cell anemia
5. Food poisoning
6. Diabetic ketoacidosis (high blood glucose)
7. Intoxication (lead, methyl alcohol, narcotic withdrawal)

Acute Cause

The abdominal organs are separated into two categories: hollow and solid. Hollow organs are the esophagus, stomach, gallbladder, bile ducts, small intestine, large intestine (including the rectum), appendix, ureters, urinary bladder, fallopian tubes, uterus, vagina, and inferior vena cava. Solid organs are the liver, spleen, pancreas, ovaries, and kidneys. Abdominal disorders fall into five main pathological categories, which affect both hollow and solid organs and produce similar symptoms in both types of organs.

Inflammation is the reaction of tissue to injury. Usually it has a history of slow onset over hours or days. Pain is usually steady. Often there is a history of fever or chills. Inflammation can be life-threatening. *Hemorrhage* may occur acutely or chronically, usually with steady pain. Usually no fever is present. Pain can radiate to one or both shoulders if the diaphragm is irritated. Watch for signs and symptoms of hypovolemia. *Perforation* is a hole in an hollow organ. Steady pain of sudden onset is felt. It is always a severe problem. Fever develops several hours following perforation. *Obstruction* is blockage in a hollow organ. Pain is usually crampy as the organ attempts to work against the obstructed area. It is moderately rapid in onset without fever. Nausea and vomiting are common. *Ischemia* is a complete or temporary lack of blood, and therefore of oxygen, to an organ. Steady pain occurs that is sudden in onset, unchanging, and often very severe.

History: Subjective Reports

1. Severity and quality. Steady pain indicates inflammation; intermittent or colicky pain indicates obstruction.
2. Location and radiation.
   a. Acute appendicitis usually begins as left-sided or mid-abdominal pain which localizes in the RLQ.

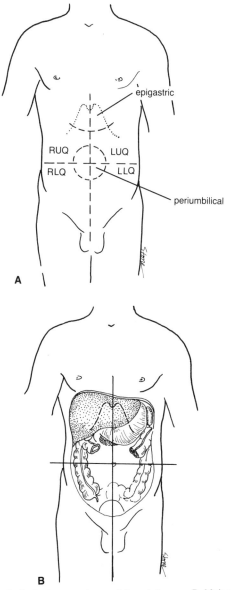

Figure 12–4. A, Surface anatomy of the abdomen. B, Major underlying organs.

   b. Renal colic may radiate to groin or testicle.

   c. Pancreatitis, posterior penetrating ulcer, or abdominal aortic aneurysm may radiate to back. Myocardial infarction, pneumonia, diaphragm irritation, inflamed gall bladder (cholecystitis) may radiate to the shoulder.

3. Prolonged vomiting may suggest obstruction.

4. Gynecologic history (missed period, discharge, and so on) may suggest an obstetrical or gynecological problem.

Examination: Objective Physical Findings

1. Vital signs. Decreased blood pressure may indicate surgical emergency; fever may indicate inflammation (appendicitis, cholecystitis).

2. Heart/lungs. Listen for rales.

3. Abdominal exam. Visually determine whether distention is present. Gentle palpation with a hand will determine whether rigidity or a pulsating mass is present and/or locate area of tenderness. Extensive physical examination in the field is not warranted, as the exam will have to be repeated in the hospital.

EMT Treatment

1. Abdominal pain should always be evaluated in the hospital.

2. If there is evidence of volume depletion (hypotension, postural rise in pulse, postural fall in blood pressure), place the patient in a supine position and elevate the lower extremities as required to maintain minimum BP; oxygen and MAST if indicated.

3. Do not give food or liquids.

4. Save a small amount of any vomited material or stool so that it may be tested for the presence of blood in the hospital.

5. Place the patient in the position of comfort. This may be flat or on the side with hips flexed.

GASTROINTESTINAL (GI) BLEEDING

Definition

Bleeding can occur in either the upper or the lower portions of the gastrointestinal (GI) tract. It can occur very suddenly, at a rapid rate, or it can occur slowly over a prolonged period. Common reasons for upper GI tract bleeding include peptic ulcer, esophageal varices, and gastritis. Upper GI bleeding is often alcohol-related. Lower GI bleeding seldom presents acutely. *Peptic ulcer* produces bleeding in the stomach, often when lack of food intake allows gastric acid to damage the stomach lining. *Esophageal varices* occur when chronic alcohol abuse causes cirrhosis of the liver. The cirrhosis causes shunting of the blood flow into the blood vessels of the stomach and esophagus, resulting in distended esophageal veins (varices). These distended veins are fragile and can rupture, causing profuse vomiting of blood. *Gastritis* (inflammation of the stomach) can be caused by overuse of aspirin or alcohol or by stress.

Acute Cause

The sudden vomiting of blood can be both frightening and life-threatening. These patients are in obvious danger of hypovolemic shock. What is less obvious is that hypovolemia can also develop in the patient who is bleeding in the GI tract at a slow rate.

History: Subjective Reports

The chief complaint of patients with GI bleeding will vary depending upon the rate of the bleeding. A loss of 4 liters over several weeks may produce only mild weakness. The rapid loss of 1 liter may produce dizziness and other symptoms of shock. When blood leaks into the stomach at a slow rate, the gastric acid turns it to brown material with a "coffee ground" appearance, and this may be what a patient will report vomiting. Abdominal pain may be reported in the epigastrium or left upper quadrant. The past medical history may include alcohol abuse and liver disease, and the history of the present incident may reveal an alcohol "binge."

Examination: Objective Physical Findings

1. Vital signs. Determine postural pulse and blood pressure unless patient's blood pressure is 80 mm Hg or less with patient supine. Weakness and fainting (syncope) occur when acute loss of blood approaches 25%. On occasion, fever may be present as a result of the blood loss.
2. Skin. Diaphoresis and pallor suggest shock. Evidence of liver disease (red palms, jaundice) may be present.
3. Abdominal exam. Tenderness, signs of peritoneal inflammation, distention, or ascites (fluid in abdomen) indicate blood in GI tract.
4. Often acute GI bleeding is obvious by vomited coffee-ground material or bright red blood passing from the rectum. Vomiting of blood indicates upper GI bleeding; bright red blood or melanotic stool may indicate bleeding from the upper or lower GI tract. On occasion, it may be difficult to distinguish GI bleeding with vomiting (hematemesis) from coughing of blood from the lung (hemoptysis). Table 12–5 compares hemoptysis with hematemesis.

EMT Treatment

1. Provide oxygen as required (4–6 liters per minute).

Table 12–5. COMPARISON OF HEMOPTYSIS AND HEMATEMESIS

	Hemoptysis (Blood from Lungs)	Hematemesis (Blood from GI Tract)
Initial symptoms	Coughing	Nausea and vomiting
Character of blood	Frothy or stringy, mixed with sputum	Never frothy, mixed with gastric contents
Subsequent sputum	Blood streaked	Usually no sputum
Color of blood	Bright red	Dark red or brown, coffee-ground appearance
Other		Food particles may be present

2. Elevate legs with patient in supine position to maintain BP.
3. Consider the use of anti-shock trousers.
4. Call for paramedic assistance if appropriate.
5. Save any vomitus.
6. Estimate blood loss.

GALL BLADDER INFLAMMATION (CHOLECYSTITIS)

Acute cholecystitis occurs when a gallstone obstructs the duct leading from the gall bladder to the gastrointestinal tract. It is an uncommon cause for an EMT call, as most patients voluntarily go to their own physicians. Occasionally, however, the pain from cholecystitis may be misinterpreted by the patient as a heart attack. Unlike the pain from MI, the pain from cholecystitis is usually located in the right lower chest and right upper quadrant of the abdomen. It may be referred to, or radiate to, the right shoulder. There is no specific EMT treatment, although naturally if there is any doubt about the patient having an MI, he or she should be treated as such.

ESOPHAGITIS

Esophagitis is inflammation of the esophagus. It is an uncommon cause for an EMT call, but on occasion, the pain is interpreted by the patient as a heart attack. Unlike the MI, the pain from esophagitis is described as "burning" and can often be relieved by antacids. EMT treatment consists of keeping the patient in a sitting position. When any doubt exists about the presence of MI, treat for MI.

MISCELLANEOUS MEDICAL CONDITIONS

ALLERGIC REACTIONS

Definition

Allergic reactions occur when the body's response to a foreign substance is not protective and defensive, but rather self-destructive. Foreign substances (antigens) can enter the body in several different ways.
1. Injection: drugs such as pencillin.
2. Ingestion: foods such as shellfish or berries, or drugs such as penicillin.
3. Insect sting: wasp, bee, yellow jacket, hornet (see Chapter 14).
4. Inhalation: pollens and other air-borne allergens.

Acute Cause

The severity of allergic reaction varies, ranging from mild symptoms of itching and burning to severe full-blown anaphylactic shock (see Chapter 9) with generalized edema, respiratory distress, cardiovascular collapse, coma, and death occurring within minutes. It can be difficult to predict which patients with allergic reactions will progress to full-blown anaphylaxis.

History: Subjective Reports

The patient with an allergic reaction may first be aware of a generalized warmth and itching, particularly of the hands and feet. Next, he or she may complain of a tightness in the throat or chest, with dyspnea and cough. This may be accompanied by nausea, vomiting, cramps, and diarrhea. The history of the present episode may reveal exposure to the foreign substance. The past medical history may include a known allergy, hypersensitivity, or asthma. Look for a medical ID tag.

Examination: Objective Physical Findings

Like the symptoms, the signs of allergic reaction will vary with the severity of the reaction. Skin signs include raised red rash; hives; and swelling (edema) of the lips, tongue, eyelids, and hands. Respiratory signs include hoarseness, mild wheezing, and stridor. Gastrointestinal signs include vomiting and diarrhea. Cardiovascular signs include weak, rapid pulse and hypotension.

EMT Treatment

1. Provide oxygen.

2. Treat hypotension, if present, with elevation of lower extremities or MAST, as needed.
3. If reaction is severe (respiratory or cardiovascular signs present), provide rapid transport to advanced life support.
4. Apply a venous tourniquet (such as a BP cuff inflated to a value between the diastolic and systolic pressures) above the site if patient was stung or injected.
5. Assist the patient with prescribed medications, if present, such as epinephrine kit (injection or inhaler).

SEPSIS

Sepsis occurs when a local infection spreads throughout the system. Most commonly it originates in bacteria from the lung or urinary tract. These patients appear very ill. The most severely affected of them will be in shock, called septic shock (see Chapter 9). This usually occurs in elderly, debilitated, or alcoholic patients. Treatment consists of oxygen and rapid transport.

DEHYDRATION

Dehydration is the loss of body fluid. Volume depletion can originate from several sources.
1. Blood loss.
2. Protracted vomiting or diarrhea (particularly in children—see Chapter 16).
3. Diabetic ketoacidosis (high blood glucose).
4. Acute debilitation (as in an alcoholic who has been lying on the floor for several days).
5. Sweating (as in heat stroke).
6. Burns (see Chapter 11).
If fluid loss is extreme, hypovolemic shock results (see Chapter 9).

KIDNEY (RENAL) DIALYSIS EMERGENCIES

Over 40,000 patients are undergoing hemodialysis in the United States. Many kidney patients have home dialysis units; most have had extensive training and many have helpers. They undergo dialysis every two to three days. The usual "run" lasts for 5 to 6 hours, depending upon size of patient, amount of kidney function remaining, and type of dialysate used. In order to "hook up" to the dialysis machine, kidney patients have either an external arteriovenous shunt or an internal arteriovenous fistula.

Kidney centers operate in most large communities and can provide valuable information over the phone.

Problems associated with dialysis generally fall into four categories.
1. Shock.
2. Potassium imbalance.
3. Pulmonary edema.
4. Machine malfunctions.

Shock

1. Extracellular volume depletion due to loss of saline. Patient becomes lightheaded, woozy, but rarely unconscious. Patient will often recognize problem and self-administer 50 ml saline or more.
2. Hemorrhage. Causes of cannula bleeding may be as follows:
   a. Intentional (suicidal). Dialysis patients have the highest suicide rate of patients with chronic disease. The patient will open the cannula and bleed out. If cannula is pumping, clamp the open cannulas and apply direct pressure. If bleeding cannot be controlled or cannual cannot be clamped shut, apply a tourniquet to limb above cannula or shunt site.
   b. Accidental.
      i. Faulty connection.
         Examination: steady leak.
         Management: establish connection and apply pressure.
      ii. Arteritis.
         Examination: oozing around arterial cannula, usually occurs soon after placement of new cannula.
         Management: direct pressure or clamping cannula may worsen hemorrhage, since it increases back pressure in the vessel.
      iii. Disconnection at vein.
         Examination: arterial hemorrhage through cannula and simultaneous venous leakage may occur.
         Management: clamp cannula. May require a great amount of pressure because of Teflon tube core. Disconnect patient from dialysis machine if leak occurred during dialysis run.
3. Cardiac (MI). Dialysis patients have a high incidence of cardiovascular complications. If patient experiences shock while on dialysis and has no apparent blood loss, then treat as for any other cardiogenic shock.
4. Duodenal ulcer. Dialysis patients have a high incidence of duodenal ulcers, which may bleed. If the patient is hypotensive with a history of tarry stools, treat for hypovolemic shock.
5. Subdural hematoma. Dialysis patients have a high incidence of spontaneous subdural hematoma because of anticoagulant therapy and usually *do not* give a history of head trauma. If the patient complains of severe headaches, especially while undergoing dialysis, stop dialysis and transport to hospital.

Potassium Imbalance

1. Hypokalemia (low potassium in the blood), found only while patient is undergoing dialysis, or immediately following it. Usually the patient is taking digoxin. Dialysis patients taking digoxin are much more likely to develop digitalis toxicity. Hypotension may be present. Arrhythmias may occur, and seizures may occur secondary to bradycardia.
2. Hyperkalemia (high potassium level). Prior to dialysis, patient may have a high serum potassium level, which may cause arrhythmias. If alert, patient will complain of profound weakness and difficulty with respiration (secondary to weakness). This patient needs dialysis as soon as possible (alert hospital so that arrangement may be made).

Pulmonary Edema

This is a common problem in dialysis patients, who usually gain two pounds per day of fluid. This fluid must be eliminated to keep weight and BP normal and lungs clear. Examination is as in pulmonary edema. Therapy is usually not effective. Tourniquets may be used with caution.

Machine Malfunctions

Power outages may occur, and during a power outage, patient may choose to stay connected to the machine and "wait it out." If the outage is short-lived, no harm is done. If the outage is prolonged, the blood will cool and the patient may then be at risk from potassium-induced arrhythmias. Management: Disconnect patient, clamp cannulas, and transport to hospital.

COMMUNICABLE (INFECTIOUS) DISEASES

Communicable (infectious) diseases are contagious: they can be transmitted from one person to another. Routes of transmission include direct contact, indirect contact via contaminated objects, and inhalation of droplets in the air. *Incubation period* is the time between exposure to infectious microorganisms and the first appearance of signs of the disease. The *communicable period* is the time during which an infected person can transmit an infectious disease to another person.

Prevention of certain communicable diseases starts with *immunization* (vaccination), in which specific antibodies are induced to develop in order to produce resistance to specific infectious disease. The EMT needs protection against certain communicable diseases through a standard up-to-date immunization series for the following:

1. Measles.
2. Mumps.
3. Rubella (German measles).
4. Polio.
5. DPT (diphtheria-pertussis-tetanus).
6. Tetanus booster (every five years).
7. Hepatitis B (serum) at local option.

In addition, personnel should be tuberculin-tested yearly for TB. The *risk of infection* depends upon whether a person has been immunized or has had the disease, and on the nature of the disease itself.

Prevention of the spread of communicable disease can start with the information that a patient who needs medical care or transportation has a known or suspected communicable disease. If possible, suitable EMTs (who have been immunized or who have previously had the disease) should be selected for the call. All unnecessary equipment and supplies should be removed from the ambulance. Disposable gowns and masks should be worn, and disposable linen used when possible. After a patient is out of the vehicle, disinfect by standard protocol:

1. Plastic bag: disposables for discard.
2. Plastic bag: contaminated linens for handling by the laundry.
3. Plastic bag: contaminated equipment for disinfection/sterilization. If necessary to do at hospital, wash once with soap and water, then again with disinfectant solution.
4. Air the ambulance for one to two hours before cleaning.
5. After airing, scrub surfaces with soap and water, following by disinfectant solution.

Often it is not known until well after the patient has been left at the hospital that a communicable disease is diagnosed or suspected. The ambulance service should have a standard protocol for dealing with that situation. It will generally consist of the following measures:

1. Decontamination of the ambulance, as above.
2. Notification of personnel involved in the case.
3. Notification of the physicians of other patients at risk for contracting the disease, such as those transported after the infectious patient.

Table 12–6. COMMUNICABLE DISEASES

Disease	Characteristics	Route of Transmission	Incubation Period	Communicable Period	Decontamination of Personnel	Decontamination of Ambulance	Risk of Infection
Chicken pox	Viral: fever, rash scabs; common in childhood	Direct contact, droplets	2–3 weeks	Day before rash to 6 days after	Shower, change of clothes	Air, scrub, boil linens	0,3
Hepatitis Infectious	Viral: fever, jaundice, loss of appetite, fatigue, dark urine	Direct or indirect contact with feces, blood, urine; contaminated water, food, syringes; contaminated needles	15–50 days	Variable	Wash hands, avoid needles	Air, scrub, clean linen	1
Serum	Same		45–160 days	Variable	Same	None	0
Measles	Viral: fever, rash, cough; common in childhood	Direct or indirect contact, droplets	8–13 days	4 days before rash to 5 days after	Mask during treatment if not immune	Air, scrub, clean linen	0,3
Meningitis	Bacterial: fever, stiff neck, headache, vomiting, coma	Direct contact, droplets	2–10 days	Variable	Mask during treatment, if close contact; see physician	Air, scrub, clean linen	1

Disease	Description	Transmission	Incubation	Communicable period	Precautions	Cleaning	
Mono-nucleosis	Viral: fever, sore throat, swollen glands	Mouth to mouth	2–6 weeks	Unknown	Standard	Clean respiratory equipment	1
Mumps	Viral: fever, swollen salivary glands, or-chitis	Direct contact, drop-lets	12–26 days	2 days before swelling to 9 days after	Mask during treatment if not immune	Air, scrub, clean linen	0,3
Pneumonia	Bacterial or viral: fe-ver, chills, cough, chest pain	Direct or indirect con-tact droplets	Variable: 1–3 days, 14–21 days	Variable	Standard	Air, scrub, clean linen	0
Pertussis (whooping cough)	Bacterial: fever, vio-lent cough, stridor; common in child-hood	Droplets, indirect con-tact	1–3 weeks	1–3 weeks	Shower, change and boil clothes	Air, scrub, boil linen	2
Rubella (German measles)	Viral: fever, rash; common in child-hood	Direct or indirect con-tact, droplets	14–21 days	7 days before rash to 4 days after	Mask during treatment if not immune	Air, scrub, clean linen	0,3
Scarlet fever (strepto-coccus)	Bacterial: fever, head-ache, vomiting, sore throat, rash	Direct contact	1–3 days	10–21 days	Mask, shower, change and boil clothes	Air, scrub, boil linen	1–2
Tuberculosis (TB)	Bacterial: cough, hem-optysis, weight loss, fatigue	Droplets	4–12 weeks	Until disease is un-der control	Mask, tuberculin skin test annually (PPD)	Air, scrub, clean linen and respi-ratory equip-ment	1

In Table 12–6, the "risk of infection" is determined as follows:
0. No risk if the EMT previously had the disease (or vaccination).
1. Mild.
2. Moderate.
3. High, especially if the EMT has never had the disease.

It should also be noted that pregnant EMTs who have not had rubella (German measles) or have not been vaccinated, and who encounter a patient with rubella on the job need medical evaluation by their personal physician.

REFERENCE

Benenson, A. S.: *Control of Communicable Diseases in Man,* 13th ed. Washington, D.C., American Public Health Association, 1980.

13

POISONING AND OVERDOSE

INGESTED POISONS

GENERAL PRINCIPLES

Definition

Overdose and poisoning mean the same thing, although by common usage, *overdose* implies an intentional ingestion of a substance, whereas *poisoning* often means an accidental ingestion. The distinction, however, between accidental poisoning and intentional overdose is sometimes blurred, and in certain situations it may be difficult to determine whether the overdose was intentional or not. Overdoses have become the most common means of attempting and succeeding at suicide. Poisonings are the fifth most common cause of accidental death, following car accidents, falls, drownings, and burns. It is estimated that 5000 deaths per year occur as a result of accidental poisoning. As one would imagine, accidental poisonings occur most commonly in children.

There are several hundred poison control centers in the United States. Their personnel are available 24 hours a day with a detailed file on toxic substances: drugs, chemicals, household products, and so on. The card for each substance contains information on chemical composition, toxic effects, and specific emergency medical treatment.

Acute Cause

An acute emergency generally develops for one of four reasons: unintended effects, often from overdose (most commonly respiratory depression); withdrawal state; panic state; or allergic reaction.

History: Subjective Reports

The symptoms will depend upon the drug. The EMT needs to obtain a past medical history, if possible, and a history of the present incident:
1. *What* was taken?
2. *When* was it taken?
3. *How much* was taken?

The EMT will need to make a list of local street terms to interpret local slang.

Table 13–1. GENERAL CHARACTERISTICS OF DRUG OVERDOSES

Clinical Presentation	Suspected Drug Type
Lethargy, slurred speech, hypotension, hypothermia	Sedatives (barbiturates), tranquilizers
Pinpoint pupils (non-reactive), hypoventilation to respiratory arrest, stupor to coma, fresh needle marks	Opiates (narcotics)
Agitation, belligerence, diaphoresis, hypertension, hyperventilation, tachycardia, dilated pupils	Stimulants (amphetamines)
Hallucinations, dry/flushed skin, fever, dilated pupils, anxiety	Hallucinogens, atropines
Dystonic posture, profound hypotension, lethargy to coma, seizures	Phenothiazines
Cardiac arrhythmias, tachycardia, agitation, coma, seizures	Tricyclics, antidepressants
Hyperventilation, fever, vomiting	Salicylates, acetaminophen

Examination: Objective Physical Findings

The signs will depend upon the drug. The primary and secondary surveys must be thorough and must include estimation of respiratory, cardiovascular, and central nervous system (CNS) status. The survey should include a search for unnoticed injury, such as compression injury (ischemia) to an extremity, as evidenced by a cold, swollen, cyanotic limb, and examination of extremities for needle marks.

Table 13–1 lists the characteristic presentations of drug overdose.

EMT Treatment

1. If patient is unconscious, assure an open airway, administer oxygen, and assist ventilation as needed. If patient is conscious and lethargic, stimulate to maintain consciousness, as respiratory depression can follow loss of consciousness. If patient is conscious and panicked, provide calm, reassuring manner.
2. Attempt to identify the agent or agents (multi-drug overdoses are common) from the history or paraphernalia. Use special caution when handling the needles from an abuser of injectable drugs, in order to avoid exposure to the infectious diseases hepatitis A and AIDS.
3. Call Poison Control with the information on what was taken, how much, and when.

4. As directed by Poison Control:
   a. Dilute poison with water or milk.
   b. Induce vomiting with ipecac.
      i. 2 tablespoons (30 ml) for adults.
      ii. 1 tablespoon (15 ml) for children 1–12 years old.
      iii. 2 teaspoons (10 ml) for infants.

      Follow with 2 to 4 glasses of water (or 1 to 2 glasses of carbonated water). Gentle rocking motion (as in an ambulance on the way to the hospital) can help the ipecac work. Repeat after 20 minutes if no results. Do not give ipecac to these patients:
      (a) Patients with decreasing levels of consciousness.
      (b) Patients who are having seizures.
      (c) Pregnant women or patients with acute MI.
      (d) Certain ingestions:
         (i) Corrosives: acid, such as toilet bowl cleaner; alkali, such as lye or drain cleaner; or any substance giving evidence of oral burns.
         (ii) Petroleum: gasoline, kerosene, lighter fluid, cleaning agents, furniture polish.
         (iii) Anti-emetics: phenothiazine drugs, such as thorazine.
         (iv) Strychnine compound: some rat poisons.

         Depending upon the policies of the receiving hospital, induced vomiting with ipecac may be withheld if transportation time to the hospital is short.
   c. Administer charcoal, 2 tablespoons (30 ml) in a glass of water.

      A commercially prepared sweet slurry of activated charcoal is available for use with children; it can be improvised with sugar water. Charcoal may be given after vomiting that was induced by ipecac but should never be used before the ipecac has worked, as the charcoal will inactivate the ipecac.
   d. Soothing agents: milk, milk of magnesia.
5. Save vomitus (save initial vomitus separately) and take associated paraphernalia and drug or chemical containers to the hospital with the patient.

Special Considerations

Consider conditions that may masquerade as drug overdose, such as head trauma, meningitis, subarachnoid hemorrhage, and brain tumor. In addition, patients who have both acute drug intoxication and head injury simultaneously present a special problem for assessment, needing an especially thorough physical examination.

ALCOHOLISM

Definition

Alcohol is the most abused drug in the United States. It is estimated that ten million Americans are alcoholic (one out of 20 people). Alcohol is associated with 50% of all arrests and 50% of all motor vehicle fatalities. Only 3% of alcoholic persons are derelicts. Alcohol is a depressant drug.

Acute Cause

Alcoholic emergencies are of three types: acute intoxication, which may be severe enough to cause central nervous system (CNS) depression and respiratory depression; withdrawal seizures; and delirium tremens (DTs). DTs can have a mortality rate as high as 15%.

History: Subjective Reports

The acutely intoxicated patient may have no complaints, but the patient's family or bystanders may relate a history of alcoholism. Withdrawal seizures usually occur 5 to 48 hours after the last drink. Delirium tremens usually occurs two to four days after the last drink. Auditory or visual hallucinations are common.

Examination: Objective Physical Findings

The acutely intoxicated patient is generally aggressive and combative, but may be comatose, with hypoventilation and dilated pupils. Vomiting or vomiting of blood (see gastrointestinal bleeding in Chapter 12) can also occur.

Withdrawal seizures are usually generalized, not partial, and cease after one or two seizures.

Delirium tremens presents with restlessness, disorientation, delusions, tremor, fever, and sweating. DTs can cause hypovolemic shock.

EMT Treatment

1. Protect patient (and self) from injury.
2. If patient is unconscious, assure an open airway, administer oxygen, and assist ventilation as necessary.
3. Treat seizures in the standard fashion. Protect from injury, use a bite block if jaws are not yet clenched, give oxygen, suction as needed, turn on side in post-ictal period, and transport. Treat status epilepticus, if seen, with high-flow oxygen, ventilatory assistance, and rapid transport.

4. Delirium tremens is a medical emergency, and all patients suspected of DTs must be transported to hospital.

DRUG/SUBSTANCE ABUSE

See Table 13–2 for specific information and management of major drug and poison categories.

INHALED POISONS

CARBON MONOXIDE

Definition

Carbon monoxide (CO) is produced by the incomplete combustion of organic materials, such as wood, gasoline, and coal. It is produced and found in harmful concentrations in poorly ventilated areas, such as a closed garage with a running automobile engine. It can also be found in heating systems, wood stoves, or camp stoves in trailers. Moderate CO levels may develop in persons in accidents on busy freeways in underpasses or tunnels. House fires and industrial fires are common sources of CO poisoning, especially for firefighters inadequately protected. Even smoking in a closed room can cause mild elevations of CO.

Acute Cause

Carbon monoxide is colorless, odorless, and tasteless. It has an affinity for the hemoglobin in the red blood cell, displacing oxygen. When the lungs do not pick up oxygen for delivery to the bloodstream, low blood oxygen level (hypoxemia) results.

History: Subjective Reports

Although suicide attempts are usually obvious, other cases of carbon monoxide poisoning may not be obvious. For the most part, CO poisoning is not perceived by the patient as a problem, because one of the results of hypoxemia is a generalized feeling of well-being. No acute discomfort occurs. The degree of symptoms is related to the length and concentration of exposure.
1. Mild exposure: lightheadedness, mild headache, dimness of vision.
2. Moderate exposure: dizziness, blurred vision, weakness.
3. Severe exposure: confusion, apathy, impaired consciousness.

Text continued on page 149

Table 13–2. MANAGEMENT OF DRUG OVERDOSE AND POISONING

Drug/Substance	Trade or Street Name	Signs/Symptoms	EMT Management	Special Comments
Household Products Acids	Toilet bowl cleaners Rust removers Metal cleaners and polishes Tile and grout cleaners	Severe pain in mouth, stomach, chest (substernal)	NEVER INDUCE VOMITING Give patient Milk Milk of magnesia Egg whites (dilutes the acid)	Have patient sit up during transport
Alkalis	Automatic dishwasher detergent Drain cleaners Oven cleaners Washing soda Ammonia Bleach	Severe pains in mouth, stomach, chest (substernal) Burns in mouth and esophagus Associated difficulty with swallowing	NEVER INDUCE VOMITING Attempt to neutralize with Citrus fruit juices (e.g., orange or grapefruit juice) Water and vinegar (mixed half and half)	Have patient sit up during transport Watch airway closely for edema causing restricted ventilation
Hydrocarbons	Petroleum products Gasoline Fuel oils Paint thinners Paint solvents Kerosene Lighter fluid Furniture polish	Most common symptoms are respiratory distress with coughing and choking Patient may develop pulmonary edema Abdominal pain may be present Convulsions (seizures) Patient may be comatose Monitor for arrhythmias	NEVER INDUCE VOMITING Treat with up to 100% oxygen depending on severity of overdose Control secretions with suction as required	Have patient sit up during transport if possible

Cyanide	Laetrile overdose Contaminated fruit Inhalation of gases from blast furnaces, seed crop fumigants	Initial stage: Confusion Rapid respirations Later stage: Depressed respirations Vomiting Seizure Comatose	Some paramedic programs have cyanide antidote kits available. Support vital signs and respiration. If antidote kit is not available, transport patient to nearest medical facility having antidote.	
Pesticides	Warfarin base: Rat killer Strychnine base: Rodenticides Arsenic base: Insect sprays Ant and roach killers Liquid insect killers DDT pesticides	Warfarin type: Severe gastrointestinal symptoms Progressive lethargy/apathy Strychnine based: Acute illness Severe nausea/vomiting Respiratory distress Tonic stiffening Arsenic based: Acute gastrointestinal symptoms DDT: Severe gastroenteritis	Warfarin poisoning: Patient must be seen at hospital for blood clotting problems Patients who are conscious with gag reflex can be given ipecac Support ventilation as required Tonic stiffening requires antiseizure medicines	Illicit drugs, e.g., heroin, are sometimes cut with strychnine Some pesticides contain anticholinergic agents
Perfumes/deodorizers	Products containing perfumes and deodorizers are too numerous to list here	Produce severe gastroenteritis Respiratory problems from aerosol products may be present	Give oxygen as required Support vital signs	

Table continued on following page

Table 13–2. MANAGEMENT OF DRUG OVERDOSE AND POISONING (Continued)

Drug/Substance	Trade or Street Name	Signs/Symptoms	EMT Management	Special Comments
Plants				
Poisonous plants	Glycosides: Foxglove Azalea Rhododendrons Alkaloidal toxins: Hemlock Nightshade GI irritants: Philodendron Deiffenbachia Holly	Glycosides: Nausea/vomiting Hypotension May have bradycardia (heart rate <55 per minute) Alkaloidal toxins: Lethargy, which may progress to seizures and coma GI irritants: Severe nausea/vomiting Diarrhea Hypotension	Support with oxygen as required Support hypotension as with hypovolemia Use cardiac monitor if available	Bring plant sample to hospital
Poisonous mushrooms	Amanita muscaria	10–30 minutes after ingestion: Severe nausea/vomiting followed rapidly by seizures; death may occur	Support with oxygen as required Support hypotension as with hypovolemia Use cardiac monitor if available	Bring plant sample to hospital
Hallucinogenic mushrooms	Psilocybin and psilocin	Severe mood disturbances Hyperventilation Nausea/vomiting Fever Reduced level of consciousness	Use ipecac if patient has gag reflex and is conscious Calm patient as necessary Support vital signs and ventilation as required	50–100 mushrooms can be fatal Onset 15–30 minutes after ingestion lasting up to 4–6 hours

Drugs, sedatives, hypnotics, tranquilizers *Barbiturates (long-acting)*			
Phenobarbital	Luminal (prescription); barbs, purple hearts (street)	Miotic pupils Respiratory depression to complete arrest Gradual onset of lethargy to coma Hypotension Hypothermia	Consult physician concerning ipecac, as drug may depress patient's gag reflex at the same time ipecac begins to work Support ventilations and blood pressure as per hypovolemia Check patient's gag reflex and level of consciousness frequently Use cardiac monitor if available	Most abused drug next to Valium and alcohol May be used to reduce effect of amphetamines causing mixed overdose Usual dose: 15–30 mg three times per day
Barbiturates (intermediate-acting)			
Amobarbital	Amytal (prescription); blue ice, blue lady, turquoise blue birds (street)	Faster onset but shorter duration than phenobarbital	Same as phenobarbital	
Secobarbital	Seconal (prescription); red birds, red devils, downers, laybacks, reds (street)	Level of consciousness from agitated to comatose		
Pentobarbital	Nembutal (prescription); block busters, nemmies, nebbies (street)			Usual dose: 30 mg 3–4 times per day; 100 mg at bedtime

Table continued on following page

Table 13-2. MANAGEMENT OF DRUG OVERDOSE AND POISONING (Continued)

Drug/Substance	Trade or Street Name	Signs/Symptoms	EMT Management	Special Comments
Pentobarbital/ Amobarbital combination	Tuinal (prescription); Christmas tree, rainbows, tootsie (street)	Brain stem reflexes may be absent Pupils may be miotic Ankle clonus may be present (grasp leg at ankle, push foot back toward patient's nose, foot will jerk)		
Other Sedatives Glutethimide	Doriden/CB,D	Rapid onset of coma (1 hour) Stupor or coma may alternate with alert or hyperactive behavior Pupils may be dilated/fixed Sudden apnea and hypotension may occur	Monitor vital signs and ventilation closely Avoid ipecac because coma may develop rapidly	Usual dose: 1 tablespoon at bedtime; repeat after 4 hours
Methaqualone	Quaalude (prescription); super/quads, soapers, roarers, ludes (street)	Sedative-hypnotic, action similar to that of short-acting barbiturates. Coma and respiratory depression most common. Possible hallucinations	Support ABCs as required	Abrupt withdrawal can cause serious side effects, including seizure, chills, general behavior change, anxiety If mixed with alcohol, drug can be fatal
Methaqualone hydrochloride Methyprylon	Parest, Somma fac Noludar	Pulmonary edema Diaphoresis Drowsiness, nausea, vomiting		Usual dose: 400 mg at bedtime

Meprobamate	Miltown, Equanil, Mepriam, Saronil, Tranmep, Meprospan	Extreme drowsiness progressing to coma Possible hypotension Possible respiratory arrest	This drug is usually slow to produce severe effects; can use ipecac if given within 15–20 min after ingestion of drug Support ABCs as required	Large quantity of alcohol makes overdose possible with smaller dose Usual adult dose: 1200–1600 mg per day in divided doses
Ethchlorvynol	Placidyl	Onset of coma in 1 hour, which can be prolonged for days Seizures Depressed ventilation Absence of response to painful stimuli	Support vital signs and respiration Be prepared for seizure Avoid ipecac, as drug has rapid action in large quantities	Combination of Placidyl and amitriptyline can cause patient to be delirious Usual adult dose: 500–1000 mg
Diazepam	Valium	Unconsciousness from Valium, Ativan and Tranxene is rapid (10–30 min) Unconsciousness from Librium, Dalmane, and Serax is slow (hours)	Do not use ipecac with Valium, Ativan, and Tranxene because of rapid action of drugs	Valium is the most widely prescribed and abused of all sedatives
Lorazepam Chlordiazepoxide Flurazepam Clorazepate Oxazepam	Ativan Librium Dalmane Tranxene Serax	Initially patient will be sleepy, confused; slurred speech with possible difficulty in controlling motor functions will progress to coma, respiratory depression, and/or respiratory arrest	Support vital signs and respiration as required	Alcohol is often used with these drugs; makes even small dose: unpredictable Usual adult dose: 2–4 mg per day

Table continued on following page

Table 13–2. MANAGEMENT OF DRUG OVERDOSE AND POISONING (Continued)

Drug/Substance	Trade or Street Name	Signs/Symptoms	EMT Management	Special Comments
Opiates and derivatives Opium Opium tincture Laudanum Morphine sulfate Codeine Diacetylmorphine Hydromorphone Oxycodone Meperidine	Numbers in parentheses indicate potency equal to 10 mg of morphine sulfate Paregoric (25 ml) Morphine Codeine (60–100 mg) Heroin (3 mg) Dilaudid (2 mg) Percodan (80–100 mg) Demerol (50 mg)	Pupils are miotic to pinpoint and are non-reactive Respiratory arrest is common, also shallow slow respirations Patients are stuporous to comatose but are often arousable to painful stimuli; will return to unconsciousness when stimulus is relaxed Patients may have pulmonary edema and/or atrial fibrillation Look for fresh injection sites in arms, legs, between fingers and toes, as well as tattoos near large veins to hide needle marks	Support vital signs and ventilation as required Patient may be talking but not have gag to protect airway Antidote is Naloxone (narcan) which is usually available from paramedics or most medical facilities These patients may have underlying communicable diseases from poor care of needles and poor living habits Treat pulmonary edema as required	Strychnine is often used to "cut" opiates; side effect is seizure and hypothermia Be alert; patients can be dangerous Do not relax vigilance in presence of patient or friends; stick to medical approach only Have police in attendance
Methadone	Dolophine (8 mg) Methadone, Amidone			Methadone often used in detoxification of heroin addicts; withdrawal symptoms are slower and less severe
Oxycodone and acetaminophen Propoxyphene Propoxyphene and acetaminophen	Percocet Darvon Darvocet, Darvocet-N	Pupils may not be pinpoint Can produce all other effects of opiates Darvocet-N may present with symptoms of hypoglycemia	Same as opiates	Can be refined and injected

Ethorphine hydrochloride	M99	Is a thousand times more potent than morphine with sedative and respiratory effects	Same as opiates. Diprenorphine hydrochloride (M50-50) counteracts. Ethorphine (antagonist as Narcan is to heroin)	Used only by veterinarians to immobilize large animals
Stimulants Amphetamine	Benzedrine (prescription); benz, bennies (street)	Agitation, flushing, perspiration, tachycardia, hypertension	Support vital signs and ventilation as required	Barbiturates often used to control "high"; therefore patient may have combined symptoms. Usual doses: 5–60 mg per day
Dextroamphetamine	Dexedrine (prescription); dexies, copilots (street)	Patient may be hyperactive, with muscle twitching	Handle patient with caution—may have rapid mood changes	
Methamphetamine	Desoxyn, Methedrine, Obedrin-L (prescription); black beauties (street)	Anxiety with visual hallucinations may occur. Nausea, vomiting, abdominal cramps. Hyperventilation. Moderately dilated pupils	May require restraints in best interest of patient. Ipecac should be considered if patient has active gag reflex and is conscious	
Amphetamine and dextroamphetamine	Biphetamine			
Methylphenidate	Ritalin (prescription); ritins (street)	When severe, can lead to seizure and coma		Ritalin used for hyperactive children to reduce hyperactivity; often injected, for street use, causing abscesses on skin and "cotton fever" from cotton ball fibers through which drug was strained for injection. Usual dose 10–60 mg per day, divided 2–3 times per day

Table continued on following page

Table 13–2. MANAGEMENT OF DRUG OVERDOSE AND POISONING (Continued)

Drug/Substance	Trade or Street Name	Signs/Symptoms	EMT Management	Special Comments
Phenmetrazine Cocaine	Preludin (prescription); snow, coke (street)	Patient often combative		
Hallucinogens, psychedelics DMT (dimethyltryptamine) LSD Mescaline Peyote Psilocybin		Pupils are large Patient is agitated, hot, flushed, delirious with hallucinations Toxic level of LSD usually lasts 12–24 hours	Protect patient from injury to EMT(s) and themselves Support vital signs and ventilation as required	Combination of hallucinogen and phenothiazines may cause cardiovascular failure, shock, and death
Phencyclidine	PCP, animal tranquilizer (prescription); angel dust, peace pill, angel fuzz, supergrass (with marijuana) (street)	Pupils may be mid-size to large Combative behavior changing to depression Respiratory arrest Effect may last 2–4 days Hallucinations	Same as above This patient can be extremely dangerous; patients have been known to break their own limbs during restraint without acknowledging injury	PCP can be easily manufactured outside the lab in large quantity, with varied composition as a result Patient may react differently to same size dose Is used in many forms
Tetrahydrocannabinol	Marijuana, grass, pot, weed, Colombian gold, Thai sticks, etc. (street)	Anxiety, agitation Large pupils with "bloodshot" whites of eyes Appears drunk Hyperventilation secondary to surprising extra effect of "good" drug	Observation is usually sufficient Occasional hypotension when used in conjunction with alcohol Treat hyperventilation as usual	

Psychotropic agents Phenothiazines Chlorpromazine Trifluoperazine	Thorazine, Promapar, Chlor-PZ Stelazine	Lethargy, which may progress to coma Orthostatic (postural) hypotension to profound hypotension	Treat hypotension with elevated extremities Support ventilation Monitor cardiac arrhythmias if monitor is available	All phenothiazines lower the seizure threshold
Thioridazine Prochlorperazine	Mellaril Compazine	Pulmonary edema (Mellaril) Cardiac arrhythmias Dystonic reactions (swollen tongue, rigid jaw with face distorted)	Be prepared for cardiac and/or respiratory arrest High-flow oxygen or bag mask assist	
Haloperidol Perphenazine	Haldol Trilafon	Limbs tonic, respiratory distress Seizures	These patients require immediate care to treat severe symptoms early	Patient can become extremely ill rapidly
Antidepressants Tricyclics Amitriptyline	Elavil, Endep	Patients are often excited but can progress rapidly to coma Tachycardia and arrhythmias are very common	Treat same as phenothiazines	Patient can become extremely ill rapidly
Imipramine	Tofranil		Cardiac arrhythmias with sudden death are the greatest danger	
Desipramine Nortriptyline Doxepin Amitriptyline and perphenazine MAO inhibitors	Norpramin Aventyl Sinequan Triavil, Etrafon Parnate Marplan Niamid Nardil	Hypertension or hypotension Seizures May have symptoms of phenothiazines and tricyclics Same as tricyclics		Foods such as cheese and wine may cause symptoms of toxicity

Table continued on following page

Table 13-2. MANAGEMENT OF DRUG OVERDOSE AND POISONING (Continued)

Drug/Substance	Trade or Street Name	Signs/Symptoms	EMT Management	Special Comments
Atropinics/ anticholinergics Belladonna	Atropine, belladonna	Classic atropine intoxication Delirious ("mad as a hatter"), flushed ("red as a beet"), dilated pupils ("blind as a bat"), absent perspiration ("dry as a bone")	Control hypotension as required Control hyperthermia as required	Jimson weed and nightshade contain belladonna
Antihistamines Diphenhydramine	Benadryl	Sedative effect with low dosage	Same as anticholinergics	Commonly used by public as antinausea medicine
Dimenhydrinate	Dramamine	Symptoms the same as anticholinergics in high dosage		
Mild analgesics Salicylate	Aspirin and others (over 400 preparations contain salicylate)	Initial symptoms: headache, nausea, hyperventilation Later symptoms: lethargy to coma Seizures Increased perspiration, hyperthermia	Use ipecac as soon as possible if patient is conscious; aspirin tends to form hard "ball" in stomach if not removed	

Acetaminophen	Tylenol, Datril, often combined with mild opiates	Same as salicylate Liver damage may occur in large quantity overdoses	Use ipecac as soon as possible if patient is conscious Administer large quantities of fluid orally to cause excretion naturally	
Other compounds Phenytoin	Dilantin	Slurred speech, hypotension Occasional dystonic posturing (see phenothiazine) Coma is rare except with massive overdose May develop AV block arrhythmia	Support vital signs and ventilation Cardiac monitor if available; be prepared to assist heart block with CPR should hypotension occur	Overdose may be accidental, as each patient's ability to metabolize this drug varies
Lithium	Eskalith Lithane	Muscle tremor, blackout spells, slurred speech, dizziness, blurred vision, dry mouth, fatigue, lethargy, confusion, stupor, coma; early signs of diarrhea, vomiting, dizziness	Support vital signs and ventilation	Lithium toxicity is closely related to serum lithium levels, and can occur at doses close to therapeutic levels Treats manic-depressive patients only
Iron Ferrous gluconate	Fergon	Nausea, vomiting, diarrhea, stomach upset, weak/rapid pulse, decreased blood pressure	Induce vomiting with ipecac Hospital must pump stomach within first hour, as stomach may perforate from treatment	

Table continued on following page

Table 13-2. MANAGEMENT OF DRUG OVERDOSE AND POISONING (Continued)

Drug/Substance	Trade or Street Name	Signs/Symptoms	EMT Management	Special Comments
Ferrous sulfate	Feosol, Mol-Iron, others	Heavy dose can cause brisk bleeding in stomach/intestine and black tarry stools (from hemorrhage) Shock		
Ferrous fumarate	Feostate, others			
Alcohol compounds Ethanol	"Alcohol"	"Drunkenness"-like symptoms, coma and respiratory depression with large quantities Loss of gag reflex Dilated, slow-reacting pupils	Normally supportive May require aggressive airway management with children and young adults (often first-time users)	Often used mixed with a variety of drugs
Methanol	Sterno	Usually takes 8-36 hours to take effect: headache, blurred vision, seizures, nausea, vomiting, abdominal cramps, to coma	Main treatment is performed by hospital Contact physician for ipecac in field	As little as 2 teaspoons can be toxic; 2-8 oz can be fatal
Ethylene Glycol	Antifreeze	Hyperventilation Coma occurs rapidly; may cause pulmonary edema seizures	Same as methanol	As little as 100 ml may cause coma

The history of the present episode may reveal clues to the source of the CO poisoning. The EMT should be especially suspicious of CO upon finding an outbreak of symptoms in several people all in the same place at the same time, such as a house or a schoolroom.

Examination: Objective Physical Findings

The degree of objective signs also depends upon the length and concentration of exposure. Low exposure produces irritability and impaired judgment. High exposures produce tachycardia, seizures, coma, and cardiovascular collapse. The classic sign of "cherry-red" mucous membranes and skin is rarely seen.

EMT Treatment

1. The EMT should be protected against any toxic environment, with breathing apparatus and/or ventilation of the area as necessary.
2. Terminate exposure of the patient, with an oxygen mask during rescue, if needed.
3. Provide 100% oxygen.
4. Support respirations as needed.
5. Hyperbaric chambers when available are used to treat serious CO poisonings.

SMOKE INHALATION

Definition

Smoke inhalation results from exposure to fire. House or industrial fires produce a number of toxic combustion products, especially from plastics such as polyvinyl chloride (PVC). The results can be life-threatening: edema of the upper airway, bronchospasm, pulmonary edema, or carbon monoxide poisoning.

Acute Cause

The smoke inhalation victim is at risk of developing these serious conditions as late as 5 to 8 hours after the exposure, even if the initial symptoms are minimal or absent.

History: Subjective Reports

Dyspnea may be the only complaint and may range in severity from mild to severe. All patients with a history of significant exposure to smoke, especially if in an enclosed space or with loss of consciousness, need hospital evaluation.

Examination: Objective Physical Findings

The victim of smoke inhalation may have hoarseness, cough, wheezing, black sputum, facial burns, or singed facial hairs. Any of these signs indicates the need for hospital evaluation.

EMT Treatment

1. Remove from the smoky environment.
2. Provide humidified oxygen.
3. If rales present, provide 100% O_2.
4. If facial burns, hoarseness, or stridor is present, provide rapid transport to hospital.

TOXIC GAS EXPOSURE: Cl_2, H_2S, CN

Chlorine Gas (Cl_2)

Inhalation of the toxic gas chlorine (Cl_2) can occur as a result of transportation accidents, leaks at swimming pools, or household mixing of bleach (sodium hypochlorite) with acid, usually in a misguided effort at cleaning a toilet bowl. Chlorine becomes a strong acid itself when it dissolves into the moisture of a person's mucous membranes, resulting in burning sensations of the eyes, nose, and throat. Other symptoms include chest tightness, headache, and nausea. Physical findings including cough, wheezing, rales, cyanosis, seizures, shock, or coma. Treatment consists of terminating exposure. Protection within a toxic environment can include makeshift masks of wet cloths. If there are several victims, those with signs of pulmonary edema have highest priority. Second priority goes to those with other forms of respiratory distress, who are treated simply with humidified oxygen. Lowest priority patients are those who require only irrigation of the eyes.

Hydrogen Sulfide (H_2S)

Inhalation of the toxic gas hydrogen sulfide (H_2S) can occur as a result of occupational or industrial exposure to sewer gas, such as that found in septic tanks. The gas is notable for its smell of "rotten eggs." Victims of H_2S exposure may complain of burning sensations of the eyes, nose, and throat; chest tightness; headache; or nausea. Physical findings include rapid respirations or sudden respiratory arrest. Treatment consists of terminating exposure and providing oxygen in high concentration. Assist ventilation as required. Irrigate eyes as needed.

Tear Gas or Mace (CN)

Inhalation of the toxic gas chloracetophenone (CN) can occur as a result of exposure to tear gas or Mace, although CN is only one of the chemical compounds used by the police and the military for crowd control or protection. Increasingly, these products are finding their way into criminals' hands as well. Exposure to high criminals' concentrations can cause pulmonary edema, and victims complain of burning sensations and dyspnea. Physical findings include tearing, salivation, cough, and rales. Treatment consists of terminating exposure and providing oxygen for respiratory distress. Victims should face into the wind and remove contaminated clothing. Irrigate eyes as needed, and caution victims not to rub their eyes. Notify the emergency department in advance, and wash down victim in shower facility outside the emergency department if possible. Decontaminate the ambulance after transport to remove traces of CN powder if present.

14

WATER

DROWNING AND NEAR DROWNING

Definition

Drowning is the fourth leading cause of accidental death. *Drowning* is death in, or under, the water. *Near drowning* is submersion under water that does not result in death.

A predictable sequence of events can occur in drowning. First, large amounts of water are often swallowed. Next, small amounts of water in the hypopharynx and larynx (upper airway and voice box) cause coughing and laryngospasm, closing off the trachea (windpipe). If the victim is rescued at this point, there will be no water in the lungs. The laryngospasm makes further breathing attempts useless, whether the victim is under water or at the surface. (It also makes rescue attempts at this stage difficult.) Lack of breathing results in hypoxia and unconsciousness.

Eventually, anoxia causes muscular relaxation. The differences that can occur in fresh water as opposed to salt water are not important to the EMT. Fresh water in the lungs is rapidly taken up into the blood stream, resulting in ventricular fibrillation. Salt water draws fluid out of the blood stream, resulting in pulmonary edema. Neither makes for any change in the rationale for treatment, as the priorities are still the basic ABCs. What does make a difference in treatment rationale is a history of near drowning in cold water. Victims have recovered completely after 40 minutes of complete submersion in cold water.

Acute Cause

The near drowning victim has been deprived of oxygen (hypoxia).

History: Subjective Reports

The patient may not be able to give any history of the incident. Bystanders are often not completely reliable for estimating the time of submersion, although that estimate should be solicited, if possible. Family or friends may relate other aspects of the incident, such as a dive into shallow water, alcohol or drug intoxication, or pertinent past medical history.

Examination: Objective Physical Findings

Assess ABCs, but do not waste time attempting to remove water from the lungs. Examine for trauma, giving special attention to possible cervical spine injury if the history is suggestive. Check for evidence of hypothermia. Give all patients thorough physical exam.

EMT Treatment

1. If rescue is needed, approach the victim carefully.
2. Assure an open airway. Avoid hyperextension if cervical spine injury is suspected.
3. Assist ventilation as necessary. Mouth-to-mouth resuscitation should be started in the water.
4. Initiate CPR (cardiac compressions) as necessary. Expect regurgitation, and suction as necessary.
5. Provide oxygen.
6. Treat immersion hypothermia, if present. If mild to moderate, remove wet clothing, insulate, rewarm the core before the extremities (heated oxygen or hot packs to chest, groin, and neck), and give carbohydrates. If severe, handle gently, give high-flow oxygen, and provide rapid transport. CPR should not be abandoned in a victim of immersion hypothermia until the victim has been rewarmed.
7. Transport all victims of near drowning to the hospital, even if they are conscious and alert.

DIVING (SCUBA)

Scuba diving (Self Contained Underwater Breathing Apparatus) is becoming increasingly popular, and untrained or inexperienced divers encounter three types of problems: descent, bottom, and ascent.

Descent Problems

A diver with existing blockage of nasal or sinus passages (such as that resulting from head cold or ear infection) has an inability to equalize the internal pressure with the increasing external environmental pressure at depth. This may result in rupture of the eardrum (tympanic membrane). The diver may experience intense pain in the ear or nasal sinuses, causing him (or her) to ascend rapidly. If the eardrum ruptures, sudden loss of balance will result. Treatment by the EMT consists of transport to hospital and treatment for ascent problems if present.

Bottom Problems

Underwater unconsciousness can occur for a variety of reasons, including carbon monoxide poisoning from an improperly filled tank, and nitrogen narcosis. *Nitrogen narcosis* is due to the effect of nitrogen on the central nervous system and results initially in mild to moderate intoxication. This sense of euphoria has been called "rapture of the deep." The diver who loses consciousness underwater may drown.

Ascent Problems

Definition

Ascent that is too rapid can cause either barotrauma to the lungs or decompression sickness. Barotrauma to the lungs occurs when rapid ascent causes the increasing pressure of air in the lungs (relative to the external environmental pressure) to rupture alveoli. Air then leaks into the chest (pneumothorax) or into the blood vessels (air embolism). An *air embolism* is an air bubble that can block the flow of blood wherever it lodges.

Decompression sickness (the bends) occurs when rapid ascent causes nitrogen gas, which had been dissolved in the blood under pressure, to suddenly form bubbles in the blood vessels as the external environmental pressure decreases on ascent. This mechanism is very similar to the sudden formation of CO_2 bubbles when a bottle of carbonated beverage is opened. To avoid the bends, SCUBA divers are trained to ascend slowly and to wait for intervals at various depths.

Acute Cause

Barotrauma to the lungs can result in respiratory distress from pneumothorax or neurological disorder from air embolism lodged in the brain. The bends results in nitrogen bubbles (nitrogen emboli), which can block circulation, usually in the muscles or joints.

History: Subjective Reports

Barotrauma to the lungs is manifested by the sudden onset of shortness of breath (dyspnea) and chest pain. An air embolism can present with disorder of the central nervous system (CNS) such as visual disturbances, dizziness, or sensory loss.

Decompression sickness is usually manifested by pain in the muscles and joints. The onset may be delayed up to 48 hours and is occasionally seen in the diver who goes on an airline flight within 12 hours of a dive.

Examination: Objective Physical Findings

Barotrauma to the lungs may produce the signs of pneumothorax: cough with bloody sputum (hemoptysis) and decreased breath sounds unilaterally. Tension pneumothorax may develop, with possible tracheal shift away from the affected side. Subcutaneous air may be present under the skin of the chest or neck. Air embolism may present with CNS disorder, such as confusion, difficulty in speaking, motor loss, loss of consciousness, or seizures.

The bends may be manifested by mottled skin, evolving rash, or muscular cramps.

EMT Treatment

Management of barotrauma to the lungs and decompression sickness requires immediate use of hyperbaric oxygen in a decompression chamber. Until arrangements for hyperbaric decompression can be made, the patient should be given as high a concentration of oxygen as possible. The patient should be placed with the head down and the feet elevated. Neurological signs should be recorded and changes monitored on a neurological check sheet (Appendix 7). If pneumothorax is suspected, position with affected side down as well, and avoid positive pressure ventilation if possible.

For information on the nearest decompression chamber, a 24-hour emergency line is operated by Brooks Air Force Base in San Antonio at (512) LEO-FAST (536–3278).

HEAT AND COLD

HEAT SYNCOPE

Heat syncope (fainting) is a transient state of unconsciousness, occurring in a hot environment, from which the victim has recovered. Heat syncope is classified as orthostatic syncope, which means that it is caused by venous pooling. The victim will usually have been standing motionless for a prolonged period, often as a spectator at an event. Upon fainting, the body becomes horizontal and the victim wakes up. The patient usually has no complaints and no physical findings unless injured while falling. Treatment consists of removing the patient from the hot environment.

HEAT CRAMPS

Heat cramps occur in the individual exercising in a hot environment, commonly while replacing sweat losses with only water and not salt. The patient complains of the sudden onset of muscular pain, which may range from mild tingling to severe pain in the extremities or abdomen. Muscle cramps will be evident. Treatment consists of rest, removal to a cool environment, salt and water replacement, and transport to hospital if evidence of heat exhaustion is present or if symptoms do not resolve rapidly.

HEAT EXHAUSTION

Definition

Heat exhaustion is a common heat illness. It occurs as a result of excessive water and/or salt loss, usually with strenuous exercise, although it may occur in the elderly or inactive. The victim may be in mild hypovolemic shock, if significant amounts of fluid have been lost through perspiration. Heat exhaustion occurs when the rate of heat loss (through vasodilation of the skin vessels and evaporation of sweat) is less than the rate of heat gain (through exercise and/or simple metabolism).

Acute Cause

In heat exhaustion, the victim collapses just when the mechanism for heat loss fails, but fortunately before the body temperature rises dangerously. (In heat stroke, on the other hand, the body temperature rises dangerously before collapse occurs.)

History: Subjective Reports

The heat exhaustion victim complains of weakness, dizziness, and nausea. It may begin gradually and often follows the exercise. The setting may be outdoors and recreational, or indoors and occupational.

Examination: Objective Physical Findings

The primary sign in heat exhaustion is skin that is of subnormal temperature. It will generally feel cold and clammy to the touch, and its color will be pale or gray. When significant fluid loss has occurred and mild hypovolemia is present, signs can include a rapid, weak pulse and postural hypotension. When significant sodium depletion has occurred, the patient may have seizures.

EMT Treatment

1. Position the patient flat with lower legs elevated.
2. Remove the patient to a cool environment.
3. Replace salt and water. Use caution if patient is nauseated and not fully alert.
4. Transport to hospital.

HEAT STROKE

Definition

Heat stroke occurs when heat loss mechanisms fail and the body temperature rises dangerously. It is the least common heat illness and the most deadly.

There are two common types of heat stroke: classic and exertional. In *classic heat stroke,* the heat loss mechanisms fail as a result of the victim's becoming too dehydrated to continue to sweat. This often occurs in the elderly during heat waves, especially in those with chronic diseases. Obesity, skin disorders, and certain drugs, such as diuretics, can also be factors. In *extertional heat stroke,* the heat loss mechanisms in the body fail to keep up with the heat produced by strenuous exercise in a hot and humid environment. High humidity reduces the effectiveness of sweating for evaporative heat loss because the rate of evaporation is decreased. Even a trained and acclimatized young adult can overexercise directly into heat stroke, which is the second leading cause of death in athletes (after trauma deaths). Excessive heat generation can also occur with certain drugs, such as an overdose of thyroid hormone.

Acute Cause

The onset of classic heat stroke can be gradual, and these patients are often discovered at home by family or friends, generally in an advanced stage of heat illness. The victim of exertional heat stroke can collapse suddenly and rapidly become comatose. Body temperatures above 41°C (105°F) are not long tolerated and must be lowered rapidly. Heat stroke has a very high mortality rate.

History: Subjective Reports

The heat stroke patient may complain of headache, weakness, dizziness, or visual disturbances.

Examination: Objective Physical Findings

For the most part, all heat stroke patients have the same signs. Delirium, seizures, or coma may be present. The primary sign in heat stroke is skin that is hot to the touch. It is usually also red (in Caucasians) and dry, although in about one third of exertional heat stroke victims, the skin is moist. The body temperature will be elevated. The pulse will be rapid, as will the respirations. Patients with classic heat stroke, with dehydration and vasodilation, will have a weak pulse and a low blood pressure. Exertional heat stroke patients may have a full pulse and a normal blood pressure.

EMT Treatment

1. Cool rapidly. This can be accomplished by immersion in a tub of cold water, if feasible. Otherwise, place cold packs at the neck, armpits, and groin, and cover with wet towels or sheets.
2. Administer oxygen.
3. Be prepared for possible seizures.
4. Assure rapid provision of, or transport to, advanced life support services.

The following table gives a comparison of the types of heat exposure emergencies.

Characteristics	Heat Exhaustion	Classic Heat Stroke	Exertional Heat Stroke
History			
Collapse	Sudden	May be gradual	Sudden
Exertion	May precede	Not present	Present
Mental status	Usually clear, may be confused	Delirium, convulsions, coma	Delirium, convulsions, coma
Skin			
Temperature	Normal or cool	Hot	Hot
Color	Pale	Red	Red
Moist/dry	Moist	Dry	Usually dry
Vital signs			
Pulse	Rapid, weak	Rapid, weak	Rapid, full
Blood pressure	May be low	Low	May be low

FROSTBITE

Definition

Frostbite occurs when localized cooling causes tissue damage. When the water within and between cells freezes, the sharp edges of the ice crystals damage the cells. Freezing can occur when the heat supply to an affected part is less than the heat loss.

Frostbite can be categorized like burns. *Frostnip,* first degree frostbite, is shallow, initial frostbite, often of the face, fingertips, or toes. *Superficial frostbite,* second degree frostbite, involves the surface and subcutaneous tissue. *Deep frostbite* additionally involves underlying muscle and bone, generally of the hands or feet.

Acute Cause

Frostbite requires rapid rewarming to avoid permanent loss of function or even tissue death and amputation of the affected body parts.

History: Subjective Reports

The patient with frostnip is generally not aware of it; the area is painless, and the onset is gradual. On rewarming, the area has a tingling sensation. The patient with superificial frostbite complains of numbness. On rewarming, the area stings initially and then throbs or aches. The patient with deep frostbite may complain of numbness, and on rewarming experiences extreme pain.

Examination: Objective Physical Findings

Frostnip appears white, turning red on rewarming. Superficial frostbite appears white and waxy. The superficial tissue is firm, but the underlying tissue is soft. On rewarming, the area becomes mottled blue and swollen, initially, and then blisters appear.

Deep frostbite appears pale or yellow. The skin is cold and hard. On rewarming, the area becomes purple or black, initially, and then blisters form.

EMT Treatment

1. If frostnip, hold against a warm part of the body, such as the armpit.
2. If superficial frostbite, rewarm with body heat, apply a dressing to protect area (especially blisters), and transport with extremity elevated.
3. If deep frostbite, keep frozen and transport to hospital unless transport time is over one hour. Keep the injured area dry and protected during transport.
4. If transport time to hospital is expected to be several hours, or if the area has previously been partially thawed, provide rapid rewarming in a warm water bath. The water should be kept carefully between 38°C and 40°C (100°F and 105°F) for 30 to 60 minutes, or until area stays red after removal from the water. Dress, protect blisters, place gauze between fingers or toes, and transport with extremity elevated. Avoid refreezing.

HYPOTHERMIA

Definition

Hypothermia, or generalized body cooling, is the term used for what was previously called "exposure." It occurs when the temperature of the core of the body (the internal organs of the trunk) is below 35°C (95°F).

Acute hypothermia occurs when a person has been immersed in cold water and becomes very quickly cooled. It is also called immersion hypothermia and can occur in water as warm as 21°C

(70°F). Thin persons, especially children, are particularly at risk for rapid heat loss from cold water immersion.

Sub-acute hypothermia occurs when a person is exposed to a cold environment, usually outdoors, without adequate preparation (insulation, shelter, food, and so on). Hikers and hunters can die in outside temperatures of 30°F to 50°F, especially if unexpected rain and wind develop, which is why this is often called the "killer of the unprepared."

Chronic hypothermia occurs when elderly persons, or persons with chronic diseases, are exposed to cold over an extended period, usually indoors in poorly heated homes. Alcoholics also can develop chronic hypothermia because of decreased sensitivity to the cold, as well as vasodilation induced by alcohol, which increases generalized cooling.

Acute Cause

Mild to moderate hypothermia exists at a core body temperature of 30°C to 35°C (85°F to 95°F). At lower temperatures (<85°F) severe hypothermia exists. The victim of hypothermia has lost the ability to maintain body temperature without medical intervention.

History: Subjective Reports

The victim of hypothermia is generally quite aware of feeling cold only when the body temperature is still above approximately 35°C (95°F). Below that temperature, although the victim may be aware of uncontrollable shivering and problems with numbness and difficulty using the fingers, the strongest feeling is that of apathy. The hypothermia victim does not care anymore.

Some severely hypothermic patients exhibit "paradoxical undressing": removal of clothes because of a sensation of heat, possibly because of failure of peripheral vasoconstriction at very low body temperatures.

The onset of hypothermia varies with its origin: minutes in acute immersion hypothermia; hours in sub-acute hypothermia; and days in chronic hypothermia.

Examination: Objective Physical Findings
EMT Treatment (see table on opposite page)

For mild to moderate hypothermia:
1. Prevent further heat loss. Remove from the cold environment. Replace wet clothing with dry clothing. Add insulation.
2. *Rewarm the core* before the extremities by insulating the arms and legs separately, not next to the body.
3. Rewarm with external heat (during transport): heated (42–46°C), humidified air or oxygen, if available; heat packs to neck, armpits, groin; electric blanket to trunk if available.

Core Temperature	Signs of Hypothermia	Mental State
>35° C (95°F)	Shivering	Withdrawn, discouraged
32–35°C (90–95°F)	Difficulty speaking ↓ Motor ability	Confused, indecisive, apathetic
30–32°C (85–90°F)	↓ Shivering Blue skin Stiff muscles	Poor judgment, lethargic
27–30°C (80–85°F) (SEVERE)	Ice cold skin Rigid muscles ↓ Pulse ↓ Respirations	Irrational
<27°C (81°F) SEVERE)	Pupils dilated/non-reactive BP unobtainable Pulse difficult to palpate Respirations as low as 2–3/min Pulmonary edema	Unresponsive, coma

4. Provide carbohydrates, if patient is able to swallow—sugar, candy, and so on.
5. Carefully examine for unperceived injuries.

For severe hypothermia:

1. Avoid further heat loss.
2. Gentle handling is vital. Ventricular fibrillation is easily induced. Cut off wet clothes. Do not use oral pharyngeal airways.
3. Provide oxygen (if heated to 42–46°C). Assist ventilation as needed, but only to about 10 per minute. Use mouth-to-mouth ventilation rather than cold oxygen.
4. Start and continue CPR, if indicated. Check for a full minute to verify the loss of a pulse. No victim of hypothermia is considered dead until after rewarming.
5. Position with head lower than body.
6. Provide rapid transport to hospital.

Special Considerations

If transport time to hospital is less than 15 minutes, do not attempt to rewarm unless warm moist oxygen is available.

In rescue situations, particularly cold water immersion, when there may be many victims, the most severely hypothermic patients will be the most quiet. Do not be distracted by those complaining most bitterly about being cold.

BITES AND STINGS

ANIMAL BITES

Animal bites from wild animals, particularly skunks, bats, raccoons, and foxes, pose a special risk of rabies. In some communities, over 10% of bats have rabies. In addition, a bite by a pet or domestic animal, *especially* if the bite is unprovoked or the animal is acting in a strange manner, may suggest rabies. Bites from mice, rats, gerbils, hamsters, squirrels, guinea pigs, or rabbits pose essentially no risk of rabies to humans.

Persons bitten by animals are often anxious and fearful. They need to be reassured that most bites are not serious. Obtain a careful history of the incident. Wash the wound extremely well, or dress with a sterile dressing and transport. All wild animal bites must be evaluated by a physician.

The EMT's responsibility is patient care. Police or animal control officers may be needed to identify or capture the animal.

SNAKEBITES

Definition

Two types of snakes are poisonous in the United States: pit vipers (rattlesnakes, cottonmouth, water moccasins, copperheads) and coral snakes. Most snake bites, however, result from non-

Characteristics	Pit Viper	Coral Snake	Non-poisonous Snake
Head	"Pits" between the eyes and nostrils, look like extra nostrils	—	—
	Large fangs	Small fangs	No fangs
	Triangular, broad flat head, wider than neck	—	
	—	Black nose	—
Eyes	Vertical pupils	Round pupils	—
Body	Thick	Small: 10–18″	—
	—	Colored bands: red on yellow	If colored bands; red on black, not red on yellow
Bite mark	Two puncture wounds, 1/2″ apart	Tiny puncture or scratch-like wounds	Teeth marks, no fang marks
		Bites on small part, such as fingers	
Speed	Quick strike	Slow, chewing action	—
Found where	Copperhead, cottonmouth: Texas to the Carolinas	South: Florida, Arizona, Texas	All states
	Rattler: all states, except Alaska, Hawaii, Maine		

poisonous snakes. The preceding table can help in the identification of snakes.

It is often difficult to identify a snake in the field, and any unidentified snake is assumed to be poisonous. Not all bites from poisonous snakes, however, result in venom deposited in the body *(envenomation)*. The EMT needs to be able to identify the signs and symptoms of envenomation in order to guide treatment.

Acute Cause

Pit viper venom is primarily toxic to the cardiovascular system. Coral snake venom is toxic to the neurological system.

History: Subjective Reports

All victims of snakebite are extremely anxious and fearful. Some may faint; others may be nauseated or vomit. All snakebites hurt. These are not specific signs of envenomation.

	Symptoms of Envenomation	
Reaction	*Pit Viper*	*Coral Snake*
Immediate/local	Severe burning pain at site of bite	Minimal pain
Delayed/systemic	Weakness	Weakness
	Faintness	Numbness at site or at lips, tongue or scalp
	Numbness at site	Visual disturbances
		Difficulty speaking

Examination: Objective Physical Findings

	Signs of Envenomation	
Reaction	*Pit Viper*	*Coral Snake*
Immediate/local	Swelling	Minimal swelling
	Discloration	Slight bruising
Delayed/systemic	Hemorrhagic blisters	Bizarre behavior
	Epinephrine response (rapid pulse, sweating)	Neurological signs
	Cardiovascular collapse	Paralysis of the eyelids and respiratory muscles
	Seizures	CNS depression
	Coma	Seizures
		Coma

EMT Treatment

1. Approach the victim cautiously. Ask, "Where is the snake? Are you *sure* it is dead?"
2. Calm and reassure the victim.
3. Quickly rinse the bite area with mild antiseptic.
4. Remove rings and bracelets.

5. Constricting bands should be applied above and below the bite site to reduce venous flow. There should be 2 to 3 inches on either side of the wound, and the band should be tight enough to restrict venous return but not reduce arterial flow. Check for an arterial pulse below the band. Remove bands for 1 minute every 10 minutes and move them slightly to stay ahead of any advancing edema. Constricting bands are of little benefit if applied more than 30 minutes after the bite.
6. Immobilize the extremity by splinting.
7. Monitor vital signs. Treat for shock and assist ventilation as needed.
8. Identify or bring the snake, if dead. The EMT's responsibility is patient care. Police or animal control officers may be needed to identify or capture live snakes. Notify the hospital of identification, if possible.
9. Transport the patient rapidly to a hospital.
10. Incision and drainage may be indicated by local protocol when transport times are prolonged. It should only be done:
    a. If ordered by physician
    b. If signs and symptoms of envenomation occur
    c. If the bite occurred less than 30 minutes earlier and
    d. If the bite is on an extremity.

The technique is performed by making a longitudinal incision, ½" long and ¼" deep, directly over the fang mark extending toward the suspected venom deposit point. Mechanical suction from a commercially available snakebite kit is then applied. If the suction device is ineffective, or not available, suction by mouth can be used. Any swallowed venom will be neutralized by stomach acid, although it is best not to swallow it and to rinse out the mouth.

Special Considerations

Do not pack the area in ice. The cooling effect can cause additional tissue damage, which can cause a greater problem than that caused by the injection of venom.

INSECT STINGS AND SPIDER BITES

Insect Stings from Hymenoptera

The class of insects known as Hymenoptera includes bees, wasps, hornets, yellow jackets, and ants. These insects inject venom. Approximately 5% of the population is allergic to Hymenoptera venom: Stings cause twice as many deaths each year as snakebites. Hypersensitivity reactions are discussed in greater detail in Chapter 12. The identification of the offender may be difficult, as the insect has often disappeared.

Local symptoms of Hymenoptera sting include a painful itching wheal. Systemic symptoms include anxiety and may include signs of allergic reaction. Local signs include a white, firm, elevated wheal, surrounded by redness and rapid swelling. Systemic signs may be seen if allergic reaction occurs (chapter 12).

Treatment is limited to removing the stinger, if it is still attached, and monitoring for any progression to signs of hypersensitivity reaction. Transport if any sign of systemic allergic reaction occurs or if the victim has multiple stings or was stung around the eye. Application of cold to the site may be comforting.

Spider Bites

The *black widow* spider, generally found in warmer climates, is a glossy, black spider about 1" in size. It may be distinguished by a red/yellow or orange marking (often in the shape of an hourglass) on the abdomen. It often inhabits pit toilets. The venom injected by its bite is toxic to the central nervous system.

The bite may be barely noticeable initially, but can cause a dull pain that rapidly spreads to result in headache, chest tightness, and dyspnea. Signs of systemic reaction include muscular cramps in the abdomen, paralysis, seizures, cardiovascular collapse, or respiratory arrest. Treatment is aimed at reducing the absorption of toxin from the site of injection and supporting basic life functions. As with snakebite, immobilize the extremity by splinting, monitor vital signs, treat for shock and assist ventilation as necessary, identify the insect if possible, and transport. Hospital treatment may include administration of antivenin.

The *brown recluse* spider, found in the south and midwest, is pale yellow or dusty brown, about ½" in size. It may be distinguished by a brown violin-shaped design on its back. It likes dark corners. The bite causes severe local effects.

The bite causes tenderness and a red swollen area, which eventually blisters. When systemic effects occur, they include weakness, fever, and shock. Treatment is limited to transportation to hospital, where surgical excision may be performed. No antivenin is available.

Scorpion Stings

Scorpions are found only in the desert, and only those in the Arizona desert are really dangerous. The Arizona "sculptured" scorpion injects a venom that is toxic to the central nervous system. Symptoms include local pain at the site and a pins-and-needles sensation. Signs include local swelling and discoloration, which can progress to muscular contractions, increased salivation, seizures, cardiovascular collapse, and respiratory arrest. Treatment is like that for snakebite: apply constricting bands, immobilize, monitor vital signs, treat for shock and assist ventilation as needed, and transport. Hospital treatment may include administration of anti-venin.

MARINE ORGANISM INJURIES

Stings

Stings can result from jellyfish, Portuguese man-of-war, ane-mone, or coral. The stinging cells (nematocysts) stick to the skin and release venom into the skin when ruptured. The stings can be lethal if the quantity is great enough or if systemic allergic reaction occurs. Occasionally, severe stings on the chest can cause cramping of the chest muscles, drowning a swimmer. Treatment consists of several steps to be done in order:

1. Pour alcohol over the wound sites. Continue to rinse with alcohol for 5 to 10 minutes. Alcohol will inactivate any stingers that have not yet fired.
2. Apply a solution of baking soda (sodium bicarbonate) to neutralize the acid venom.
3. Apply a dry powder to make the nematocysts stick together. Talcum powder is adequate, but meat tenderizer contains an enzyme (papain) that can also inactivate venom.
4. Scrape the nematocysts off with a knife and wash in salt water.

Punctures

Punctures can result from stepping on spiny animals such as sting rays, sea urchins, or salt water catfish. Systemic allergic reactions are rare. Look for broken-off pieces of spine in the wounds. Place the injured part in hot water for at least 30 minutes to inactivate venom. Avoid burning a numbed foot by placing both feet in the hot water, if feasible.

Poisons

Rarely, poisoning can be caused by the eating of a marine organism such as pufferfish, scombroids, ciguatera, or contami-nated shellfish ("red tide"). Treat as for any poison. Signs of laryngeal edema (hoarseness or stridor) indicate the need for rapid transport.

MAN-MADE HAZARDS

RADIATION EXPOSURE

Definition

Radioactive material releases ionizing radiation. This can be in the form of alpha rays, beta rays, gamma rays, x-rays, or neutron

Roentgens	Effects of Short-term Whole-Body Radiation Exposure
20–100	Blood cell changes
200–400	Nausea, vomiting, hair loss
	Marked reduction in white blood cells, leading to some deaths from infections
300–600	Diarrhea, destruction of bone marrow, sterility
	50% chance of death within 30 days
1000–2000	Severe diarrhea
	Death likely within two weeks
over 2000	CNS damage
	Death within hours

radiation. Radiation sources include isotopes used in hospitals or industry for research or treatment, radioactive wastes from research or nuclear power plants, radiation leaks from nuclear power plants, and materials used in the production of nuclear weapons. Trucks or other vehicles transporting radioactive materials are always clearly marked with purple and yellow signs and are heavily protected. The possibility of leakage of radiation material from a well-packed container is slight, though real.

Accidents involving radioactive materials generally occur where radiation experts are present to direct safe procedures, and often any needed decontamination will be done before the EMT arrives. (These are called "clean" accidents.) If not, the risk from exposure is estimated by measuring the radiation with a Geiger counter, which registers units of r (roentgens) per hour. Local protocol will determine how the EMT dispatcher obtains advice in the case of the "dirty" accident.

Acute Cause

Ionizing radiation causes changes in the ways all the body cells function. Some effects are immediate (hours to days), and some effects are delayed (years). Exposure is cumulative over one's lifetime. Biological effects include hair loss, cataracts, sterility, birth defects, bone necrosis, and cancer. There is no known treatment for recovery from the long-term effects.

Several factors will influence the outcome of exposure to ionizing radiation. They are the type and strength of the radiation, the duration of exposure, the distance from the source, and the protective shielding in place.

History: Subjective Reports

Ionizing radiation cannot be heard, seen, or felt.

Examination: Objective Physical Findings

Patients exposed to ionizing radiation can be divided into two groups: those posing no risk to the EMT and those posing some risk. The first group consists of persons exposed to a source of radiation that has subsequently been shielded, and persons who have inhaled or swallowed radioactive material. Patients exposed to a source of radiation do not become radioactive themselves. However, clothing and skin may become contaminated with radioactive particles or liquids if a fire or explosion has occurred. This second group of patients poses some risk to the EMT.

Patients exposed to radiation usually have no external signs of injury. Therefore, external injuries associated with accidents during transportation are generally the result of the vehicle accident and are not due to exposure to radioactive materials. At the scene of a transportation accident, do not allow the presence of radioactive materials in the vehicle (such as low level wastes) to delay initiation of examination of the accident victim.

EMT Treatment

1. Assess the danger of radiation exposure. Ask the radiation safety officers, if they are on the scene. Look for the color-coded labels that indicate the surface radiation level.
2. Obtain expert help if they are not already present on scene.
3. Minimize self-exposure if the patient or the area is suspected of being contaminated. Protection is based upon decreasing the time of exposure, increasing the distance from the source, and increasing the protective shielding.
   a. Park the ambulance away and upwind.
   b. Rescue, if needed, should be well-planned. It should be quick; victims may have to be moved without regard for injuries. Older rescuers are preferred. If extrication is required for a person trapped near a radiation source, the work should be divided so that no one rescuer receives more than 100 r.
   c. Protective clothing, including hoods, masks, gowns, gloves, and shoe covers, should be worn.
   d. Avoid dust and smoke by staying upwind whenever possible.
4. Medical care consists of the standard ABCs. In addition, flush wounds well with saline solution at the scene.
5. Avoid the spread of contamination.
   a. Remove contaminated clothing from the patient, wrap it in plastic bags, and leave it at the scene. If at all possible, the "dirty" victim should be washed or hosed with water at the scene. Wrap the patient well in a blanket.
   b. Notify the hospital while en route.
   c. Transfer at the emergency department according to its protocol for decontamination.
   d. Decontaminate the ambulance as directed by the radiation safety officer. EMTs may need to shower before returning to service.

ELECTRICITY

Injuries due to *electricity* can occur from downed power lines, malfunctioning of home appliances, or improper use (as when a child chews through an electric wire). Similar injuries are seen when a person is struck by *lightning*. The sudden surge of electricity through the body can cause extensive burns, cardiac or respiratory arrest, or fractures. Examination must be particularly thorough and must include a search for entrance and exit wounds, signs of spinal fracture or shoulder dislocation, and neurological signs such as motor or sensory loss.

The first priority is to approach the victim safely. Ask, "Is the power still on?" Be *sure* it is shut off before proceeding. Advise victims trapped in cars by downed power lines to stay put until electric company experts arrive. The next priority is the standard ABCs. Assume that the unconscious patient has a spinal injury, and use the jaw thrust if necessary. Dress burn wounds, splint fractures, and transport on a backboard.

15

OBSTETRIC AND GYNECOLOGIC EMERGENCIES

EMERGENCY CHILDBIRTH

UNCOMPLICATED DELIVERY

Definitions

Delivery prior to arrival at a hospital may occur despite the most careful plans. Although emergency childbirth is a challenge, it can also be wonderfully gratifying for an EMT to assist a prospective mother in the delivery of her child.

Mothers deliver babies, not EMTs (or MDs). A *primigravida* is a woman having her first pregnancy. A *multipara* is a woman who has had two or more previous deliveries. The *fetus* is the developing baby while in uterus. *Labor* is rhythmic contractions. *Bloody show* is the mucous plug expelled at the start of labor. *Breaking water* is the gush (or occasionally slow trickle) of watery fluid from the vagina when the amniotic sac ruptures. *Presentation* refers to the part of the baby that comes out first.

Acute Cause

Delivery can be precipitous if the process is unexpectedly abrupt. Transportation difficulties, such as a storm or ambulance break-down, may also cause unplanned out-of-hospital birth.

History: Subjective Reports

To determine whether there is time for transportation to hospital, ask three questions:
1. "Is this the first baby?" For the primigravida the stages of labor are generally prolonged. For the primipara or multipara the stages of labor are more rapid.
2. "How advanced is the labor?" To answer this question, ask the woman, "How frequent are the contractions?" Contractions that are less than 2 minutes apart are a sign that delivery is imminent. "Has the water broken?" (rupture of the amniotic sac). This is not necessarily a sign of imminent delivery, but it does indicate that the woman is in the final stages of labor.
3. Is there a sensation of rectal fullness? If the woman feels as though she has to move her bowels, this is another sign of

imminent delivery. This sensation results from the fetal head pressing against the rectum through the vagina.

Examination: Objective Physical Findings

If the answer to any of the above questions indicates that delivery may be imminent, then the EMT needs to examine the woman for crowning (Fig. 15–1, *A*). *Crowning* is the bulging out of the presenting part (usually the fetal head) at the vaginal opening.

EMT Treatment

In some instances, it is obvious that delivery will occur promptly, and arrangements should be made for delivery at the scene. When there is some doubt, local protocol may call for contacting the hospital for advice. For delivery at the scene:

1. *Reassure the woman:* an unplanned delivery causes anxiety in addition to the normal strain of childbirth. Tell the primigravida that rectal pressure is normal and does not indicate that she needs to move her bowels. One person (a family member or EMT) should stay at the woman's head for the duration, to provide reassurance and hold her hand. An emesis basin should be present. Coaching her about her breathing involves giving these instructions:
   a. Pant through the mouth during contractions.
   b. Avoid bearing down or pushing.
   c. Rest between contractions.

2. *Prepare the environment* for delivery. Position the woman on her back or side with a clean sheet beneath her buttocks. The woman should be positioned so that the knees are bent and can be spread apart. For sterile supplies, open the OB kit first, then wash hands well before putting on gloves. If there is time, the sterile drapes can be placed under the buttocks, between the legs, across the abdomen, and over each thigh.

3. *Assist with birth of the head.* Place the palm of the hand over the head of the baby and exert very gentle pressure to prevent an explosive delivery. This reduces the chance of tearing of the area around the vagina and/or losing control of the baby. Avoid placing fingers over the fontanelles, which are the soft spots on the midline near the front and near the back. Release pressure when the contraction ends and reapply when it starts again. Support the head from beneath as it emerges (Fig. 15–1, *B*).

4. *Look and feel for the cord around the neck* (Fig. 15–1, *C*). If the umbilical cord is wrapped around the neck, gently loosen it and slip it over the head carefully. If it is too tight to be easily slipped over the head, the cord should be clamped at two sites 2″ apart and cut between the clamps.

5. *When the face is visible,* look for and puncture the amniotic

Text continued on page 176

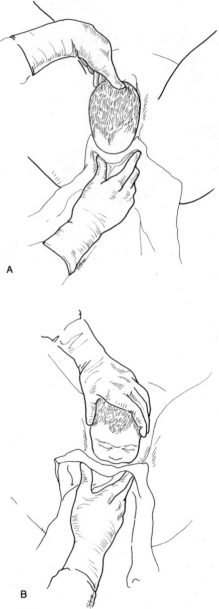

Figure 15–1. Delivery. *A*, Initial presentation. *B*, Emergence of the head.

Illustration continued on opposite page

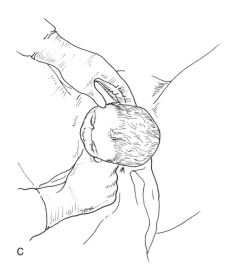

C

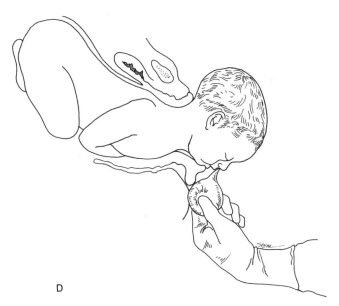

D

Figure 15–1 *Continued. C,* Checking for the cord around the neck; 90°
rotation. *D,* Initial suctioning of nostrils.

Illustration continued on following page

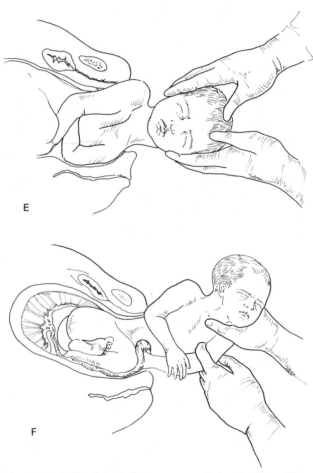

E

F

Figure 15–1 *Continued. E,* Emergence of the shoulder with gentle downward traction. *F,* Gentle upward traction to free both shoulders.

Illustration continued on opposite page

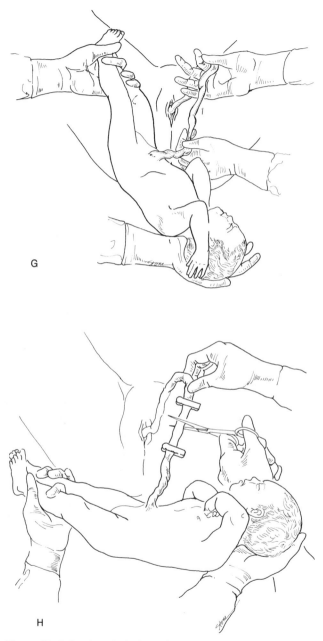

Figure 15–1 *Continued. G,* Preparing to clamp the cord. *H,* Clamping and cutting the cord. Notice that the infant's head is lower than the feet.

sac if it is present. *Suction with the bulb syringe* (compress, insert, release) two to three times (Fig. 15–1, *D*). In suctioning the mouth, insert syringe about 1 to 1½"; and in suctioning each side of the nose, insert syringe about ½".

6. *Assist with birth of the shoulders.* Support the baby with both hands (Fig. 15–1, *E*). Guiding the head downward can assist with delivery of the upper shoulder. Guiding the head upward can assist delivery of the lower shoulder (Fig. 15–1, *F*).

7. *Position the baby* on the table or bed between the mother's legs at the level of the vagina or lower, with the baby's head slightly lower than its body. Wipe the baby's face and *repeat bulb syringe suction* of the mouth and nostrils. Wrap the baby well in blankets or towels. Evaluation of the newborn infant's condition at this point and at 5 minutes after birth may include calculation of the APGAR score (see Appendix 6). Feet that are initially blue are not abnormal.

8. *Clamp and cut the umbilical cord.* Wait for the pulsations to cease first and then clamp roughly halfway between the baby and the mother (Fig. 15–1, *G*). Try to leave at least 6" of cord attached to the baby, and have 2" to 3" between the clamps. Cut with sterile scissors (Fig. 15–1, *H*). Local protocol may call for the addition of an umbilical tape tied on the baby's end of the cord, about ½" from the clamp toward the baby. Apply umbilical tape very slowly and carefully.

9. *Wait for the placenta to deliver.* This usually occurs 15 to 20 minutes after the birth of the baby. Evaluate the mother's condition during this time, and transport if there is heavy bleeding (postpartum hemorrhage) or if 20 minutes pass without delivery of the placenta. If the baby is all right, it can be put to breast during this period, and this will aid in contraction of the uterus. When the placenta is delivered, wrap it in a plastic bag and take it to the hospital for examination. After the placenta is delivered, the lower abdomen can be massaged by gentle rubbing in a circular motion.

10. *Record* the time of birth.

11. *Prepare for transportation* to hospital with clean linen, a sanitary napkin over the vaginal opening, and direct pressure on any lacerations to stop bleeding.

PROLONGED DELIVERY

Prolonged delivery is defined as labor lasting more than 20 minutes after contractions have become 2 to 3 minutes apart. The fetus may be too big to deliver vaginally, although there are other causes. Appropriate management is transport to hospital.

COMPLICATIONS OF DELIVERY

PROLAPSED UMBILICAL CORD

The term prolapsed cord refers to the situation that exists when the umbilical cord comes out of the birth canal before the fetus (Fig. 15–2). It can occur at the same time as the breaking of the waters (rupture of the membranes) and usually occurs early in labor, so that delivery is not imminent. The danger in a prolapsed cord is that the cord can be compressed between the fetal head and the sides of the birth canal. The result of this compression is that the flow of oxygenated blood to the fetus can be diminished or totally blocked.

If the cord is visible coming out of the vagina before the fetus, the EMT treatment is aimed at keeping the fetal head out of the birth canal and away from the cord.

1. Place the woman on her side and elevate her hips so that they are higher than her shoulders.
2. Using a gloved hand, try to push the fetus back into the vagina several inches. Never attempt, however, to push the cord itself back. This (along with complicated breech delivery) is the only instance in which it may be necessary to insert a hand into the woman's vagina.
3. Transport rapidly to hospital.
4. En route to hospital, administer oxygen to the mother. This increases the oxygen supply to the fetus.
5. Keep the cord moist en route to hospital by wrapping in a moistened, sterile towel from the OB kit.
6. Notify the receiving hospital of the prolapsed cord while en route.

BREECH PRESENTATIONS

There are two types of breech presentation, the buttocks presentation and the limb presentation (Fig. 15–3). With the *buttocks presentation,* delivery is usually slow, allowing time for transport to hospital. When delivery is too rapid to allow time for transport, a special problem may occur. After the buttocks and trunk have been delivered, the head may be delayed in the birth canal. The pressure of the fetal head in the birth canal against the umbilical cord can diminish or totally block the flow of oxygenated blood to the fetus. At the same time, once the chest has been delivered, the baby will attempt to breathe spontaneously. However, the face is still in the birth canal, and thus the airway is blocked.

If delivery of the head does not occur within 3 minutes after delivery of the trunk, the following procedure is followed:

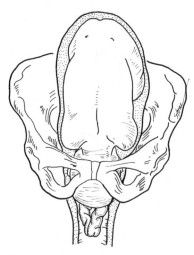

Figure 15–2. Prolapsed umbilical cord.

1. Using a gloved hand, the EMT should place two fingers into the vagina, forming a V with the fingers on either side of the baby's nose. The vaginal wall should be pushed away from the baby's face until the head emerges spontaneously, which it will usually do. *Do not* pull on the baby at any time. If possible, the cord should pass through the opening created by the fingers. This (along with prolapsed cord) is the only instance in which it may be necessary to insert fingers into the mother's vagina.
2. If the head is not delivered within 2 to 3 minutes, rapid transport to hospital is indicated. Continue to maintain the open airway. En route to hospital, administer oxygen to the mother and notify the hospital.

With the *limb presentation,* delivery in the field is not possible. Rapid transport to hospital is indicated. Elevate the woman's hips higher than her shoulders and notify the receiving hospital in advance.

MULTIPLE BIRTHS

In general, the birth of two or more infants is handled in the same fashion as delivery of a single infant. Usually, the woman is aware of carrying twins, although the EMT should suspect multiple birth if the mother's abdomen is unusually large after the birth of the (first) baby.

Twins are usually small and may be premature. Therefore, they deserve special handling, as described under premature births.

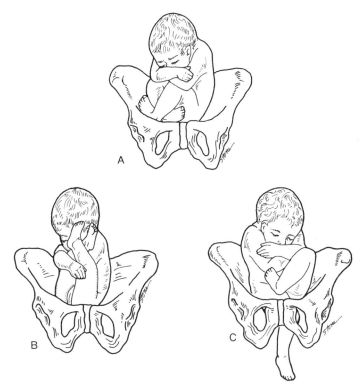

Figure 15–3. Breech presentations. *A,* Complete. *B,* Frank. *C,* Incomplete (single footling).

PREMATURE BIRTHS

A baby is considered premature if it weighs less than 5½ pounds; this often occurs in infants born before seven months of pregnancy. Although babies weighing as little as 1 pound have been known to survive, premature infants have major problems with heat loss and respiratory distress.

A premature infant looks smaller, thinner, and redder than the normal baby, with a disproportionately large head. Its skin may seem particularly wrinkled, and creases on the soles of the feet may be absent. EMT treatment is as follows:

1. Keep the infant warm, to about 32° C (90° F) in an infant carrier if available. Protection against heat loss can be improvised by wrapping the baby well, first in a blanket, then in aluminum foil. Avoid burning a premature infant's tender skin by direct contact with hot water bottles.

2. Assure an open airway. Keep the air passages, especially the nostrils, clear by suctioning with the bulb syringe.
3. Administer humidified oxygen at 2 to 3 liters per minute into a tent improvised from a sterile towel or aluminum foil.
4. Be especially careful with the umbilical cord. Observe it closely for bleeding from the cut cord, and apply an additional clamp or tie if indicated.
5. Avoid contamination. A surgical mask (on the EMT) can prevent the transmission of infection.
6. Contact the hospital and transport, or call for the neonatal transport service, if one is available and situation requires it.

MECONIUM-STAINED NEWBORN

Meconium is the first bowel discharge of the newborn infant. When meconium is released by the fetus while still in the uterus, it can create problems. The meconium-stained newborn is at risk for respiratory complications, and the mortality rate can be as high as seven times normal. Particularly ominous is dark green or black, thick fluid appearing on rupture of the amniotic sac (breaking of water) early in labor. EMT treatment involves special care of the newborn's air passages (suctioning with the bulb syringe) and rapid transport to hospital.

STILLBIRTH

Most newborns are healthy and start breathing within 30 seconds of birth. Some do not and require infant resuscitation (CPR). The stillbirth is a fetus that has been dead for some time in the uterus before birth. The stillborn baby is easily recognized by a foul odor, skin covered with blisters, and soft head. CPR is not indicated for a stillbirth. If there is any doubt, opt in favor of the patient; assume that some possibility for life exists, and attempt resuscitation.

POSTPARTUM HEMORRHAGE

Excessive bleeding after delivery is called postpartum hemorrhage. It may result from internal or external bleeding and is defined as bleeding resulting in more than four to five soaked pads in the 30 minutes following delivery. Internal bleeding may be caused by retained placenta. External bleeding usually results from tears of the perineal area. Blood loss can be severe enough to cause shock.

EMT treatment involves adding sanitary napkins as needed. Save soaked pads in a plastic bag so that blood loss can be estimated by hospital personnel. Elevate the mother's legs. Encourage the baby to suck at the mother's breast, which will aid in contraction of the uterus. The lower abdomen can be massaged by gentle rubbing in a circular motion (uterine massage). When signs of shock are present, treat as usual with oxygen, anti-shock trousers (MAST) if indicated, and rapid transport.

UTERINE INVERSION

Uterine inversion is a rare complication following delivery in which the uterus turns inside out. It can occur either spontaneously or as a result of pulling on the umbilical cord. It is a very serious condition, and shock may occur rapidly. Wrap the inverted uterus in moistened sterile towels and transport patient rapidly to hospital.

PULMONARY EMBOLISM

Pulmonary embolism is a very rare complication of childbirth. It can be caused by amniotic fluid escaping into the woman's circulatory system and lodging in a blood vessel in the lungs. Symptoms, signs, and treatment are as described in Chapter 12.

COMPLICATIONS OF PREGNANCY

TOXEMIA OF PREGNANCY (ECLAMPSIA)

Definition

Toxemia occurs when the pregnant woman's body produces poisons in the blood stream, for reasons that are unknown. It is more common in the first pregnancy and often appears at about the 24th week. The advanced stage, *eclampsia,* is marked by seizures.

Acute Cause

Eclampsia seizures have a high mortality rate.

History: Subjective Reports

The pregnant woman with toxemia generally complains of headache, visual disturbances, or epigastric pain.

Examination: Objective Physical Findings

Signs of toxemia of pregnancy include a high blood pressure and swelling (edema) evident in the face, hands, or feet.

EMT Treatment

1. Administer oxygen.
2. Reduce external stimuli that could precipitate a seizure. Keep lights dim before and during transport. Keep noise to a minimum; avoid using the siren unless absolutely necessary.
3. Position the woman on her side.

ECTOPIC PREGNANCY

An ectopic pregnancy occurs when the fertilized egg implants outside the uterus, for example, in the fallopian tube. Early in the first trimester it can rupture, causing internal bleeding. Shock may result. The woman will complain of acute abdominal pain of sudden onset. Ask her if she has missed a period and could be pregnant. Physical findings may include slight or no vaginal bleeding and signs of shock. When postural signs are found or other signs of shock, treat as usual for shock: oxygen, anti-shock trousers (MAST) if indicated, and rapid transport.

FIRST TRIMESTER VAGINAL BLEEDING

Definition

The medical term *abortion* refers to the termination of a pregnancy within the first 20 weeks. It may be spontaneous or induced. The term *miscarriage* is the word most non-medical people use for spontaneous abortion. Induced abortions can be done safely in a medical setting.

Acute Cause

When an abortion is incomplete and some portion of the placenta remains, uterine bleeding can be profuse. In addition, self-induced or criminal abortion can result in perforation of the uterus, causing massive hemorrhage.

History: Subjective Reports

The woman may complain of abdominal pain, often similar to menstrual cramps.

Examination: Objective Physical Findings

Vaginal bleeding may be minimal or profuse. Tissue may be passed.

EMT Treatment

1. Save any tissue passed or protruding from the vaginal opening.
2. Observe closely for signs or symptoms of shock.
3. Transport priority is determined by clinical condition: routine if vital signs are stable, rapid if shock is present.

THIRD TRIMESTER VAGINAL BLEEDING

Definition

There are several causes of third trimester vaginal bleeding. *Placenta previa* occurs when the placenta is abnormally located over the opening of the uterus into the birth canal (cervix) (Fig. 15–4). When the cervix dilates early in delivery, the blood vessels in the placenta tear and bleed. *Abruptio placentae* is premature separation of the placenta from the wall of the uterus (Fig. 15–5). *Uterine rupture* can occur in a woman who has previously undergone delivery of a baby by cesarean section (surgery).

Acute Cause

Vaginal bleeding in the third trimester can be minimal or can be severe enough to be a life-threatening emergency for both the woman and the fetus.

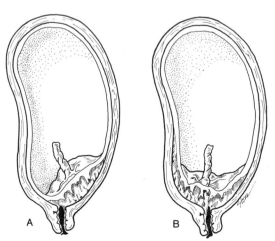

Figure 15–4. Placenta previa. *A,* Partial. *B,* Complete.

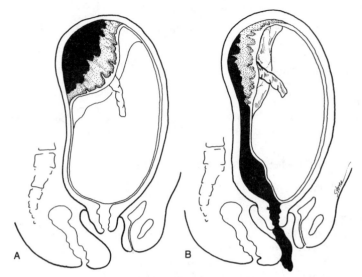

Figure 15–5. Abruptio placentae. *A,* Concealed. *B,* Apparent.

History: Subjective Reports

Although placenta previa is painless, abruptio placentae presents with abdominal pain. The ruptured uterus presents as "tearing" pain in a specific area, with abdominal tenderness, and the uterine contractions of childbirth may stop.

Examination: Objective Physical Findings

Vaginal bleeding may be minimal or massive. In some cases of abruptio placentae the bleeding may be concealed, hidden inside the uterus. When blood loss is significant, signs of shock will be present.

EMT Treatment

1. Place sanitary napkins over the vaginal opening as needed. Save soaked pads in a plastic bag so that blood loss can be estimated by hospital personnel.
2. Position the woman on her side.
3. Administer oxygen.
4. Notify the hospital and provide rapid transport, especially when signs of shock are present.

SEXUAL ASSAULT

History of Sexual Assault

"Rape" and "sexual assault" are legal terms, not medical terms. Medical personnel should use the term "history of sexual assault." The victim's treatment should be similar to treatment for any other victim of violent assault. This particular type of violence produces both physical and emotional trauma. The victim who relates a history of sexual assault thus needs both physiological and psychological care.

1. Provide a soothing and calming professional manner. Do not display personal curiosity, and do not moralize.
2. Control obvious bleeding, and treat other injuries in the standard fashion. Do not examine the genital area, unless considerable bleeding is obvious.
3. Inform the victim of the need for medical care for treatable injury, infection, or pregnancy. Advise her not to wash, urinate, or defecate until after she has been seen by a physician, in order to preserve evidence. The victim may choose to ignore this advice, and that is her right.
4. If the victim refuses transport to hospital, advise her of the local rape crisis/counseling center telephone number. Try not to leave a victim alone; encourage her to contact a friend who can come be with her. If that is not possible, call the local rape center and then put the victim on the line.
5. Record details carefully. Use the victim's own words, in quotes, in the report.

INTRODUCTION

Many of the specific emergencies that can occur in childhood are the same as emergencies that occur to adults. The difference is that they have occurred to children. However, children are not just small adults. Other types of specific emergencies that occur primarily in childhood are the subject of this chapter.

For discussion of other causes of injury or illness that can be seen in children, see Obstructed Airway, Chapter 8; Burns, Chapter 11; Asthma, Abdominal Pain, Chapter 12; and Poisoning, Chapter 13. Examination of the child is covered in Chapter 2, Assessment of Patient.

RESPIRATORY DISTRESS

CROUP

Definition

Croup is a viral infection that often follows a cold or other upper respiratory illness. The common age is 6 months to 3 years.

Acute Cause

Acute attacks often occur at night. Swelling of the tissues around the larynx, just below the epiglottis, can restrict the flow of air, causing respiratory distress.

History: Subjective Reports

The patient may not be old enough to provide any history, but the parents may relate the history of recent respiratory illness.

Examination: Objective Physical Findings

The three most notable signs are high-pitched stridor or a wheezing sound on inspiration, a barking cough (called "seal bark"), and hoarseness. A low grade fever may be present. Signs of respiratory distress may include flaring nostrils or intercostal and supraclavicular retractions. Signs of hypoxemia may include restlessness and tachycardia.

EMT Treatment

1. Provide cool, humidified oxygen. Both the humidification and the coolness are beneficial.
2. Place in the position of comfort, which may be sitting.
3. Gentle handling includes avoiding looking in the mouth. Croup can be difficult to distinguish from epiglottitis.

EPIGLOTTITIS

Definition

Epiglottitis is a bacterial infection, commonly seen in children 2 to 7 years old. There is usually a history of recent upper respiratory illness.

Acute Cause

Epiglottitis is a life-threatening emergency because the swollen larynx can go into spasm at any time, causing total obstruction of the airway.

History: Subjective Reports

The patient will complain of pain on swallowing. The patient (or the parents) will usually relate a history of sudden onset of the acute symptoms.

Examination: Objective Physical Findings

The patient with epiglottitis is usually frightened and prefers to remain still. The position of comfort is upright and leaning forward with the chin thrust out. Drooling will be evident. Stridor will be present. Other signs may include a high fever, cough, or hoarseness.

EMT Treatment

1. Allow to remain in position of comfort.
2. Provide humidified oxygen.
3. Avoid any stimulation of the mouth or throat. Do not use airways. Do not use suction.
4. Provide rapid transport to hospital. Notify while en route.

MISCELLANEOUS PEDIATRIC EMERGENCIES

SUDDEN INFANT DEATH SYNDROME (SIDS)

SIDS is the leading cause of death in infants between 1 month and 1 year old. Seven thousand five hundred to 10,000 deaths occur each year, which is roughly two to three SIDS deaths per 1000 live births. The cause is unknown, and no early warning signs have yet been identified. The infants usually die during sleep in their cribs at night. In about 10% of crib death cases, autopsy reveals a previously unsuspected abnormality or an infectious disease, such as meningitis or pneumonia. These particular children are not victims of SIDS and some of them may be resuscitable.

EMT treatment for crib death is standard BLS (basic life support), CPR, and rapid transport to hospital. Although the first priority is the infant, crib death is a family disaster, and the parents will be panicked and grief-stricken. Some parents will have intense guilt feelings. Provide reassurance that everything possible is being done for the baby. Hospital personnel may want to initiate special counseling for the parents, once SIDS has been diagnosed.

FEBRILE SEIZURES

Definition

Fever can be seen in a variety of common childhood illnesses. It is defined as a body temperature greater than 39°C (103°F). Causes of fever in children include infection (viral or bacterial) or exposure to a particularly hot environment (classic heat stroke). About 5% of children with fever develop seizures. Seizures in children can also result from epilepsy.

Acute Cause

Febrile seizures are not life-threatening, although the panicked family may think they are. Febrile seizures are generally limited to a single event. Multiple seizures suggest some other cause.

History: Subjective Reports

The children will generally be too young (less than 2 years) to relate complaints, but the family may be able to give details about the character of the seizure. Febrile seizures are usually generalized, with symmetrical tonic-clonic motor activity, whereas the finding of focal motor activity may indicate a more serious condition, such as meningitis.

Examination: Objective Physical Findings

By the time the EMT arrives, the seizure will usually have stopped, and the only physical findings on examination may be the post-ictal state and warm, red skin. A stiff neck may be suggestive of meningitis.

EMT Treatment

1. Standard approach to seizures involves the following measures:
   a. Protect patient from injury.
   b. Give oxygen, and suction as necessary.
   c. Position patient on side when post-ictal, and transport.
2. If skin temperature is particularly hot, remove the clothing to aid natural cooling. Sponging with lukewarm water may be indicated in cases of heat stroke. Do not use alcohol or ice water.

DEHYDRATION AND HYPOVOLEMIA

Volume depletion in infants and children may result from acute blood loss due to trauma or from dehydration due to fever, vomiting, or diarrhea. Relatively small amounts of fluid lost can be catastrophic, since there is proportionately less fluid reserve in children than in adults. Although signs of acute blood loss may be obvious, signs of dehydration may be subtle. They include lethargy, dryness of lips and oral mucosa, decreased skin turgor with tenting, tachycardia, and a depressed fontanelle. EMT treatment includes humidified oxygen and transport. Treat for shock as required.

CHILD ABUSE (BATTERED CHILD)

Definition

Child abuse is a social disease that affects all socioeconomic groups. There are four types of abuse: physical, emotional, sexual, and neglect. It is not a rare problem; as many as 10% of all children under age 5 seen in hospital emergency departments are battered children. Although 90% of these children are abused by their parents, about 10% are abused by others, such as babysitters or friends of the family.

Acute Cause

Child abuse incidents can progress from minor injury to increasingly severe injury. The battering parent is likely to abuse the child again unless some intervention occurs. One in every 500 battered children dies. About 35% may be permanently damaged. When child abuse is suspected, therefore, it is important to protect the child from further abuse and to assist the family in seeking treatment.

History: Subjective Reports

When child abuse is suspected, the EMT has *two* patients: the physically (and/or emotionally) injured child *and* the emotionally disordered parent.

The Child. Get down on the same level as the child by kneeling or sitting down. The child may be too young or too fearful to voice complaints, so adopt a reassuring and comforting manner. Do not ask detailed questions about what happened, especially if the suspected abuser is still in the same room.

The Parent(s). Do not question the parent in front of the child. Do use supportive interview techniques. Although a history of multiple "accidents" in the past is suggestive of child abuse, do not contradict the history given by the parent (or by the child, for that matter). That history may seem odd; the parent(s) may be vague or evasive, and they may have waited an excessive amount of time before calling for emergency help.

Examination: Objective Physical Findings

The Child. The child may not be crying despite an obvious injury and may be withdrawn and fearful. Carefully explain the need for examination before touching the child. Trauma that may seem bizarre, especially if the history does not match the injury, is suggestive of battering. Unexplained burns, especially cigarette burns, are suggestive of abuse as well. "Glove-like" or "sock-like" scald injuries or patterned burns (such as iron-shaped) are also suggestive. Unexplained fractures are suggestive. Multiple injuries at different stages of healing, such as old and new bruises, are particularly suggestive.

The Parent(s). The parent's (or parents') behavior may seem odd. They may seem detached or unconcerned and may make little attempt to comfort the child. Occasionally, the parents may show signs of substance abuse or be openly hostile or uncooperative.

EMT Treatment

1. Transport to hospital, even if injuries seem trivial, if battering is suspected. Do not give the parents the option of transporting the child by themselves.
2. Maintain a calm, professional, non-judgmental manner toward the parents. They may be asking for help in a fashion that is difficult to recognize.

3. When making plans for transport, be aware that the child may react negatively to the idea of separation from the parents, even if only for the trip to hospital.
4. If parents refuse to allow transport, do not argue over the child, but contact the EMS medical director (or hospital physician) before leaving the scene. Use a telephone rather than the radio, if possible.
5. Observe state and local laws on reporting cases of suspected child abuse.

17

BEHAVIORAL EMERGENCIES

GENERAL PRINCIPLES

A behavioral emergency is the sudden appearance of unusual, disordered, or socially inappropriate behavior. "Unusual" refers to the behavior or lifestyle that is not normal or "usual" for the person in question. "Disordered" behavior lacks pattern or purpose. Behavior is "inappropriate" when it does not match the setting (the time or place) or the particular cultural group or age group.

Behavioral emergencies can vary in severity. A *life-threatening emergency* exists when an individual is dangerous to self or others. This can occur when the person is out of control, acutely suicidal, or acutely homicidal. In addition, patients can present with a behavioral emergency that is related to an acute life-threatening medical emergency. This can occur in the context of substance abuse or some other medical condition. The way in which the EMT handles such a patient can convert a life-threatening situation into a non-life-threatening one, or vice versa.

To identify a life-threatening emergency, the EMT needs to observe the person's appearance and behavior, listen to the person, and assess the physical (medical) status. Appearance and behavior observations include the person's posture, facial expressions, speech, motor activity, and mannerisms. Listening includes being aware of sensitive topics that increase the person's agitation, focusing on the ability to distinguish what is real from what is not, and noting an erratic mood, poor impulse control, or questionable judgment. Assessment of medical status must be particularly thorough if there is reason to suspect a medical emergency and if the patient is irrational or uncooperative.

Management of a life-threatening behavioral emergency includes, first, treatment of any medical condition, second, psychological management, third, controlling the environment, and fourth, physical restraint when necessary. *Medical treatment* starts with assessment of the patient for a medical cause for the behavioral disorder, such as hypoxemia or drug overdose, as discussed below. *Psychological management* starts with establishing rapport by active listening—reflecting feelings by paraphrasing, acknowledging, and validating those feelings (fear, sadness, or anger). Clarify misperceptions of external reality, without contradicting the person's internal reality. Set limits by labeling inappropriate behavior, and ask the person to cooperate.

Controlling the environment involves using trusted family or friends when possible but removing them from the immediate environment when they are contributing to the crisis by further agitating the person. Removing the person from a hostile or frightening environment may also be helpful. Police may be required to help with managing the environment, especially when crowd control may be a problem. The overall goal of controlling the environment is to enable the person to feel safe. The EMT must keep a safe distance, not crowding or cornering the person.

Physical restraint is the treatment of last resort. Local laws and policies may dictate specific actions, but the person who is out of control is generally acknowledged to be in danger. Special training can allow EMTs and others to use a minimum of force in restraint. The basic principles are adequate personnel, good coordination (team leader), securing the extremities one at a time, using padded leather restraints, and especially careful observation to avoid aspiration if the patient vomits while restrained.

Most behavioral emergencies are *non–life-threatening*. However, as mentioned above, the actions of the EMT can convert a non–life-threatening situation into a life-threatening one. Therefore, the EMT needs to be continually aware of the signs of dangerousness while assessing the person's mental status.

Assessment proceeds as usual. Obtain a chief complaint, a history of the present illness, past medical (and psychiatric) history and medications; and record the symptoms and signs. Use the person's own words (in quotes) to describe thought content and mood. Objective findings include such descriptions as these:

1. Appearance: posture, facial expression, actions, motor activity, mannerisms.
2. Speech: rate, volume, quantity.
3. Thought flow: logical sequence.
4. Affect: apparent mood.
5. Perception: illusions, hallucinations.
6. Reasoning: orientation, attention span, memory, judgment, coherent expression.

MEDICAL CAUSES

Medical causes of behavioral emergencies are similar to the range of causes of coma listed in Chapter 5, which are either structural or metabolic. Structural causes include head injury and cerebral vascular accident (CVA). Metabolic causes include low blood sugar (hypoglycemia), oxygen deficit (hypoxemia), toxic state from substance abuse (drug or alcohol), and fever or infection (such as meningitis). In any of these conditions a life-threatening state may exist that is primarily medical, not behavioral. The behavioral disorder may indeed be only a transitional state, preceding the onset of unconsciousness and death. However, the delerious patient may be out of control and dangerous to others, which also creates a life-threatening emergency.

Some findings in the patient assessment are typical of medical causes of behavioral emergencies. The history may reveal hallucinations (visual or auditory) or problems with memory or orientation. Objective physical findings may include a decreased level of consciousness, an empty facial expression, slurred speech, or motor deficits. These, or any other signs of an acute medical condition, indicate that medical treatment takes the first priority. Treat life-threatening emergencies as is medically appropriate.

When the condition is not life-threatening, treatment is supportive: provide reassurance and transport to hospital. Special reassurance is required for *senile dementia,* which is marked by decreased reasoning power and memory loss in the elderly. Unlike *delirium* (the acute confusional state described earlier), dementia is slow and insidious in onset.

SITUATIONAL ANXIETY

REACTIONS TO INJURY OR ILLNESS

Fear and anxiety are common reactions to acute illness or injury. Patients are often fearful about pain and the possibility of future disability or death. The feeling of helplessness, or loss of personal control, naturally causes anxiety. Some fearful patients will react with denial and some will react with anger, occasionally directed at the EMT. In some patients, the reaction to injury or illness is "regression" to child-like behavior, such as demanding or whining. The EMT treatment (beyond whatever is medically necessary) is supportive: provide reassurance and transport. Give a realistic appraisal of the situation in order to help patients cope. Do not confront the patient with denial, but be concerned and supportive.

GRIEF AND REACTIONS TO DEATH

Both sudden death and anticipated death cause great emotional reactions in people. By virtue of their profession, EMTs frequently encounter death. It is difficult for families to cope with sudden death, particularly suicide. Anticipated death, as in the patient with a known terminal disease, presents the EMT with both family reactions and the emotional reactions of the patient.

The person expecting to die may go through a number of phases: denial, anger, bargaining, depression, and acceptance. Family reactions are very similar. The EMT may encounter individuals in any of these phases. Family members are not as frequently exposed to death as is the EMT; therefore, their initial response to sudden death may be one of disbelief and dismay. Some people, particularly in some cultural groups, become wildly hysterical. In cases of suicide, family members may be overcome with feelings of guilt and self-blame. As family members realize what has happened, emotions of depression or anger may become evident. Anger may be directed at the EMT. Realistic coping comes later. Some individuals react quickly; others react slowly over weeks.

The EMT may also react emotionally in this type of emotionally charged situation. To provide efficient care, the EMT must control these feelings. At the same time, sensitivity as a human being needs to be maintained. The EMT must not become immune to his or her own deep-felt emotions as well as to the grief and emotion experienced by others.

The EMT can play a comforting role in situations of grief by expressing empathy. Empathy involves responding on a feeling level, using active listening skills to paraphrase, acknowledge, and validate others' feelings. This giving of "emotional permission" for venting of intense feelings is very important. In addition, try to be realistic in the use of language about death, particularly with children. Do not confront the fear of death in patients or family, but instead acknowledge those feelings of denial and fear in a straightforward empathetic manner.

DISASTERS AND MASS CASUALTY INCIDENTS

Strongly emotional reactions occur in natural disasters (earthquake, storm, flood) or man-made disasters (explosion, crash, fire, building collapse). The EMT will be faced with both physical injuries and psychological distress. People may be suddenly isolated from their families and other supports, as well as possibly losing the security of their homes.

Most people react with initial numbness, followed by anxiety ranging from nervousness to blind panic. A few people (a minority) stay "numb" for prolonged periods. Many may resist transport from the scene because of concern about their homes or other family members. It can occur that only a small minority of individuals involved in a mass casualty incident remain calm. In this context, the EMT or other rescuer may also be overwhelmed.

The EMT needs to concentrate on the task at hand: safety and control of the scene, and triage and medical treatment according to established protocol. When individuals are resistant to transport from the scene, balance the need for transport with other needs. Children, especially, do better if reunited with family before transport. When persons are confused, agitated, and uncooperative, set limits on their behavior. Assign nervous people specific tasks to accomplish. Isolate the panicky individual by physically removing him or her and assigning a calm individual to remain with the panicky one to avoid the spread of panic.

PSYCHIATRIC CAUSES

ACUTE ANXIETY

Everyone experiences anxiety as a response to stress. When the level of anxiety is such that it interferes with the ability to function, then it becomes a psychiatric disorder. The term "acute anxiety" is used here to cover a wide variety of disorders.

Anxiety neurosis describes the patient who is nervous, fearful, and hyperalert with various physical symptoms such as a rapid pulse, pale cool clammy skin, dry mouth, and nausea.

Panic attack occurs unpredictably and usually lasts only minutes. The patient has feelings of terror and fear of losing control or "going crazy," with physical symptoms such as faintness, sweating, and shaking.

Phobic disorder is the irrational fear of a specific object, situation, or activity.

Hyperventilation syndrome is marked by numbness and tingling in the fingers, toes, and lips; dizziness; diffuse chest pain; contractions of the fingers (carpopedal spasm); and, of course, rapid breathing.

Conversion reaction occurs when the reaction to stress is converted into physical symptoms such as blindness, paralysis, or sensory loss.

Pseudo-coma is a type of conversion reaction, often recognized by fluttering eyelids, especially when they are touched lightly.

Hysterical seizures are another type of conversion reaction, appearing as bizarre thrashing motions.

In general, acute anxiety is a "diagnosis of exclusion," which is to say that it is considered only when other possible causes of the behavior, whether medical or psychiatric, have been reasonably ruled out. For example, it is important to consider alternative causes of hyperventilation, such as CHF, before treating the condition as acute anxiety (see Chapter 3).

EMT treatment of acute anxiety is generally supportive: provide reassurance and transport. Separate family members from the patient if they are contributing to increased agitation (but let them stay if the patient becomes more agitated at the suggestion that they leave the room). Provide realistic information, and identify or label the disorder if it is certain. Explain what will happen, and involve the patient in decisions, if possible. Set limits on behavior when necessary.

Hyperventilation syndrome can be treated by the use of a paper bag or a rebreather mask. Local policy and procedures may govern the use of noxious stimulants in suspected pseudo-coma; ammonia inhalants in particular may be contraindicated in hypertensive patients. Patients with hysterical seizures can be controlled by wrapping their forearms together. This is done by holding the arms together overlapping, so that the fingers of the hand are at the elbows of the other arm, and wrapping both forearms together with elastic gauze, such as Kerlix.

DEPRESSION AND SUICIDE

Definition

Everyone experiences sad or depressed feelings as a response to the frustrations and disappointments that are an inevitable part of daily life. When these depressed feelings are persistent and oppressive, they constitute a psychiatric disorder. Suicidal behavior can range from an active threat (such as the person standing on a ledge) to a minor overdose. Suicide is the ninth leading cause of death.

Acute Cause

The person with a major depressive illness is at risk of suicide. All suicidal patients are treated as being in life-threatening emergencies for two reasons: first, suicide "gestures" can be unintentionally fatal; and second, intense suicidal feelings are generally short-lived. Thus, if the EMT can intervene and prevent suicidal behavior, the patient can benefit.

History: Subjective Reports

The depressed patient will report feeling "blue" and despairing. He or she commonly feels hopeless, helpless, and worthless. A major depressive illness is marked by symptoms lasting over two weeks, such as these:
1. Disorders of sleep or eating.
2. Lack of interest in usual activities.
3. Overwhelming fatigue.
4. Guilt feelings.
5. Difficulty concentrating.
6. Persistent thoughts of death or suicide.

All depressed patients should be asked about suicidal ideas and behaviors. Suicide gestures are generally cries for help, although death can accidentally occur. A suicide attempt may be ambivalent or serious. The following table gives a profile of suicidal patients.

Types	Age	Sex	Method	Setting
Suicide gesture (death accidental)	15–35	Male:female—1:3	Overdose (minor) Wrist lacerations	In presence of others Impulsive act Overly manipulative Lovers' quarrel History of gestures
Ambivalent suicide attempt (mixed motivations)	35–45	Male:female—1:1	Overdose (serious) Wrist lacerations	Help available Ambivalent wish to die Wants relief from suffering, not necessarily death Usually not impulsive act
Serious suicide attempt (survival accidental)	35–45	Male:female—2:1	Hanging Gunshot wound Drowning	Isolated setting Expressed wish to die Discovery and survival accidental
Completed suicide	45+	Male more common	Gunshot wound Jumping	Isolated setting History of serious attempts Recent loss of loved one, status, health

To evaluate the seriousness of suicidal thoughts or behavior, ask the patient about the following:
1. Previous suicide attempts.
2. Recent loss (death, divorce, job).
3. Plans: vague or specific.
4. Means available (highly lethal, such as guns or jumping).
5. Family history of suicide.
6. Chronic medical illness.

Examination: Objective Findings

The patient may appear very sad, may be crying, and may appear despairing and hopeless (flat affect). Scars may be present from previous suicide gestures or attempts.

EMT Treatment

1. The first concern is safety. The out-of-control person with a weapon, even if seemingly only threatening suicide, presents a danger to all in the immediate vicinity. Disarming the person is a police responsibility, not the EMT's.
2. Life-threatening medical emergencies are treated in the standard fashion, starting with the ABCs.
3. Treatment of the depressed patient is supportive. It may be helpful to have only one EMT talk to the patient privately. Ask others to leave the room.

4. Ask all depressed patients about suicidal ideas and behaviors.
5. Prevent further suicidal actions. Do not leave these patients alone. Remove pill bottles and potential weapons from the immediate vicinity.
6. Be definite in the plan of action. Indicate that the patient is expected to go to hospital by phrases such as "let's go to the ambulance now," rather than asking for the patient to agree.
7. When the acutely depressed or suicidal patient adamantly refuses transport, local laws may apply. Most states have an involuntary treatment act that allows hospitalization against the person's will if he or she is at risk for suicide. States differ regarding who is empowered to carry out these laws—they may be local police, physicians, or specially trained mental health professionals. Physical restraint and transport by the EMT may be indicated (or prohibited). Obey local policy.

PSYCHOSIS AND VIOLENCE

Definition

The term "psychosis" covers a wide range of psychiatric disorders, all of which commonly involve a loss of contact with reality. The psychotic patient has difficulty with the activities of daily living, distorted thoughts and perceptions, and confusion between subjective ideas (internal reality) and what is objective (external reality). The psychotic patient is fearful, mistrustful, and sometimes angry. Psychotic disorders range from the harmless recluse who acts and dresses bizarrely to the violently wild and out-of-control person who thinks everyone is trying to kill him.

Acute Cause

The psychotic patient can be dangerous to self or others.

History: Subjective Reports

The psychotic patient may have a history of hospitalizations for psychosis and be taking anti-psychotic medications. The psychotic may report hearing voices or believing that others can hear his or her thoughts or control those thoughts. The mood may be reported to be elevated (euphoria) or depressed. Hallucinations may also be reported, which are visual, tactile, olfactory (smell), or gustatory (taste).

Examination: Objective Findings

Some types of psychosis have a medical cause, and every patient should be carefully examined for medical conditions. In general, the patient with psychosis from a *medical* cause has disorientation, memory loss, short attention span, or fluctuating levels of consciousness. These signs are not usually seen in the psychosis which is primarily psychiatric.

Objective findings in psychosis include the following:

1. Appearance: bizarre dress, odd mannerisms, inappropriate behavior.
2. Speech: talking to self, monotone.
3. Thought flow: lacking logical sequence.
4. Affect: mood appears inappropriate or blunted (flattened).
5. Perception: false beliefs, confusion of internal reality with external reality.
6. Reasoning: lacking insight or judgment.

EMT Treatment

1. The first concern is safety. The out-of-control psychotic person can be dangerous, especially if armed and paranoid. Disarming the person is a police responsibility.
2. If the hostile psychotic patient is aggressive and menacing, verbal restraint should be attempted before physical restraint.
   a. Emphasize the EMT identity and purpose as helpful and professional.
   b. Remain at least 8 feet from the patient to avoid the patient's feeling pressured or controlled. Move closer to patient as rapport is established. Avoid touching patient until given permission.
   c. Listen actively and indicate interest. "Not being heard" is a common precipitant of violent outbursts.
   d. Paraphrase and feedback to patient what is heard, especially reflecting back the patient's feelings. This helps to correct misunderstandings.
3. Physical restraint is indicated when verbal restraint is unsuccessful or risk of violence is high. As indicated in the introduction to this chapter, it is the last resort.
   a. Show of force: A group is organized before confronting the patient. Specific limbs are assigned to avoid confusion. The patient is confronted with the choice of the "easy" versus the "hard" way of accepting necessary transport and medical evaluation at hospital.
   b. Human restraint: Patient's limbs and head are immobilized in a coordinated effort by the group on command of the team leader.
   c. Mechanical restraint: All four extremities and waist are restrained. Secure one arm above the head, place the other at waist level and secure. Padded leather restraints give better security than cloth and cause less injury to the patient.
   d. Observe carefully to avoid aspiration if the patient vomits while restrained.

4. Most psychotic patients are not violent or dangerous and need supportive therapy—reassurance and transport. Carefully explain EMT identity and purpose. Maintain a stance of concerned neutrality. Do not confront fantasies or illusions.
5. The psychotic patient who is not dangerous and refuses transport to hospital presents a peculiar problem. In our society, one has the right to be different. However, many states have laws that allow psychotics who are "gravely disabled" (or other similar wording) to be treated against their will under provisions of an involuntary treatment act. States differ in who is empowered to carry out these laws—they may be local police, physicians, or specially trained mental health professionals. Physical restraint of these patients and transport by the EMT may be indicated (or prohibited). Obey local policy.

Special Considerations

The patient receiving antipsychotic drugs may present with a common side effect called *dystonic reaction:* involuntary contraction of the muscles in the head and neck. The patient appears oddly distorted, with facial grimacing and neck muscle contraction causing the head to tilt backward. The patient may also have drooling and difficulty in talking or swallowing. Dystonic reactions can be life-threatening if air exchange is affected by laryngospasm (which occurs rarely). Assure rapid provision of, or transport to, advanced life support.

IV

PROCEDURES AND MEDICAL EQUIPMENT

The procedures in this section are included as refreshers for EMTs and other persons who are trained and certified in their use. Instructions with the illustrations are advised by the manufacturer of the device or are standards already accepted in the emergency care field by sources such as the American Heart Association. Local methods and procedures should supersede those indicated in this section.

18

ASSESSMENT

BLOOD PRESSURE MEASUREMENT*

Measurement of blood pressure (BP) with a sphygmomanometer and stethoscope can be reliable with proper technique or highly unreliable with improper technique. The principles are straightforward enough. An inflatable cuff is wrapped snugly around the arm and rapidly inflated beyond the systolic arterial pressure, blocking all flow through the artery. With stethoscope in place over the antecubital fossa (popliteal if using the thigh), the cuff is slowly deflated. The sound produced by the blood beginning to rush through the distorted artery as the cuff pressure falls below the systolic pressure marks that measurement (palpation of the radial or pedal pulses at this point marks the palpatory systolic pressure). The sound produced by the blood flowing through this distorted artery becomes abruptly muffled or disappears when the cuff pressure drops below the diastolic pressure (the artery is no longer distorted) and this marks that measurement. (No change in the pulse is palpable at this point, so that palpatory method yields only a systolic value.) Although the principles are straightforward, errors of technique can occur that are related to the equipment, the patient, and the observer.

Equipment

1. The blood pressure cuff must be the proper size for the patient. It should cover roughly two thirds of the distance between the elbow and the shoulder. In smaller individuals, or children, if the choice is between a cuff that may be too small or one that may be too large, it is better to choose the larger of the two. The diameter of the arm is also important—obese individuals will need a larger size. (If an oversized cuff is not available for a markedly obese individual, a palpatory systolic pressure can be obtained by applying the cuff on the forearm below the elbow.) Overall, if the cuff is too small, falsely high readings will result; if the cuff is too large, falsely low readings will result.
2. The cuff must be snugly applied around the arm. A loosely applied cuff will reduce the effective surface contact as the inflated cuff balloons, resulting in falsely high readings.

---

*Macdonald, S. C., Butman, A. M., Wayne, M. A., et al.: *Using Anti-Shock Trousers (MAST): A guide for the EMT.* Emergency Training, Westport, Conn., 1982. Reprinted with permission of publisher.

3. Anaeroid manometers are sturdy only to a certain point and should be calibrated yearly. This can be done simply with a mercury manometer by the use of a Y-connector.

The Patient

1. The patient's arm must be positioned at the level of the heart, such as in normal supine or sitting position. If the arm is positioned below the level of the heart, falsely high readings will result; if above the heart, falsely low readings will result.
2. Overly anxious patients will have a falsely elevated systolic pressure.
3. In some hypertensive patients, an auscultatory gap exists (a silent period between systolic and diastolic pressures) that can be misleading. This is why it is often recommended that determination of systolic pressure by palpation precede the auscultatory method. The gap may cover as much as 40 mm Hg and can lead to falsely low systolic estimations or falsely high diastolic estimations.
4. Quiet Korotkoff sounds (or weak pulses), such as those found in clinical shock, can lead to falsely low estimations of systolic pressure or falsely high estimations of diastolic pressure.

The Observer (Technique)

1. The speed of deflation must be roughly 3 mm Hg per second (range of 2 to 5). Too rapid deflation can result in falsely low readings.
2. The stethoscope head must be placed firmly, but with as little pressure as possible, over the fossa. Heavy pressure will distort the artery, producing falsely low diastolic readings.
3. The bounce of the aneroid gauge must be disregarded. The vibrations produced by the blood rushing through the distorted artery, which cause the audible sound, also cause the needle to bounce upward with each pulsation. The position of the needle before the bounce is the accurate reading.
4. Other possible sources of error include those from viewing the gauge at an angle, too great a distance between the edge of the cuff and the stethoscope, the cuff bladder not being centered over the artery, sensory impairment, and, of course, inattention or carelessness.

It can occur that a clinical picture of shock emerges in the primary assessment, but measurement of the systolic pressure yields a value greater than 90 mm Hg. This patient may be in the stage of compensatory shock, and the variant of blood pressure measurement called *postural signs* or *tilt test* is useful in this situation. Blood pressure that is normal in the supine position may drastically fall when the patient is elevated to either a sitting or a standing position. This condition, called *postural hypotension* or *orthostatic hypotension,* occurs because gravity makes the body do more work to maintain normal pressure when it is upright. This is the same phenomenon that occurs when one stands quickly after resting and feels dizzy. Blood pressure drops suddenly, and it takes a number of body mechanisms to readjust to the body's new position. The normal healthy person compensates quickly for the postural change. The patient in shock may be at the limit of his ability to compensate. To check for postural signs, the supine pulse and BP are recorded and the patient raised into a sitting position with feet dangling (assuming this is not contraindicated by specific injuries). After roughly 30 seconds, the pulse and BP are rechecked. A 15-point change (increased pulse or decreased systolic) is taken as a positive tilt test.

Another diagnostic test that can be of importance in the recognition of shock is the *capillary refill test.* This test quickly reveals whether the patient is severely hypovolemic. When pressure is applied to the thumb, the flesh under the nail blanches. When the pressure is released, the flesh will appear normal in 2 seconds or less if the patient is normovolemic. If the capillary refill takes longer, the patient is probably hypovolemic. This can be a particularly useful test in revealing internal bleeding.

USE OF THERMOMETERS

The medical thermometer is a device used to measure the heat of the body. It can be purchased calibrated in degrees Fahrenheit or Centigrade.

Body temperature may be measured by one of three methods by placing a thermometer in (1) the mouth (oral), (2) the rectum (rectal), or (3) under the arm (axillary).

The normal temperature taken orally is 98.6° F (37° C). The rectal temperature is usually from 0.5° to 1.0° F (0.25° to 0.50° C) higher than oral and is the most accurate. Axillary temperatures are 0.5° F (0.25° C) lower than oral.

The oral thermometer is held for 3 minutes under the patient's tongue with the lips closed if possible. The temperature should not be taken for at least 10 minutes after ingestion of a hot or cold liquid. Oral thermometers are not advisable for infants, mouth breathers, or comatose or extremely ill patients.

Rectal temperatures are obtained by inserting the thermometer into the anal canal to a depth of approximately 1 inch and allowing it to remain for 3 minutes.

Axillary temperature is obtained by placing the thermometer for 3 to 5 minutes in the apex of the axilla with the patient's arm held close to the side of the body.

Before using the thermometer, be sure to "shake down" the fluid in it to a level a few degrees lower than normal body temperature.

The term "fever" is used to describe a body temperature greater than 99.5° F. The term "hypothermia" describes a body temperature that falls below 95° F (35° C).

19

VENTILATION AND RESUSCITATION

GAG REFLEX

1. The gag reflex is an automatic reflex that closes the epiglottis over the opening to the trachea if a foreign substance, such as food or drink, is introduced.
2. A patient who has a reduced level of consciousness, or who is unconscious because of trauma, excessive alcohol use, or excessive drug intake, loses the gag reflex and may aspirate food or liquid into the lung.
3. All patients with an altered level of consciousness or suspected neurological impairment should have the presence of the gag reflex checked.
4. To test a patient's gag reflex, place a blunt thin object (wooden tongue depressor or oropharyngeal airway is most commonly used) on the tongue and carefully advance it to the posterior (back) of the oral pharynx. Often a reflex may be elicited by applying gentle downward pressure on the most posterior aspect of the tongue. If that is not successful, advance the device to the area around the tonsils. If that is not successful, assume that a gag reflex is not present.
5. When checking for a gag reflex, it is not necessary to "jam" the testing advice into the patient's mouth. Careless use of the testing device may cause the patient to vomit.
6. Pay close attention to patients with decreased or absent gag reflex. Use suction as required to reduce aspiration of secretions.

OROPHARYNGEAL AIRWAYS

1. Oropharyngeal airways are used in unconscious patients to control the airway and keep it open. The initial steps in controlling the airway involve the head tilt, supplemented by either the neck lift or the chin lift.
2. The oropharyngeal airway comes in several sizes. Judge the correct size by measuring the distance between the patient's lips and the angle of the jaw. It should be inserted upside down or sideways, then rotated. A tongue blade can assist placement.
3. The partially conscious patient will reject the airway, and when the gag reflex is present the person can vomit and aspirate. Caution is advised if the level of consciousness is uncertain.

POCKET MASK

1. The pocket mask is a small collapsable plastic resuscitation mask. It is generally used with an oropharyngeal airway in the non-breathing patient. Some come with oxygen inlets, allowing delivery of up to 50% oxygen.
2. Use of the pocket mask allows a good sense of lung resistance/compliance, good visualization of the rise and fall of the chest, and good volumes. With the EMT positioned at the top of the patient's head, the mask is held in place with two hands, allowing for a good seal to the patient's face.

BAG-VALVE MASK

1. The bag-valve is mask used for patients who are not breathing (Fig. 19–1, A). It is useful to support respirations in patients who are semiconscious with slow, shallow respirations (<8 respirations per minute) and signs of cyanosis.
2. Oxygen concentration can be varied from approximately 20% (without supplemental oxygen) to approximately 40% using 10 to 12 liters per minute flow of supplemental oxygen. A concentration of up to 90% can be achieved with the addition of an oxygen reservoir (Fig. 19–1, B).
3. The bag-valve device is a useful adjunct for the treatment of pulmonary edema.
4. It is important to maintain a tight fit of face to mask in order

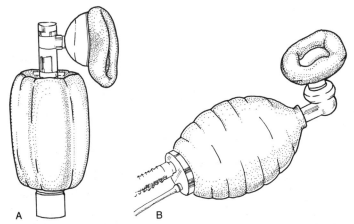

Figure 19–1. *A* and *B*, Bag valve masks. *B*, Mask capable of delivering 90% oxygen with secondary oxygen source and reservoir tubing or bag reservoir.

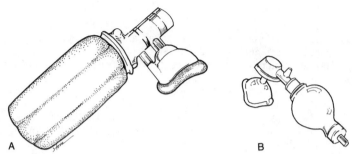

Figure 19–2. *A* and *B,* Bag valve masks for infants and children. Pressure relief valves and smaller volume bags *(B)* protect lungs from overinflation.

   to provide maximum efficiency. An oropharyngeal airway should be used in conjunction with the bag-valve mask in unconscious patients to maintain proper position of the tongue and ensure an open airway.
5. The bag should be squeezed firmly to force oxygen into the trachea and lungs. Patient's head should be placed in an extended "sniffing" position (except for patients with possible cervical spine injury). Watch for gastric distention caused by air forced into the stomach.
6. Special small bag-valve masks should be used with infants to prevent overinflation of their lungs (Fig. 19–2).
7. Suction vomit, blood, and extra secretions from the mouth and upper airway.

DEMAND VALVE

1. The demand valve can be used with both the conscious hypoxemic patient in whom air is not moving well, and with the unconscious hypoxemic patient in whom air is not moving well. Its primary value is in the conscious patient who needs respiratory assistance.
2. Oxygen flow is triggered automatically by slight inspiratory pressure. Flow rates range from 100 to 150 liters per minute during inspiration. Flow ceases at a pre-set pressure limit of 40 mm Hg. This automatic triggering is clearly advantageous. However, the demand valve has the disadvantage of delivering only dry, non-humidified oxygen. Humidified oxygen is particularly necessary for the asthma patient.
3. The high flow rate of the demand valve can overcome the esophageal tone and inflate the stomach. This is a significant disadvantage, as air in the stomach promotes vomiting, with the attendant risk of aspiration.

4. To assist ventilation with the demand valve in the conscious hypoxemic patient, start by explaining the procedure to the patient. Chose the appropriate mask size, and make a good seal with the thumb and fingers on the sides of the mask. Allow the patient's inspiratory effort to trigger oxygen flow. Gauge effectiveness by watching the chest expand.

5. The demand valve can also be used to provide positive pressure ventilation for the unconscious hypoxemic patient who is not breathing. The manual override button allows the EMT to generate high pressures and fill the lungs even during CPR. Unfortunately, overinflation is a common complication, leading to gastric distention. Thus, the bag-valve mask is a better device for use during CPR.

OXYGEN DELIVERY DEVICES

Venturi Mask

1. The Venturi mask is designed to deliver a fixed percentage of oxygen concentration (Fig. 19–3). This is accomplished by an adjustable flow rate dial or specific oxygen flow restrictors, which are inserted into the mask. The percentage of flow is not affected by the rate of depth of a patient's respirations.

2. Oxygen percentages normally are 24, 28, 35, and 40%.

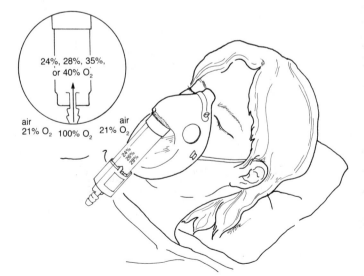

Figure 19–3. Venturi mask, in which 100% oxygen is mixed with room air, making accurate selection of oxygen concentration possible. The mask is especially useful in the treatment of patients with chronic lung disease.

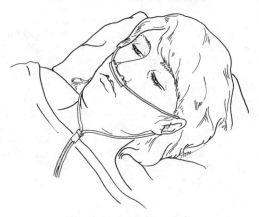

Figure 19–4. Nasal cannula.

Nasal Cannula

1. The nasal cannula is the most commonly used oxygen delivery device (Fig. 19–4). It is used for patients who are breathing spontaneously and require supplemental oxygen.
2. It has the advantage of allowing the patient to talk. The patient usually does not feel smothered or claustrophobic.
3. It delivers from 20 to 40% oxygen concentration depending upon the oxygen flow rate (liters per minute). For example, 4 liters per minute is a routine setting, except for patients with COPD, who should be given 2 liters/minute.
4. The nasal cannula is not affected by mouth breathing, but the actual percentage of oxygen concentration is variable.

Oxygen Delivery Device	Flow Rate *(l/min)*	Concentration Delivered *% of Oxygen*
Nasal cannula	1–2	24–28
	4–6	36–44
Venturi mask		
24%	4	24
28%	4	28
35%	8	35
40%	8	40
Simple face mask	6–10	35–55
Partial rebreathing mask	6–10	40–60
Reservoir (non-rebreathing) mask	10–12	90–100

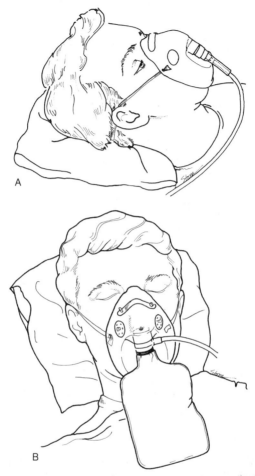

Figure 19–5. Face masks. *A*, Simple mask. *B*, Face mask with oxygen reservoir for higher concentration of oxygen.

Face Masks

1. Face masks may deliver 35 to 60% oxygen concentration (Fig. 19–5). They often give the patient a feeling of suffocation.
2. Face masks combine unused air in the upper airway with new oxygen.
3. Flow rates of oxygen should be at least 5 liters per minute to exceed 20% oxygen (which is available in room air).
4. The mask should have a tight seal for proper function.

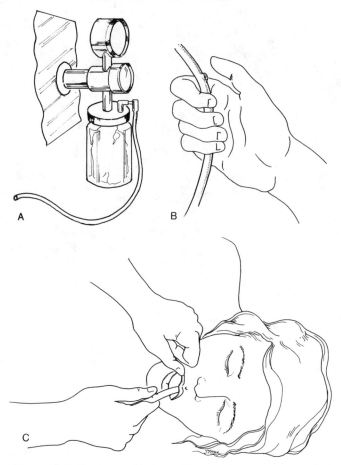

Figure 19–6. Suction. *A,* Typical wall-mounted vacuum suction device with a vacuum gauge and jar with a disposable plastic container. *B,* "Whistle tip" suction tip, thumb operated. *C,* Turn the patient's head to one side when possible, place the suction tip in one side of the patient's mouth, and do not suction for more than 10 seconds at a time.

SUCTION DEVICES

1. A suction device should be capable of clearing blood, vomitus, or secretions from the upper respiratory system. Various portable devices are available; they may be hand- or foot-operated, or battery-powered.
2. The suction device includes a plastic bag or bottle to trap the aspirate, flexible tubing, and "whistle tip" or Y-connector type

catheters of various sizes (Fig. 19–6, *A*). Control over the amount of suction applied is done by placing a thumb over the open Y-connector (Fig. 19–6, *B*).

3. Steps for proper suctioning techniques:
   a. Select the proper catheter size for the size of the patient and for the type of secretions to be suctioned.
   b. Insert the tip of the catheter, but do not apply suction until the catheter is in the desired location (Fig. 19–6, *C*). It is difficult to advance the catheter while suction is applied.
   c. Do not suction the airway for periods of longer than 5 to 10 seconds, as the suction impedes the patient's ability to breathe.
   d. When the airway is cleared, assist the patient's respiration, using oxygen concentrations.
   e. Be careful not to cause additional gagging and vomiting during suctioning.
      Note: Suctioning may cause increased intracranial pressure if patient has head injury. Therefore, use it sparingly.
4. Clear secretions from the catheter using water or saline by applying suction until clear fluid reaches the trap.

20

ANTI-SHOCK TROUSERS (MAST)

1. Anti-shock trousers, also called Military Anti-Shock Trousers (MAST), increase the circulation to the vital parts of the body (brain, heart, lungs) by decreasing the capacity of the circulatory system in the areas under the suit (legs and abdomen). In addition, the MAST suit effectively controls bleeding in areas under the suit (particularly internal bleeding into the abdominal cavity) and serves as an effective splinting device for fractures of the pelvis and lower extremities (Figure 20–1).
2. Local protocol will determine whether anti-shock trousers are used only under direct physician direction (over the radio) or under the direction provided by written (standing) orders. Generally speaking, the trousers are applied to hypotensive patients with a systolic pressure less than 90 mm Hg and a clinical picture of shock (cool, pale, clammy skin, rapid pulse, nausea, anxiety, and thirst). Local medical protocol will also determine the use of MAST in special situations, such as the presence of cardiogenic shock, pulmonary edema, pregnancy, or evisceration.
3. To apply anti-shock trousers:
   a. Patient assessment must be thorough. Physical examination of areas under the suit will not be possible once the suit is applied and inflated.
   b. Remove the patient's pants, or empty pockets and remove belt.
   c. Lay out the suit.
   d. Place the patient on the suit.
   e. Fasten the suit around the patient, connect the foot pump, and open the stopcock valves.
   f. Inflate the suit (legs first, then abdomen) until there is a clinical response (level of consciousness, skin color, vital signs) or until full inflation at about 100 mm Hg.
   g. Monitor vital signs closely, and adjust the suit pressure as required.
   h. Do not deflate the suit in the field. Deflation will have to be accompanied by fluid replacement in the hospital.

WOUND CARE

Occlusive Dressings

An occlusive dressing is used in two different conditions: sucking chest wound and abdominal evisceration. Materials that can be used to make occlusive dressings include sterilized aluminum foil, sterilized plastic wrap, and sterile Vaseline gauze. Although aluminum foil can also be used as an insulator for the premature infant, it is difficult to work with to create an occlusive dressing because it will not easily conform to the skin surface.

To make an occlusive dressing for a sucking chest wound:
1. Look for an exit wound.
2. Size the dressing to be several times greater than the wound.
3. Seal the wound at the end of forced exhalation.
4. Tape on all four sides.
5. Turn the patient onto the injured side.
6. Observe carefully for the possible development of tension pneumothorax. If tension pneumothorax is suspected, test by releasing the seal on one side to see if air rushes out. If it is present, the occlusive dressing can be left taped on three sides, as the occlusive dressing will seal against the wound on inspiration, but allow air to escape during expiration.

To make an occlusive dressing for abdominal evisceration:
1. Cover the eviscerated bowel completely.
2. Tape on four sides.

Tourniquets and Constricting Bands

It is important to distinguish between the need for tourniquet(s) and constricting bands(s).

Tourniquet(s)
1. Tourniquets completely occlude the flow of venous and arterial blood.
2. Other methods of controlling the hemorrhage should be attempted prior to application of a tourniquet.
3. The tourniquet is applied as close to the wound as possible.
4. A blood pressure cuff makes the best tourniquet, when possible. Inflate to higher than systolic pressure.
5. Once applied, the tourniquet must not be released until the patient is under care at a medical facility.
6. Note the exact time the tourniquet is applied. Relate this information immediately to the receiving medical personnel.

Constricting Band(s)
1. Constricting bands reduce venous return. They are used in management of snake bites, allergic reaction to insect sting, and severe congestive heart failure.
2. Blood pressure cuffs make the best constricting bands, when possible. Inflate to a value between diastolic and systolic pressures.
3. Arterial pulses distal to the constricting band must be assessed and the bands adjusted to maintain distal pulses at all times.
4. When used for congestive heart failure, the bands should be rotated every 15 to 20 minutes to allow for normal venous flow.

Text continued on page 222

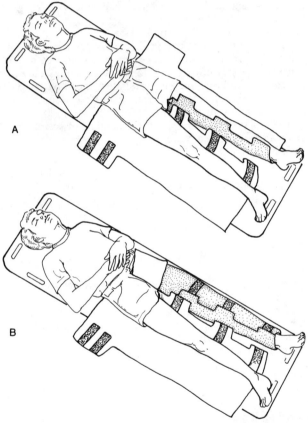

Figure 20–1. Antishock pants. *A, B, C,* and *D,* Successive steps of log-rolling patient onto pants and fastening first the legs and then the abdomen.
Illustration continued on opposite page

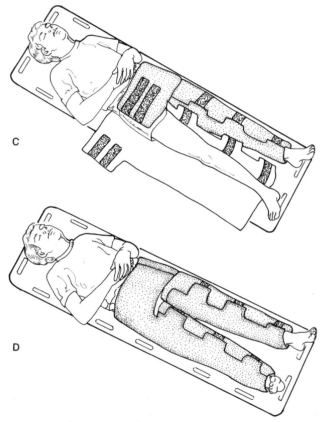

Figure 20–1 *Continued.*

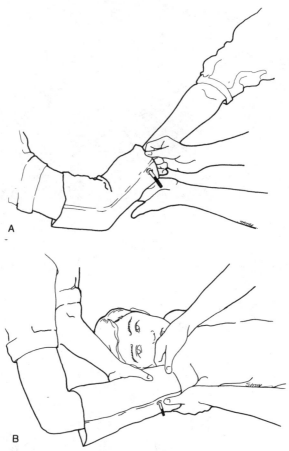

Figure 20–2. Air splints. *A,* EMT, who is going to maintain traction on the fractured extremity, should place the hand and arm inside the splint and grasp the wrist or ankle of the extremity to be splinted. *B,* With the extremity in proper alignment, slide splint from EMT's arm onto the fractured extremity. *C,* Maintain traction and alignment, and inflate the splint by mouth until it is moderately firm.

Illustration continued on opposite page

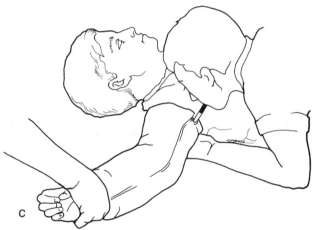

Figure 20–2 *Continued.*

Extremity Splints

1. The management of fractures and dislocations is a challenge to patience and common sense. There are few hard-and-fast rules.
2. Most musculoskeletal injuries are not life-threatening. Exceptions include hemorrhage from open fractures, fractures to the thorax with insults to respiratory organs or large vessels, fractures to the pelvis, and fractures of the femur. Usually, the EMT has time to prepare a systematic approach to the problem and thus prevent additional injury to the surrounding tissue.
3. The goal of the EMT is to stabilize, immobilize, and, if possible, realign the extremity(ies) to near-normal anatomical position.
4. There are numerous devices available for splinting (Figs. 20–2, 20–3, and 20–4). When selecting a device for splinting, consider the following factors:
   a. The location of the part to be stabilized.
      i. Splint joint injuries with moldable splints (such as a ladder splint) in position found.
      ii. Use traction devices for heavy-muscled long bones.
      iii. Splint to one joint above and the joint below the injured part.
   b. Consider the ease and comfort of application of the splint. Pillows and blankets are useful padding for simple rib fracture and ankle or foot injuries, and for elevation of extremity fractures during transportation. Vacuum splints, although extremely effective, can be slightly uncomfortable to a conscious patient.
   c. Leave access to distal pulses (Fig. 20–5).

Figure 20–3. Pillow splint, an especially comfortable and stable method of splinting fractures of the ankles and feet.

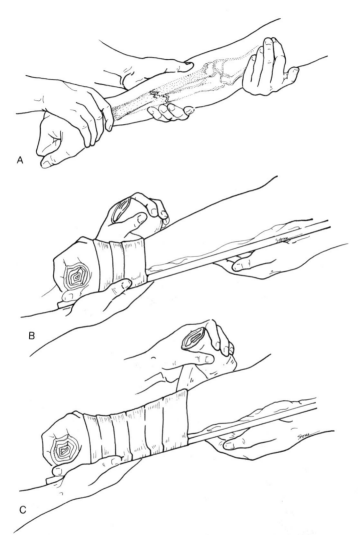

Figure 20–4. Board or ladder splint. *A,* Align fractured extremity with gentle traction. *B,* After padding the board to fill the contours of the arm, place splint along inside of forearm with roll of padding in palm of extremity. *C,* Secure extremity to splint with roll of bandage material.

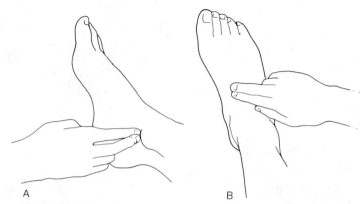

Figure 20–5. Pedal pulses. Distal pulses of lower extremities must be checked before and after splinting of fracture. *A,* Posterior tibialis pulse. *B,* Dorsalis pedis pulse.

  d. Pneumatic anti-shock trousers should be large enough to surround the pelvic girdle.
5. Rules of splinting:
  a. Always work with a partner and predetermine the role each rescuer will perform during treatment.
  b. Inform patient of all treatment before beginning, including the possibility of when to expect pain.
  c. Remove clothing, debris, and boots/shoes.
  d. Control hemorrhage with direct pressure
  e. Cover open wounds and exposed bones with sterile, dry dressings. Rinse exposed bones with saline before applying traction if end is likely to slip back in.
  f. Assess arterial pulses, sensations, and movement distal to the site of injury, and record them.
  g. Assemble necessary materials required for splinting. Place padding on splint before beginning treatment.
  h. Have partner stabilize the joint above splinting site. Gently apply traction in the direction of angulation. Move limb very slowly to normal anatomical position. It is not necessary to replace bone ends together. Align them parallel to each other.
  i. Reassess distal pulses, sensations, and movement after splinting is completed. If pulses or sensation have changed, do not reposition limb. Check adequacy of traction. Record results, and advise receiving physician of the time of loss of pulse or sensation.
  j. The splint must immobilize at least one joint above and one joint below the fracture site.
  k. Elevate the injured limb before transport.

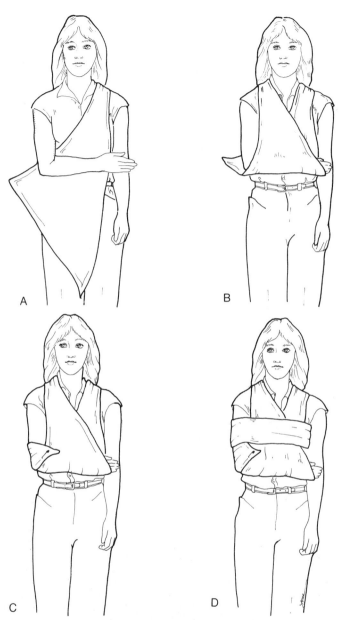

Figure 20–6. Sling and swathe used with injuries of the humerus and shoulder. *A,* Place patient's forearm across chest. *B,* Secure both ends of the sling with a knot in a comfortable position at the shoulder. *C,* Secure elbow flap of sling. *D,* Tie swathe around chest just tight enough to prevent arm from swinging away from patient's body.

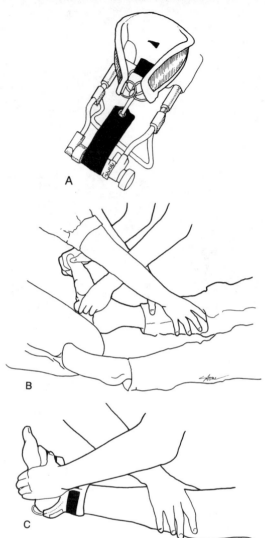

Figure 20–7. Installing Hare traction splint. *A*, Proper position of ankle hitch to windlass. *B*, Remove shoe, sock, and all clothing from fractured extremity. Determine whether distal pulse is present. *C*, Install ankle hitch while immobilizing fracture at joints above and below the fracture site. *D*, Pull traction manually, using ankle hitch, while still maintaining immobilization at knee joint. *E*, Position splint in place firmly against the buttock and apply thigh strap. Use padding under the strap as necessary in the groin area. Splint should be adjusted to proper length before placing it on the patient. Be sure to leave extra length for windlass action. *F*, Attach ankle hitch rings to windlass and apply traction according to patient's comfort. Close the leg straps, starting at the ankle and working toward the fracture. Raise the stand to keep the heel off the surface.

Illustration continued on opposite page

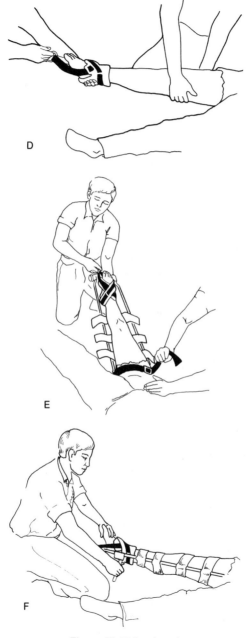

Figure 20–7 *Continued.*

6. Remember, when using air splints or MAST pants and moving from a cold to a warm environment or changing altitudes, that the pressure in the splint increases with increases in temperature and/or altitude.
7. Avoid concentrating on obvious fractures at the expense of neglecting the ABCs.
8. Apply sling and swath to injuries of the humerus and shoulder (Fig. 20–6).
9. Devices for splinting the lower extremity are shown in Figures 20–7 and 20–8.

Neck and Spine Immobilization

1. Injuries to the neck (cervical spine), mid-back (thoracic spine), and lower back (lumbar spine) may be subtle. The patient may complain of minor pain. Deformity may not be palpable. For this reason, it is vital for the EMT to get as clear a mental picture as possible of the mechanism and the force of the mechanism of injury.
2. General considerations for use of cervical collar (Fig. 20–9) and spine board immobilization:
   a. All persons with head injuries and all unconscious trauma victims have associated cervical injury until proved otherwise.
   b. Any complaint of pain in any portion of the spine.
   c. Decreased sensation, numbness or tingling, reduced or complete loss of motion of any or all extremities after trauma, even if it has resolved.
   d. Palpable deformities or tenderness in any portion of the spine after trauma.
   e. Lacerations and/or hematomas to the head from another moving object, or a blow to the head from heavy or fast-moving source.
   f. Deceleration injuries such as those resulting from a vehicle accident or fall.
   g. A forceful blow to any portion of the spine.
3. There have been cases of patients with fractures of the spine that have gone unnoticed and were discovered hours later when severe symptoms began to develop. Often this circumstance can be avoided if EMT treatment is based upon the mechanism of injury. Rely on your initial impression: "If you think about the need for neck and spine immobilization, do it."
   a. Align the head and neck along the long axis of the skeleton *before* assessing any other limb/injury.
   b. Should the patient's head/neck be rotated, provide initial traction, then rotate to anatomical position.
   c. Should the patient's head/neck be rotated and flexed or extended, first initiate traction on the head (this achieves a normal anatomical position and has the effect of straightening

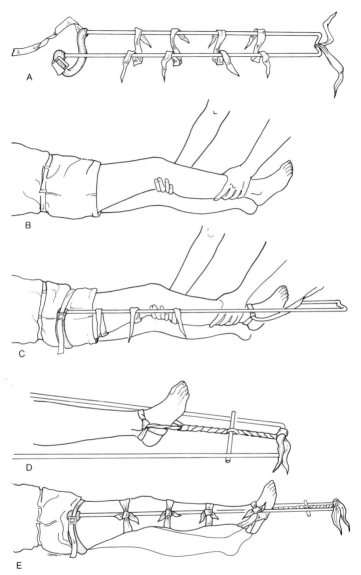

Figure 20–8. Thomas half-ring splint. *A,* Buckle of thigh strap is always positioned on outside of extremity. *B* and *C,* Follow the same steps to apply the splint as with the Hare splint, except that this splint does not have a built-in windlass and leg straps. Cravats are normally used for those purposes. *D,* Sample ankle strap and windlass. *E,* Splint in place.

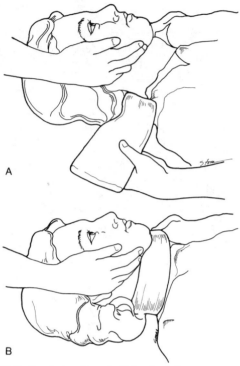

Figure 20–9. Cervical collar. *A,* Using both hands, placed under the patient's ears on the mastoid processes, pull traction in a straight line with the spine. Slide the collar under the patient's neck until the notch is positioned under the chin. The collar should be snug. *B,* The head should be held stable during any movement of the patient until sandbags are placed on both sides of the head and the head is secured to a backboard.

    the neck). Next, rotate the head into a normal position (the result should be a forward-facing position with the neck and head in a neutral position).

4. Cervical immobilization devices include commercially available hard collars such as Philadelphia collars, rolled blankets, and taped sandbags.

APPENDIX 1: COMMONLY PRESCRIBED DRUGS

GENERAL DRUG TYPES AND HOW THEY WORK

Antihypertensive Drugs

Usually, drugs for hypertension are a mixture of two or more or a combination of drugs from the three basic categories used to reduce hypertension. The type of drug used is determined by the severity of the hypertension.

1. Vasodilators directly affect the muscles in the arterial walls and relax them, thereby reducing blood pressure.
2. Diuretics reduce blood pressure by reducing fluid volume in the vascular system.
3. The third category of antihypertensive drugs affects various parts of the central nervous system, which in turn cause a relaxation of the muscles in the blood vessels.

Cardiac (Heart) Drugs

These drugs have a direct effect on the heart and the heart's electrical conduction system.

1. Antiarrhythmia drugs correct irregularities in the electrical impulses that cause the heart to beat in even cycles (Dilantin, Pronestyl, Inderal, Quinidine).
2. A special drug category is members of the digitalis family, which have the effect of increasing the force of the heart's contractions and slow the heart rate, making the heart a more efficient pump.
3. Antianginal drugs, such as the nitrate group, i.e., nitroglycerin, cause a relaxation of the arteries supplying the heart, thereby providing an increase in blood and oxygen to the heart. The drug propranolol (Inderal) is often used for its ability to slow down the heart rate, reducing the requirement for extra oxygen by not allowing the heart to increase its activity.

Anticoagulants

Used to prevent blood from clotting, they are often described as "blood-thinning" drugs.

Antihistamines

1. Used to counteract the stuffy, runny nose; itchy eyes; and scratchy throat caused by the release of the body chemical histamine.
2. The itching and other reactions constitute an allergic response to pollen, an insect bite, or a virus (common cold).

Analgesics

1. Used to relieve severe to mild pain.
2. Strong analgesics are the drugs in the narcotic family such as morphine, Demerol, opium, Percodan, and Talwin.
   a. Are used cautiously, as they are habit forming.
   b. Have serious side effects, including respiratory depression or arrest.
3. Mild analgesics are broken down into two categories: codeine and Darvon; and drugs that also reduce fever (antipyretic), such as aspirin and acetaminophen.
4. Aspirin and acetaminophen are the two most widely used drugs around the world, as they also work as an anti-inflammatory medicine in addition to correcting mild pain and fever.

Psychotropic Drugs

These drugs been found to be useful in managing day-to-day stress by relieving the symptoms of psychiatric disorders. Psychotropic drugs are separated into three categories:

1. Antianxiety drugs are the minor tranquilizers of the benzodiazepines: Valium, Librium, Serax, and Meprobamate.
   a. Anxiety neurosis is characterized by panic, apprehension, tension, and fatigue.
2. Antidepressant drugs are separated into tricyclics and MAO inhibitors.
   a. Depressed patients are brooding, suffer feeling of extreme helplessness, tend to be self-critical.
   b. Often complain of loss of appetite, headache, tiredness.
3. Antipsychotic drugs are divided into three categories: the phenothiazines, the butyrophenones, and the thioxanthenes, and because of their side effects are saved for the most severe situations. These drugs have direct effect on the brain to control paranoid or schizophrenic disorders.

The following table is an alphabetical list by brand name and generic name (in capital letters) of the most commonly used drugs, the usual indications for use, and the basic families from which they are derived. Only the medicines that are used on a long-term basis are included, and short-term or occasionally used drugs such as antibiotics, hormones, birth control pills, and medicines for colds have been excluded. Also, many of these drugs have been selected to assist the EMT to recognize pertinent chronic disease by the medicine taken by the patient. The medicines in the table are usually potent and have serious side effects when not used as prescribed. This table of drugs is established from a list of drugs used over the entire United States. EMTs should become familiar with the drugs used in their own locales.

Drug	Indications for Use	General Drug Type
ACETAMINOPHEN	Tylenol, Datril	Pain, fever, inflammation	Mild analgesic
ACETAZOLAMIDE	Diamox	Seizures, glaucoma	Weak diuretic
Adapin	DOXEPIN	Depression	Tricyclic antidepressant
ALBUTEROL	Proventil	Asthma, COPD	Bronchodilator
Aldactazide	HYDROCHLOROTHIAZIDE	High blood pressure	Potassium-sparing diuretic
	SPIRONOLACTONE	High blood pressure	Potassium-sparing diuretic
Aldactone	SPIRONOLACTONE	High blood pressure	Combined with other diuretic to spare potassium
Aldoril	HYDROCHLOROTHIAZIDE	High blood pressure	Diuretic with CNS relaxant of vascular system
	METHYLDOPA	High blood pressure	Diuretic with CNS relaxant of vascular system
ALLOPURINOL	Zyloprim	Gout, high uric acid blood level	Prophylactic for gout
AMITRIPTYLINE	Elavil	Depression	Tricyclic, antidepressant
Anaprox	NAPROXEN	Pain, inflammation, arthritis	Non-narcotic, non-steroid analgesic
Anhydron	CYCLOTHIAZIDE	High blood pressure	Diuretic
Apresoline	HYDRALAZINE	Essential hypertension	Vasodilator
Artane	TRIHEXYPHENIDYL	Parkinson's disease	Synthetic antispasmodic—works like atropine
ATENOLOL	Tenormin	Angina, hypertension	Beta-adrenergic blocker—action is to slow heart rate
Ativan	LORAZEPAM	Anxiety, for sleep	CNS tranquilizer
Azolid	PHENYLBUTAZONE	Arthritis, other inflammations	Anti-inflammatory
BECLOMETHASONE	Vanceril	Asthma	Anti-inflammatory
Benadryl	DIPHENHYDRAMINE	Allergic reaction	Antihistamine
Benemid	PROBENECID	Gout, high uric acid blood level	Prophylactic for gout
Bentyl	DICYCLOMINE	For nausea and vomiting	Anticholinergic
Blockadren	TIMOLOL MALEATE	Angina, hypertension	Beta-adrenergic blocker—action is to slow heart rate
Brethine	TERBUTALINE	Asthma	Bronchodilator
Bricanyl	TERBUTALINE	Asthma	Bronchodilator
Butazolidin	PHENYLBUTAZONE	Arthritis	Short term anti-inflammatory
Calan	VERAPAMIL	Effort angina, coronary artery spasm, PAT	Calcium channel blocker

Table continued on following page

233

	Drug	Indications for Use	General Drug Type
Cardioquin	QUINIDINE	Cardiac arrhythmia	Antiarrhythmic
Cardizem	DILTIAZEM	Effort angina, coronary artery spasm	Calcium channel blocker
Catapres	CLONIDINE	High blood pressure	Neuro effect vasodilator
CHLORDIAZEPOXIDE	Librium	Anxiety	Tranquilizer
CHLORPROPAMIDE	Diabinese	Diabetes	Oral antidiabetic
CHLORPROMAZINE	Thorazine	Psychosis	Antipsychotic/phenothiazine
CHLORTHALIDONE	Hygroton	Congestive heart failure, hypertension	Diuretic
CHLORTHIAZIDE	Diuril/Diupres	High blood pressure	Vasodilator
CIMETIDINE	Tagamet	Ulcer disease	Histamine H_2
Clinoril	SULINDAC	Arthritis	Non-steroid anti-inflammatory
CLONIDINE	Catapres	High blood pressure	Neuro effect vasodilator
Clonopin	CLONAZEPAM	Seizures	CNS depressant
CLORAZEPATE	Tranxene	Anxiety	CNS tranquilizer
COLCHICENE	—	Gout	Prophylactic for gout
Compazine	PROCHLORPERAZINE	Nausea, psychosis	Antipsychotic/phenothiazine
Corgard	NADOL	Angina, hypertension	Beta-adrenergic blocker—action is to slow heart rate
Coumadin	WARFARIN	Blood thinner	Anticoagulant
CROMOLYN	Intal	Asthma	Inhibits the release of histamines
CYCLANDELATE	Cyclospasmol	Nightime leg cramps, thrombophlebitis	Vasodilator
Cyclospasmol	CYCLANDELATE	Nightime leg cramps, thrombophlebitis	Vasodilator
CYCLOTHIAZIDE	Anhydron	High blood pressure	Diuretic
CYPROHEPTADINE	Periactin	Colds, allergies	Phenothiazine
Dalmane	FLURAZEPAM	Sleep medicine	Benzodiazepine
Darvon	PROPOXYPHENE	Pain	Mild analgesic, mild narcotic
Darvon, Darvocet	PROPOXYPHENE NAPSYLATE	Pain	Mild analgesic, mild narcotic
Datril	ACETAMINOPHEN	Pain, fever, inflammation	Analgesic
Demerol	MEPERIDINE	Severe pain	Strong narcotic
Diabinese	CHLORPROPAMIDE	Diabetes	Oral antidiabetic
Diamox	ACETAZOLAMIDE	Seizures, glaucoma	Diuretic
DIAZEPAM	Valium	Seizures, anxiety	Benzodiazepine, CNS tranquilizer

DICYCLOMINE	Bentyl	Nausea, vomiting	Anticholinergic
DIFLUNISAL	Dolobid	Pain, inflammation, arthritis	Non-narcotic, non-steroid analgesic
DIGOXIN	Lanoxin	CHF, cardiac arrhythmia	Antiarrhythmic
Dilantin	PHENYTOIN	Seizures	Anticonvulsant
DILTIAZEM	Cardizem	Effort angina, coronary artery spasm	Calcium channel blocker
DIPYRIDAMOLE	Persantine	Cardiac chest pain	Antianginal
DISOPYRAMIDE	Norpace	Cardiac arrhythmia	Antiarrhythmic
Diuril, Diupres	CHLOROTHIAZIDE	High blood pressure	Vasodilator
Dolene, Darvon	PROPOXYPHENE	Pain	Mild analgesic, mild narcotic
Dolobid	DIFLUNISAL	Pain, inflammation, arthritis	Non-narcotic, non-steroid analgesic
Donnatal	—	Stomach spasm	Anticholinergic
Doriden	GLUTETHIMIDE	Sedative for insomnia	Non-barbiturate hypnotic
DOXEPIN	Adapin, Sinequan	Depression	Antidepressive
Dyazide	HYDROCHLOROTHIAZIDE	High blood pressure	Diuretic
Dyrenium	TRIAMTERENE	High blood pressure	Potassium-sparing diuretic
Edecrin	ETHACRYNIC ACID	High blood pressure	Diuretic
Elavil	AMITRIPTYLINE	Depression	Tricyclic antidepressant
Elixophylline	THEOPHYLLINE	Asthma	Bronchodilator
Enduron	METHYCLOTHIAZIDE	CHF	Diuretic
EPHEDRINE	Marax	Asthma	Broncholidator
Equanil	MEPROBAMATE	Anxiety, tension, promotes sleep	Tranquilizer
Esidrix	HYDROCHLOROTHIAZIDE	High blood pressure	Diuretic
ETHACRYNIC ACID	Edecrin	High blood pressure	Diuretic
ETHCHLORVYNOL	Placidyl	Sedative	Hypnotic
ETHOSUXIMIDE	Zarontin	Petite mal seizures	Anticonvulsant
Feldene	PIROXICAM	Pain, inflammation, arthritis	Non-narcotic, non-steroid analgesic
FENOPROFEN	Nalfon	Arthritis	Non-steroid anti-inflammatory
Feosol	FERROUS SULFATE	Iron deficiency	Iron
FERROUS SULFATE	Feosol	Iron deficiency	Iron
Fiorinal	Aspirin combination	Pain	Analgesic
Flagyl	METRONIDAZOLE	Vaginal infection	—
FLURAZEPAM	Dalmane	Sleep medicine	Benzodiazepine
FUROSEMIDE	Lasix	High blood pressure, CHF	Diuretic

235

Table continued on following page

	Drug	Indications for Use	General Drug Type
Gantanol	SULFASOXAZOLE	Urinary tract infection	Sulfa drug
GLUTETHIMIDE	Doriden	Sedative for insomnia	Non-barbiturate hypnotic
GUANETHIDINE	Ismelin	High blood pressure	Neuro effect vasodilator
Haldol	HALOPERIDOL	Psychosis	Antipsychotic
HALOPERIDOL	Haldol	Psychosis	Antipsychotic
HYDRALAZINE	Apresoline	High blood pressure	Vasodilator
HYDROCHLOROTHIAZIDE	Esidrix, Hydrodiuril, Oretic	High pressure pressure, CHF	Diuretic
Hydrodiuril	HYDROCHLOROTHIAZIDE	High blood pressure, CHF	Diuretic
HYDROFLUMETHIAZIDE	Salutensin	High blood pressure	Neuro effect vasolidator
Hydropres	HYDROCHLOROTHIAZIDE/ RESERPINE	High blood pressure	Neuro effect vasolidator
HYDROXYZINE	Vistaril, Atarax	Nausea, vomiting, anxiety, tension	Antihistamine
Hygroton	CHLORTHALIDONE	CHF, high blood pressure	Diuretic
IBUPROFEN	Motrin	Arthritis	Non-steroid anti-inflammatory
Imavate	Imipramine	Depression	Antidepressant
IMIPRAMINE	Imavate, Tofranil	Depression	Antidepressant
Inderal	PROPRANOLOL	Angina, cardiac arrhythmia, hypertension	Beta-adrenergic blocker—action is to slow heart rate
Indocin	INDOMETHACIN	Arthritis	Non-steroid anti-inflammatory
INDOMETHACIN	Indocin	Arthritis	Non-steroid anti-inflammatory
INSULIN	Ilentin, Lente, Semilente, Ultralente NPH, NPH Ilentin, Protamine Zinc Insulin	Diabetes	"U" is units per ml, comes in fast-acting form (½ to 1 hr), and short-, intermediate-, and long-acting (6 to 36 hr)
Intal	CROMOLYN	Asthma	Inhibits the release of histamines
Ismelin	GUANETHIDINE	High blood pressure	Neuro effect vasodilator
Isoptin	VERAPAMIL	Effort angina, coronary artery spasm, PAT	Calcium channel blocker
Isordil	ISOSORBIDE DINITRATE	Angina	Antianginal (nitrates), vasodilator
Isosorb	ISOSORBIDE DINITRATE	Angina	Antiangnal (nitrates), vasodilator

236

ISOSORBIDE DINITRATE	Isordil, Isosorb, Sorbitrate	Angina	Antianginal (nitrates), vasodilator
ISOXSUPRINE	Vasodilan	Relief from chronic organic brain disease	Vasodilator
K-Lyte	POTASSIUM CHLORIDE	Replacement of potassium in the body	Potassium supplement
Lasix	FUROSEMIDE	CHF, high blood pressure	Diuretic
Librium	CHLORDIAZEPOXIDE	Anxiety	Antianxiety
Lomotil	DIPHENOXYLATE	Diarrhea	Antidiarrheal anticholinergic
Lopressor	METOPROLOL	High blood pressure	Beta blocker
LORAZEPAM	Antivan	Anxiety, for sleep	CNS tranquilizer
Luminal	PHENOBARBITAL	Seizure, sedative	Anticonvulsive
Marax	EPHEDRINE, THEOPHYLLINE	Asthma	Bronchodilator, sedative
Mellaril	THIORIDAZINE	Psychosis	Antipsychotic, phenothiazine
MEPERIDINE	Demerol	Severe pain	Narcotic (opiate)
MEPROBAMATE	Miltown, Equanil	Anxiety, tension, promotes sleep	Tranquilizer
Metahydrin	TRICHLORMETHIAZIDE	High blood pressure	Diuretic
METHIMAZOLE	Tapazole	Hyperthyroidism	Inhibits synthesis of thyroid hormones
METHYCLOTHIAZIDE	Enduron	CHF	Diuretic
METHYLDOPA	Aldomet	High blood pressure	Used in combination with other hypertensive medications
METHYLPHENIDATE	Ritalin	Narcolepsy, hyperactivity	CNS stimulation
METOLAZONE	Zaroxolyn	High blood pressure	Diuretic
METOPROLOL	Lopressor	High blood pressure	Beta blocker
METRONIDAZOLE	Flagyl	Vaginal infection	—
Miltown	MEPROBAMATE	Anxiety, tension, promotes sleep	Tranquilizer
Minipress	PRAZOSIN	Hypertension	Beta-adrenergic blocker—action is to slow heart rate
Motrin	IBUPROFEN	Arthritis	—
Mysoline	PRIMIDONE	Seizure	Anticonvulsive
NADOLOL	Corgard	Angina, hypertension	Beta-adrenergic blocker—action is to slow heart rate
Nagua	TRICHLORMETHIAZONE	—	Diuretic
Nalfon	FENOPROFEN	Arthritis	Non-steroid anti-inflammatory
Naprosyn	NAPROXEN	Arthritis	Non-steroid anti-inflammatory
NAPROXEN	Naprosyn, Anaprox	Arthritis	Non-steroid anti-inflammatory

Table continued on following page

237

	Drug	Indications for Use	General Drug Type
Navane	THIOTHIXENE	Psychosis	Antipsychotic, thioxanthene
NIFEDIPINE	Procardia	Effort angina, coronary artery spasm	Calcium channel blocker
Nitrobid, Nitrostat	NITROGLYCERIN	Cardiac chest pain	Antianginal
Nitro-Dur	NITROGLYCERIN	Cardiac chest pain (angina)	Nitro paste—chest pad
Norpace	DISOPYRAMIDE	Cardiac arrhythmia	Antiarrhythmic
Oretic	HYDROCHLOROTHIAZIDE	High blood pressure, CHF	Diuretic
Orinase	TOLBUTAMIDE	Diabetes	Antidiabetic
Oxalid	OXYPHENBUTAZONE	Arthritis, rheumatoid spondylitis	Anti-inflammatory, analgesic (potent)
OXAZEPAM	Serax	Anxiety	Tranquilizer
OXYCODONE	Percodan	Severe pain	Narcotic (opiate)
OXYPHENBUTAZONE	Oxalid, Tandearil	Arthritis, rheumatoid spondylitis	Anti-inflammatory (dangerous drug)
PAPAVERINE	Pavabid	Relief of arterial spasm	Vasodilator
Paregoric	—	Symptomatic treatment of diarrhea	Narcotic (opiate)
PENTAZOCINE	Talwin	Severe pain	Narcotic (opiate)
PHENOBARBITAL	Luminal	Seizure, sedative	Anticonvulsive
PHENYLBUTAZONE	Azolid, Butazolidin	Arthritis	Anti-inflammatory
PHENYTOIN	Dilantin	Seizures, cardiac arrhythmia	Anticonvulsive
Percodan	OXYCODONE	Severe pain	Narcotic (optiate)
Periactin	CYPROHEPTADINE	Colds, allergies	Phenothiazine
Persantin	DIPYRIDAMOLE	Cardiac chest pain	Antianginal
PINDOLOL	Visken	Angina, hypertension	Beta-adrenergic blocker—action is to slow heart rate
PIROXICAM	Feldene	Pain, inflammation, arthritis	Non-narcotic non-steroid analgesic
Placidyl	ETHCHLORVYNOL	Sedative, promotes sleep	Sedative-hypnotic
POTASSIUM	Slow-K, K-Lyte	Replaces potassium	Potassium supplement
PRAZOSIN	Minipress	Hypertension	Vasodilator
PREDNISONE	—	Asthma, arthritis	Anti-inflammatory
Pro-Banthine	PROPANTHELINE BROMIDE	Gastrointestinal distress	Anticholinergic
PROBENECID	Benemid	Gout, high uric acid blood level	Prophylactic for gout
PROCAINAMIDE	Pronestyl	Cardiac arrhythmias	Antiarrhythmic
Procardia	NIFEDIPINE	Effort angina, coronary artery spasm	Calcium channel blocker

Proloid	THYROGLOBULIN	Thyroid hormone
Pronestyl	PROCAINAMIDE	Antiarrhythmic
PROPANTHELINE BROMIDE	—	Anticholinergic
PROPOXYPHENE	Darvon, Dolene, SK-65	Narcotic
PROPRANOLOL	Inderal	Beta-adrenergic blocker—action is to slow heart rate
PROPYLTHIOURACIL	—	Inhibits synthesis of thyroid hormones
Proventil	ALBUTEROL	Bronchodilator
Quibron	THEOPHYLLINE	Bronchodilator
Quinaglute	QUINIDINE	Quinine (controls potassium)
Quinidex	QUINIDINE	Quinine (controls potassium)
QUINIDINE	Quinaglute, Quinidex, Cardioquin	Quinine (controls potassium)
Regroton	RESERPINE, CHLORTHALIDONE	Diuretic
RESERPINE	Serpasil, Sandril, Regroton, Hygroton	Diuretic, vasodilator
Ritalin	METHYLPHENIDATE	CNS, stimulant
Sandril	RESERPINE	Diuretic, vasodilator
Salutensin	RESERPINE, HYDROFLUMETHIAZIDE	Diuretic, vasodilator
Seconal	SECOBARBITAL	Barbiturate
Seconal	SECOBARBITAL	Barbiturate
Ser-Ap-Es	RESERPINE, HYDROCHLOROTHIAZIDE	Diuretic, vasodilator
Serpasil	RESERPINE	Diuretic, vasodilator
Serax	OXAZEPAM	Tranquilizer
Sinequan	DOXEPIN	Antidepressive
SK-Pramine	IMIPRAMINE	Antidepressive
SK-65	PROPOXYPHENE	Narcotic
Slow-K	POTASSIUM	Potassium supplement
Sorbitrate	ISOSORBIDE DINITRATE	Antianginal (vasodilator)
SPIRONOLACTONE	Aldactone	Potassium-sparing diuretic
Stelazine	TRIFLUOPERAZINE	Phenothiazine
SULFAMETHOXAZOLE	Gantanol	Sulfa drug

Proloid	Thyroid replacement	
Pronestyl	Cardiac arrhythmias	
PROPANTHELINE BROMIDE	Gastrointestinal distress	
PROPOXYPHENE	Mild pain	
PROPRANOLOL	Angina, hypertension, cardiac arrhythmia	
PROPYLTHIOURACIL	Hyperthyroidism	
Proventil	Asthma, COPD	
Quibron	Asthma	
Quinaglute	Cardiac arrhythmia	
Quinidex	Cardiac arrhythmia	
QUINIDINE	Cardiac arrhythmia	
Regroton	CHF, high blood pressure	
RESERPINE	CHF, high blood pressure	
Ritalin	Narcolepsy, hyperactivity	
Sandril	CHF, high blood pressure	
Salutensin	High blood pressure	
Seconal	Sleep medication	
Seconal	Sleep medication	
Ser-Ap-Es	High blood pressure	
Serpasil	High blood pressure	
Serax	Anxiety, sleep medication	
Sinequan	Depression	
SK-Pramine	Depression	
SK-65	Mild pain	
Slow-K	Replaces potassium	
Sorbitrate	Angina	
SPIRONOLACTONE	High blood pressure	
Stelazine	Antipsychotic	
SULFAMETHOXAZOLE	Urinary tract infection	

239

Table continued on following page

Drug		Indications for Use	General Drug Type
SULINDAC	Clinoril	Arthritis	Non-steroid anti-inflammatory
Synthroid		Thyroid replacement	Thyroid hormone
Tagamet	CIMETIDINE	Ulcer disease	Histamine H_2
Talwin	PENTAZOCINE	Severe pain	Narcotic
Tandearil (oxalid)	OXYPHENBUTAZONE	Arthritis	Anti-inflammatory (extremely toxic)
Tapazole	METHIMAZOLE	Hyperthyroidism	Inhibits synthesis of thyroid hormone
Tenormin	ATENOLOL	Angina, hypertension	Beta-adrenergic blocker—action is to slow heart rate
TERBUTALINE	Brethine, Bricanyl	Asthma	Bronchodilator
THEOPHYLLINE	Quibron, Elixophylline, Aminophylline	Asthma	Bronchodilator
THIORIDAZINE	Mellaril	Psychosis	Antipsychotic-phenothiazine
THIOTHIXENE	Navane	Psychosis	Antipsychotic-thioxanthene
Thorazine	CHLORPROMAZINE	Psychosis	Antipsychotic-phenothiazine
THYROGLOBULIN	Proloid	Thyroid replacement	Thyroid hormone
Tigan	TRIMETHOBENZAMIDE	Control of nausea and vomiting	Antiemetic
TIMOLOL MALEATE	Blockadren	Angina, hypertension	Beta-adrenergic blocker—action is to slow heart rate

Tofranil	IMIPRAMINE	Depression, tranquilizer	Antidepressant
TOLAZAMIDE	Tolanase	Diabetes	Oral antidiabetic
TOLBUTAMIDE	Orinase	Diabetes	Oral antidiabetic
Tolectin	TOLMETIN	Arthritis, pain	Anti-inflammatory
TOLMETIN	Tolectin	Arthritis, pain	Anti-inflammatory
Tranxene	CLORAZEPATE	Anxiety	Tranquilizer
TRIAMTERENE	Dyrenium	High blood pressure, CHF	Potassium-sparing diuretic
Triavil	AMITRIPTYLINE	Depression	Tricyclic-antidepressant
TRICHLORMETHIAZIDE	Methahydrin, Naqua	CHF, hepatic cirrhosis	Diuretic
TRIHEXYPHENIDYL	Artane	Parkinson's disease	Synthetic antispasmodic—works like atropine
Tylenol	ACETAMINOPHEN	Pain, fever, inflammation	Mild analgesic
Valium	DIAZEPAM	Anxiety, seizures	Benzodiazepine
Vanceril	BECLOMETHASONE	Asthma	Anti-inflammatory
Vasodilan	ISOXSUPRINE	For chronic organic brain disease	Vasodilator
VERAPAMIL	Calan, Isoptin	Effort angina, coronary artery spasm, PAT	Calcium channel blocker
Visken	PINDOLOL	Angina, hypertension	Beta-adrenergic blocker—action is to slow heart rate
Vistaril	HYDROXYZINE	Anxiety, nausea, vomiting, tension	Antihistamine
WARFARIN	Coumadin	Blood thinner, post CVA, blood clot	Anticoagulant
Zaroxolyn	METOLAZONE	High blood pressure	Diuretic
Zyloprim	ALLOPURINOL	Gout, high uric acid blood level	Prophylactic for gout

APPENDIX 2: LEGAL CONSIDERATIONS

Legal action against members of the health professions increases each year. The EMT should be aware that he/she is included in this group and should understand the type of circumstance that could result in legal action against him/her.

Maintaining a professional, compassionate, considerate attitude is the best way to prevent the patient and/or family members from becoming unhappy with the treatment provided. The discontented patient is the one most likely to institute legal action. Patients will often overlook certain mistakes in treatment if they feel that the health professional has a general attitude of real concern and truly has their best interests in mind, regardless of the circumstances.

FOUR ELEMENTS OF A LEGAL ACTION

Duty

In a suit, the plaintiff (person who is suing) must prove the duty of the person or agency to perform actions involving him/her.

1. If it is the duty of the EMT to provide transport of an ill patient, it is also the duty of the EMT to take all reasonable precautions to protect the patient and others on the street by avoiding reckless and/or careless handling of the vehicle so as not to cause additional harm to the patient or others.

2. It is the duty of EMTs to provide the appropriate care whenever necessary, according to the standards to which they are certified, as long as they are identifiable by virtue of uniforms, patches, marked vehicles, and so on. During off-duty hours, care is provided by the EMT according to best judgement of the EMT at the time, but it should be remembered that the element of liability still exists regardless of good intentions of the EMT when off duty. EMTs under the influence of drugs or alcohol should consider the consequences of a possibly impaired ability to function normally.

Breach of Duty

EMTs who fail to perform expected actions or whose actions exceed the training and skills for which they are certified would be considered in breach of duty.

Example: EMTs performing intravenous therapy, endotracheal intubation, and so on, when not certified to perform these actions.

Damage or Harm

The harm or damage must be proved to have occurred.

Proximate Cause

The EMT must be proved as the proximate cause of the damage or injury.

1. Rib fractures occurring while CPR is being given to a patient without respirations and who is pulseless would not usually be considered a case of proximate cause.
2. But injuries during treatment that could have been prevented by normal prudent care by the EMT are cause for a charge of proximate cause.

RECORD-KEEPING

Two key factors in record-keeping can provide the EMT with a professional "track record" that may assist in defending against suit.

1. Accurate records of all ongoing training, commendations, and proof of proper performance in the role of EMT establish competence level and can be for reference.
2. Concise and complete medical field reports of patient examination and treatment also demonstrate concerned professionalism.
   a. Accurate reporting of subjective statements by patient, patient's family, or witnesses without embellishment by the EMT.
   b. Objective statements that include only known facts about the patient, including *all* tests performed during the patient examination. All statements should be specific and pertinent to the patient's medical or emotional problems and should include both negative and positive results. Report should indicate a logical approach to the problem and treatment.
   c. Abbreviations used in the report should be generally recognized by the medical profession. As a general rule, the report should be written so that the EMT will not have difficulty reciting specifics of the incident up to a year from the time of the incident.

PATIENT CONSENT FOR TREATMENT

1. Local laws regarding emergency consent of minors and the patient's right to refuse treatment should be explicitly understood. Local law officers are an excellent source of precise information concerning this subject. Read the law. Do not rely on word of mouth.
2. Most states have implied consent laws for emergency settings by which minors may be treated without parents or guardians available for consent, and for patients who are not rational.

Special care must be exercised, however, when physical force and/or restraints are considered, so as to avoid the act of false imprisonment of the patient.
3. Any injury inflicted to the patient during the course of treatment or transportation, against the will of the patient, may be legal grounds to sue the EMT responsible.

CHILD ABUSE

1. It is the obligation of the EMT to report all suspicious acts of possible child abuse. When this suspicion is reported in a professional manner, the reporting EMT is considered immune to legal action.
2. In some states, reporting suspected child abuse is considered the legal duty of the EMT, and the EMT can be construed negligent if further abuse of the child occurs after failure to report.

SUMMARY

1. It is not the intent of this section to scare the EMT into thinking that everyone he/she treats is looking for a reason to institute legal action. Instead, it is a reminder that the law does not provide a "blank check" to health professionals just because they are involved in assisting with medical emergencies.
2. As a general rule, if EMTs treat their patients as though they were their own family members, the appropriate level of concern and treatment will be provided, and situations that may cause legal action will be avoided.
3. It is vital that EMTs be familiar with all legal positions regarding the field EMT in their working areas.

APPENDIX 3: FAHRENHEIT-CENTIGRADE CONVERSION TABLE

Fahrenheit Degrees	Centigrade Degrees
32	0
41	5
50	10
68	20
77	30
86	35
95	35.56
96	36.11
97	36.67
98	37.22
99	37.78
100	38.33
101	38.89
102	39.44
103	40.00
104	40.56
105	41.11
106	41.67
107	

APPENDIX 4: UNIVERSAL ANATOMICAL POSITIONS

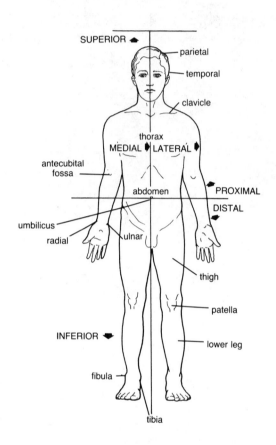

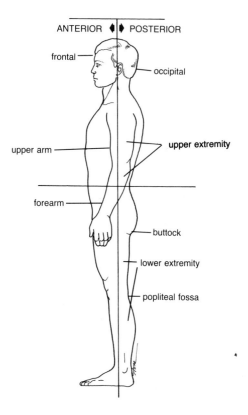

ANTERIOR ◀|▶ POSTERIOR

frontal

occipital

upper arm

upper extremity

forearm

buttock

lower extremity

popliteal fossa

APPENDIX 5: ABBREVIATIONS

.abd	.abdomen/abdominal
A/O	alert/oriented
AOB	alcohol on breath
@	at
ASAP	as soon as possible
amb	ambulance
ax	axillary
B/P	blood pressure
bilat	bilateral
cap	capsule
C-spine	cervical spine
cl	clear
CNS	central nervous system
c̄	with
c/o	complaining of
c/c	chief complaint
conj	conjugate
diff	difficulty
DOA	dead on arrival
dsg	dressing
Dx	diagnosis
E&R	equal and reactive
EKG	electrocardiogram
ETOH	ethyl alcohol
est	estimated
ext	extremity
F&D	fixed and dilated
fx	fracture
GSW	gunshot wound
h/a	headache
Ht	height
HTN	hypertension
Hx	history
HEENT	head, eyes, ears, nose, throat
jt	joint
Ⓛ	left
lac	laceration
lg	large
liq	liquid
LLQ	left lower quadrant
LUQ	left upper quadrant
LOC	level of consciousness
L-spine	lumbar spine
M = R	mid, equal, reactive
MCA	motorcycle accident
med(s)	medicine(s)
mg	milligrams
ML	midline

.mod	.moderate
multi	multiple
NKA	no known allergies
NC	nasal cannula
neg	negative
NROM	normal range of motion
N&V	nausea and vomiting
ō	no/none
occ	occasional
OD	overdose
P	pulse
P.D.	police department
PE	pulmonary embolis
P.E.	physical examination
PMD	private medical doctor
PND	paraoxysmal nocturnal dyspnea
POV	private vehicle
ped	pedestrian
po	by mouth
poss	possible
prox	proximal
pt	patient
p̄	past/after
pHx.	past history
®	right
re	regarding
req	request
RLQ	right lower quadrant
RUQ	right upper quadrant
R/O	rule out
Rt	routine
Rx	treatment
s̄	without
STH	said to have
STHH	said to have had
STHB	said to have been
SOB	short of breath
sl	slight
sm	small
s̄s̄	half
S-spine	sacral spine
SW	stab wound
Sx	sign/symptom
T	temperature
Tab	tablet
TIA	transient ischemic attack
T-Spine	thoracic spine
Tx	transport
unc	unconscious
unk	unknown
WD/WN	well developed/well nourished
WNL	within normal limits
wt	weight

y/o	year old
+	plus, positive
=	equal
−	negative
×	times
≈	approximately
♂	male
♀	female
↑	increasing up, above
→	carry thought on
↓	decreasing, down, below
>	greater than
<	less than
/	per
⚬—⌐	supine
⌐⌐	semi reclining
⌐	sitting
⚬	standing

APPENDIX 6: SEVERITY INDICES

TRIAGE INDEX

Variable	Definition	Score
Respiratory effort (visual inspection of chest wall movement)	Normal	3
	Shallow	1
	Retractive	1
	None	0
Capillary refill (nail bed or finger pad pressure)	Immediate (less than 2 sec.)	2
	Delayed (more than 2 sec.)	0
Eye opening (spoken or shouted verbal commands or standard pain stimulus)	Spontaneous	3
	To voice	2
	To pain	1
	None	0
Verbal response (conversational ability, *e.g.*, sentences, words only, sounds only)	Oriented	4
	Confused	3
	Inappropriate words	2
	Incomprehensible sounds	1
	None	0
Motor response (spoken or shouted verbal commands or standard pain stimulus)	Obeys command	4
	Withdrawal	3
	Flexion	2
	Extension	1
	None	0

A score of less than 7 is critical. Scale developed by Drs. Champion and Sacco in 1976 at Washington Hospital Center, Washington, D.C.

NELSON SCALE FOR CHILDREN

		Score	
Variable	*0*	*1*	*2*
Respiratory effort	Labored or absent	Some distress	No distress
Skin color	Cyanotic	Pale, flushed, mottled	Normal
Activity	Delirium, stupor, coma	Lethargy	Normal
Play	Refuses to play	Decreased	Normal
Temperature (°F)	<97.4 or >104	101.1-104	97.4-101

10 points is *not* sick; 8 or 9 is *moderately sick;* 7 points or less is *very sick.* Scale developed by Dr. Kathleen Nelson in 1975 at Yale University School of Medicine, New Haven.

APGAR SCORE

The Apgar score is useful in evaluating the status of the infant. The Apgar score should be determined immediately after birth and 5 minutes after delivery. This score is determined by assessing the appearance, pulse, reflexes, activity, and respiration of the infant according to the following table:

		Score	
Sign*	0	1	2
A: Appearance (color)	Blue, pale	Body pink, extremities blue	Completely pink
P: Pulse (heart rate)	Absent	Less than 100	Greater than 100
G: Grimace (reflexes)	No response	Grimace	Cough, sneeze
A: Activity (muscle tone)	Limp	Some flexion of extremities	Active motion
R: Respiration	Absent	Slow, irregular	Strong cry

*Each sign is evaluated individually and scored from 0 to 2 at both 1 and 5 minutes of life. The final score at each time is the sum of individual scores.

A score of 7 to 10 indicates adequate function of the infant. A score of 4 to 6 indicates moderate depression. Infants with scores less than 4 will often require active resuscitation. Remember that babies are often blue or extremely pale 1 minute after delivery, with flaccid muscles and poor respirations; hence it is important to reassess the infant's score at 5 minutes after delivery.

GLASGOW COMA SCALE

EYES	Open	Spontaneously	4
		To verbal command	3
		To pain	2
	No response		1
BEST MOTOR RESPONSE	To verbal command	Obeys	6
	To painful stimulus°	Localizes pain	5
		Flexion – withdrawal	4
		Flexion – abnormal (decorticate rigidity)	3
		Extension (decerebrate rigidity)	2
		No response	1
BEST VERBAL RESPONSE°°		Oriented and converses	5
		Disoriented and converses	4
		Inappropriate words	3
		Incomprehensible sounds	2
		No response	1
TOTAL			3–15

The Glasgow Coma Scale, based on eye opening, verbal and motor responses, is a practical means of monitoring changes in level of consciousness. If response on the scale is given a number, the responsiveness of the patient can be expressed by the sum of the figures. Lowest score is 3; highest is 15.

°Apply knuckles to sternum; observe arms.

°°Arouse patient with painful stimulus if necessary.

APPENDIX 7: NEUROLOGICAL CHECKLIST*

Instructions. Record vital signs in Unit I. If the patient can talk, check (✔) one subdivision in units II, III, and IV. An oriented patient should know his name, age, etc. A moan can be checked as "garbled" speech. If unable to talk, check (✔) "none" in Unit III and one block in Unit V. In an "inappropriate" response, the patient is not effective in removing the painful stimulus; when "decerebrate," the extremities reflexly extend and/or hyperpronate. In Unit VI, draw the size and shape of each pupil and check (✔) for a reaction to light. Under Unit VII, normal strength is scored as "4," slight weakness "3," a 50 percent reduction in strength "2," marked weakness and without spontaneous movement "1," and complete paralysis "0."

---

*Reproduced courtesy of American College of Surgeons.

UNIT	TIME					
I Vital signs	blood pressure					
	pulse					
	respirations					
	temperature					
II Conscious and	oriented					
	disoriented					
	restless					
	combative					
III Speech	clear					
	rambling					
	garbled					
	none					
IV Will awaken to	name					
	shaking					
	light pain					
	strong pain					
V Nonverbal reaction to pain	appropriate					
	inappropriate					
	"decerebrate"					
	none					
VI Pupils	size on right					
	size on left					
	reacts on right					
	reacts on left					
VII Ability to move	right arm					
	left arm					
	right leg					
	left leg					

APPENDIX 8: MOTORCYCLE HELMET REMOVAL*

The varying sizes, shapes, and configurations of motorcycle helmets necessitate some understanding of their proper removal from victims of motorcycle accidents. The rescuer who removes a helmet improperly might inadvertently aggravate cervical spine injuries.

The Committee on Trauma believes that physicians who treat the injured should be aware of helmet removal techniques. A gradual increase in the use of helmets is anticipated because many organizations are urging voluntary wearing of helmets, and some states are reinstating their laws requiring the wearing of helmets.

---

*Reproduced with permission of the American College of Surgeons.

Types of Helmets

A

Full face coverage—motorcycle, auto racer

B

Full face coverage—motocross

C

Partial face coverage—motorcycle, auto racer

D

Light head protection—bicycle, kayak

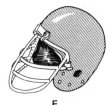

E

Football

Helmet Removal

One rescuer applies inline traction by placing his or her hands on each side of the helmet with the fingers on the victim's mandible. This position prevents slippage if the strap is loose.

1

The rescuer cuts or loosens the strap at the D-rings while maintaining inline traction.

2

A second rescuer places one hand on the mandible at the angle, the thumb on one side, the long and index fingers on the other. With his other hand, he applies pressure from the occipital region. This maneuver transfers the inline traction responsibility to the second rescuer.

3

The rescuer at the top removes the helmet. Three factors should be kept in mind:

1. The helmet is egg-shaped, and therefore must be expanded laterally to clear the ears.

2. If the helmet provides full facial coverage, glasses must be removed first.

3. If the helmet provides full facial coverage, the nose will impede removal. To clear the nose, the helmet must be tilted backward and raised over it.

4

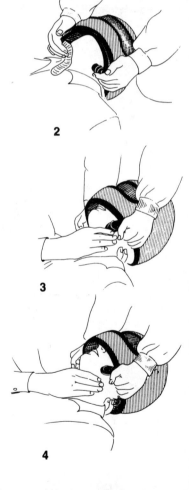

Throughout the removal process, the second rescuer maintains inline traction from below in order to prevent head tilt.

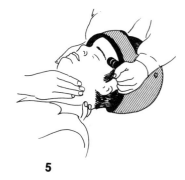

5

After the helmet has been removed, the rescuer at the top replaces his hands on either side of the victim's head with his palms over the ears.

6

Inline traction is maintained from above until a backboard is in place.

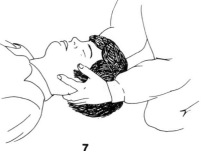

7

Summary

The helmet must be maneuvered over the nose and ears while the head and neck are held rigid.

1. Inline traction is applied from above.
2. Inline traction is transferred below with pressure on the jaw and occiput.
3. The helmet is removed.
4. Inline traction is re-established from above.

INDEX

Note: Page numbers in *italics* refer to illustrations; page numbers followed by (t) refer to tables.